EDUCATING THE URBAN NEW SOUTH

EDUCATING THE URBAN NEW SOUTH

ATLANTA AND THE RISE OF GEORGIA STATE UNIVERSITY

1913–1969

Merl E. Reed

Mercer University Press
Macon, Georgia

MERCER
UNIVERSITY PRESS

Endowed by
TOM WATSON BROWN
and
THE WATSON-BROWN FOUNDATION, INC.

MUP/H784

© 2009 Mercer University Press
1400 Coleman Avenue, Macon, Georgia 31207
All rights reserved

First Edition.

Book design: burt&burt

Books published by Mercer University Press are printed on acid free paper
that meets the requirements of American National Standard for Information
Sciences—Permanence of Paper for Printed Library Materials.

Mercer University Press is a member of Green Press initiative
(greenpressinitiative.org), a nonprofit organization working to help publishers
and printers increase their use of recycled paper and decrease their use of fiber
derived from endangered forests. This book is printed on recycled paper.

Library of Congress Cataloging-in-Publication Data

Reed, Merl Elwyn, 1925-
Educating the urban new south : Atlanta and the rise of Georgia State
University, 1913-1969 / by Merl E. Reed.
p. cm.
Includes bibliographical references and index.

ISBN-13: 978-0-88146-148-0 (hardback : alk. paper) ISBN-10: 0-88146-148-2

1. Georgia State University—History.
2. Education, Urban—Georgia—Atlanta—History. I. Title.

LD1965.R44 2009   378.758'231—dc22

2009021723

PREFACE

Work on this history began shortly after then-academic Vice President Thomas Brewer inaugurated the undertaking in the late 1980s and turned the project over to Gary M. Fink, the history department chair, recently deceased. Fink invited the author to participate and researched the extensive papers of President Noah Langdale, Jr., before withdrawing for personal reasons. Yet Fink's continuing encouragement and counsel, and his careful critique of every chapter, have been extremely important in shaping the final account. The author acknowledges the indispensable released time from teaching that made the research possible.

The author also is indebted to the late George E. Manners, a 1935 Evening College graduate and former dean of the business school. A trained historian with a prodigious memory, he gave generously of his time and knowledge. Ellen L. Evans was particularly helpful, as were Gerald H. Davis and the late Charles B. Pyles, all of whom waded through the then over 900 pages to make useful comments. Wayne J. Urban carefully critiqued the manuscript for the Mercer University Press before its publication. Of course, all of their efforts relieve the author of none of the responsibility for the book's failings or shortcomings. Finally, the author is especially appreciative of the enthusiastic support given by Hugh Hudson, Georgia State University history department chair.

The Pullen Library's Department of Special Collections, with its extensive university archive, provided the major share of the research material. The author is grateful to Leslie S. Hough, the head of Special Collections, and his successor, Julia M. Young. They and their staffs were always helpful and cooperative. Special thanks go to university archivist Laurel G. Bowen, who generously applied her intimate knowledge of the material, and to Peter Roberts for his special expertise in photography. The author also acknowledges the cooperation of the archival staffs at the University of Georgia, the Georgia Department of Archives and History, Georgia Tech, and the Woodruff Library at Atlanta University.

Of course, prolonged involvement in a work such as this exacts sacrifices from family. The author is extremely grateful to Germaine (Gerry) Memelo Reed for her encouragement and patience.

INTRODUCTION

By fall 2007, Georgia State University (GSU) had become a major urban institution. Its location in Atlanta, the state's capital and one of the South's most dynamic cities, greatly facilitated this progress. The majority of GSU's traditional and nontraditional students, numbering over 27,000, commuted from the Atlanta area, but hundreds more came from all of Georgia's counties, the fifty states, and over 100 countries. The six colleges offered over 200 majors in 217 fields of study, with fifty nationally accredited programs leading to bachelors, masters, specialists, and doctoral degrees. Its two libraries contained some 1,476,610 volumes and 9,832 periodicals. Significantly, the Carnegie Foundation in 2000 classified GSU as a "Doctoral/ Research University-Extensive," a ranking then applicable to only 151 other institutions, or nearly four percent of the nation's universities. Such a placement required a wide range of baccalaureate programs, a commitment to graduate work through the doctorate, and the awarding of fifty or more doctoral degrees per year across at least fifteen disciplines. GSU's research activities also were expanding. In 2007, support from federal, state, and private sources exceeded well over $64,000,000.[1]

The college's symbiotic relationship with Atlanta had been fundamental to its existence and growth, and its promotional literature in 2007 continued to recognize this "close-knit relationship." As the Southeast's cultural and economic center, the city provided an atmosphere in which "traditional education" could be enhanced through internships and guest lectures. Employment opportunities, unavailable in smaller communities, always had existed in Atlanta businesses, law and insurance offices, banks, three levels of government, and the health and entertainment industries. In turn, Georgia State responded to a variety of urban needs through its flexible academic programs and its division of continuing education, which offered noncredit services through workshops, conferences, and short courses.[2]

Such a multi-purpose institution would have been inconceivable to the founders in 1913 when they established a small commerce department at the Georgia Institute of Technology to teach the engineers some rudiments of business. A short time later, in rented, shabby rooms, a downtown branch called the Tech Evening School began offering courses primarily to the nontraditional students employed in Atlanta's thriving businesses. The first class graduated from Tech with three-year commerce degrees in 1915. Toward the end of World War I, women began matriculating, receiving their degrees from the all-male Tech. In offering college work in business, Tech entered a relatively new and undeveloped field. At the same time, until the post-World War II period, no other major Southern city had an institution like the Evening School, a public college offering degrees in business to working young adults.[3]

As Atlanta's economy boomed in the 1920s, the Evening School also thrived. The booster spirit pervading the business community also infected higher education. The deft financial management of its director, George M. Sparks, strengthened the school during the late 1920s and helped save it during the Depression; he even found money to purchase a downtown building in the early 1930s. While surviving the severe economic downturn, the Evening School was separated from Georgia Tech in 1932, an act that brought on other serious problems. Placed directly under the chancellor and regents in a centralized

x

University System of Georgia (USG), the newly named System Center, or Atlanta Center, faced immediate challenges to its accreditation because of insufficient state financial support and questions about its academic standing. Unloved and unwanted except by its Atlanta supporters, the Center continued to grow slowly in the 1930s as the city recovered and prospered. World War II and the GI Bill established the institution, once and for all, as an indispensable player in Atlanta higher education.

The Center's postwar role in the university system, however, still faced serious challenges. When the Center's lack of accreditation threatened the entire system, the regents in 1947 turned it over to Athens as the Atlanta Division of the University of Georgia (UGA). For the next eight years, aggressive UGA administrators and supportive regents worked assiduously to restrict the division. They confined its academic activity to one four-year degree in business administration, denied advanced work in the arts and sciences, blocked all graduate programs, and sought to limit its public service activities to the Atlanta area. Supported by Atlanta businesses, state legislators, and citizens in need of higher education, the school achieved its independence in 1955 as the Georgia State College of Business Administration, changed to Georgia State College in 1962. Facing closure at any time, it somehow survived the segregation crisis of the late 1950s that played out in a more tolerant Atlanta, the emerging "city too busy to hate." Nevertheless, pressure from accrediting agencies as well as businesses, government employees, and ordinary citizens forced the regents in 1958 to add new functions, including four-year arts and sciences degrees and masters programs in business. As additional masters and doctoral programs were authorized during the ensuing decade, the college achieved university status in 1969.

The Evening School's founding and subsequent evolution into a major urban university would have been impossible outside of dynamic Atlanta. In view of this relationship, Georgia State's past must be approached as a part of an urban as well as institutional history. The city's economic, business, and entrepreneurial developments also affected the college. While Atlanta became well known for its boosters and promoters, Georgia State produced its own able educational entrepreneurs, such as Sparks and George E. Manners. Director Sparks applied financial wizardry and political contacts to the college's benefit, while Dean Manners of the business school established close ties to important Atlanta businesses, especially insurance and banking. Of course, the college also was a part of the University System of Georgia, and an analysis of this relationship invites a reinterpretation of Georgia higher education between 1932 and 1969.

EDUCATING THE
URBAN NEW
SOUTH

1

PROGRESSIVE ATLANTA AND GEORGIA TECH'S DOWNTOWN EVENING SCHOOL

In 1912, the Georgia Institute of Technology began offering daytime lectures in commerce to give "the BUSINESS MAN a college training...and the ENGINEERING STUDENT a business training." The Tech School of Commerce came into existence the next year with forty-four enrollees. Perhaps half of them were nontraditional students employed in Atlanta's central business district. Their enthusiastic response encouraged Tech in 1914 to open the Tech School in the downtown area. Operating at several locations over the next two decades, the Evening School separated from Georgia Tech in 1933 under the newly created University System of Georgia (USG). Thenceforth, this struggling public urban college went through several name changes and at times nearly faced extinction before becoming Georgia State University in 1969.[4]

Although a few commerce schools existed when Tech's program began, only two operated in the South: Louisiana State University (1898) and Washington and Lee (1906). The University of Georgia's school of commerce began a year after Tech's. With some 155,000 people, Atlanta in 1913 was scarcely a metropolis, and Georgia Tech had no plans of becoming an urban college. Yet in establishing an evening school in downtown Atlanta, Tech unwittingly laid a tenuous foundation for what became Georgia State University. The few Northern city, or urban, colleges at that time had no counterparts in the South.[5] Nevertheless, the Evening School became an urban college as Atlanta grew and prospered.

As Tech began offering commerce courses, Atlanta was making impressive strides forward. With fifteen railroads providing access to the entire Southeast and links to the Northeast and Midwest, the groundwork existed for thriving banking and commercial activity around cotton and other raw materials. Three successful expositions in the late nineteenth century enhanced Atlanta's image as a convention center. Around 1900, a steel plant began fabricating bale hoops for the cotton trade. Seventeen new buildings complemented the city's skyline by 1910 along with an auditorium armory to host conventions. In the succeeding decade, as Atlanta's population rose above 200,000, nine more edifices costing over $5,000,000 went up, mostly in the six-block area along Peachtree Street north of the railroad. Spurred by the Chamber of Commerce, a $3,000,000 bond issue extended the city's sewer system from eighty-nine to over 250 miles, erected a sewage disposal plant, lengthened the water mains, built Grady Hospital, and constructed school buildings. Amidst opportunity, wealth, and jobs, baseball and other recreational activities thrived, and some Atlantans also had time for the fine arts, including regular spring visits by the Metropolitan Opera beginning in 1910.[6]

Yet Atlanta scarcely could be seen as a cultural mecca. Indeed, historian David Levine pictured that era's Atlanta as an "educational desert." Besides Georgia Tech, two small colleges, Agnes Scott and Oglethorpe, served Caucasians, along with a few questionable proprietary schools. African Americans attended colleges around the struggling Atlanta University. Emory College opened for instruction in 1918 and shortly established a business school.[7]

While the business community supported bond issues for infrastructures, taxes for quality public education aroused little enthusiasm. Only four high schools provided creditable training for white, mostly middle- and upper-class families. No high school for blacks existed until 1924. In fact, education officials earlier had attempted to end seventh- and eighth-grade African American classes. In 1922, a study team headed by Columbia University's George D. Strayer evaluated Atlanta's schools as so "woefully lacking" that the children's "health is being menaced."[8]

In addition, poor housing and inadequate public health programs plagued the city. A fetid, overcrowded slum immediately south of the Tech campus greeted faculty headed downtown to the Evening School. Despite the new sewer lines, outdoor privies served the poor. Illnesses, such as diphtheria, rampant in black neighborhoods, led the *Atlanta Constitution* in 1914 to label as nearly criminal the city's attitude about "Negroes and diseases." The central city itself often choked from factory smoke and railroad soot, while the softwood and coal in residential stoves and fireplaces polluted the air in Atlanta's lower lying areas, known as "bottoms."[9]

3

Certain social aberrations cast an even darker shadow over the city's image—the bloody 1906 race riot, a bitter 1915 Fulton cotton mill strike, and two other labor conflicts on the public transit system. All raised the specter of class warfare and exposed the business community's ethnic divisions. Atlanta endured additional blemish when a mob in nearby Marietta lynched Leo Frank, a Jewish employer accused of murdering a factory girl, and when Atlanta's Fulton County issued a charter to the rejuvenated Ku Klux Klan. Nature ravaged an eastern residential area during the devastating 1917 fire.[10]

Nevertheless, throughout such misfortunes, growth and prosperity continued to propel the city forward. When Tech President Kenneth G. Matheson decided to offer commerce courses, support came from some eighty businessmen, many of them Tech alumni who viewed the newly graduating engineers as "babes in the woods." They needed business science supplemented by lectures from business people. With alumni raising $25,000, several became the commerce school's "guarantors," with partial funding for nearly four years. Tech offered its first course in winter 1912. Commerce programs everywhere, still relatively new to academia, suffered from ambiguous course content and the lack of clearly defined disciplines and fields of concentration. Tech had no trained teaching staff. The first course, entitled Business Education, revolved around the lectures of six Atlanta businessmen selected by a faculty committee.

In planning for the upcoming 1912–1913 school year, Tech gave contracts to two nonacademic professionals. Joel Hunter, a respected accountant, volunteered. Other lecturers included an Atlanta law firm's senior member, a banker with a North Carolina master's degree in corporate finance, and various local experts who taught accounting, commercial law, buying, and selling. This activity led directly to the establishment in 1913 of the School of Commerce, which offered both daytime and evening classes. A few Tech faculty, all retooling, also participated. Wayne Sailley Kell, in metallurgy and geology, took up accounting, finance, and the title of dean. He worked to improve his own business training and by one account was the third Georgian to become a certified public accountant.[11]

Competent part-time instructors strengthened such programs. Other nonacademic professionals in fields, such as law, accounting, finance, and banking, increasingly flocked to larger urban communities like Atlanta for jobs in business and government. Many made significant pedagogical contributions to Tech's Evening School, to its successors, and to rising commerce

4

Wayne Sailley Kell, Dean 1913–1918. Courtesy of GSU Archives.

schools all over the country. The original Tech volunteer, Joel Hunter, chaired the Georgia board of CPA examiners and later gave free lectures at the University of Georgia (UGA), where, in the small city of Athens, qualified accountants were hard to find.[12]

Initially, Tech offered a three-year bachelor of commercial science (B.C.S.) degree followed by two years of approved work in business. A certificate of proficiency went to "irregular" students who did not complete all the courses. All campus collegiate requirements applied to the downtown Evening School. In 1916, Tech switched to a four-year degree program, the bachelor of science in commerce (B.S.C.), which had a much more demanding curriculum. This change coincided with the founding of the American Association of Collegiate Schools of Business (AACSB). Nevertheless, Tech failed in joining this organization until 1921 because it demanded higher admission standards and other criteria. Downtown Evening School students could receive the four-year degree only by taking additional daytime campus courses.[13]

5

As the downtown Evening School opened, the United States census affirmed the existence of a viable Atlanta business clientele with more than 270 proprietors, 647 salaried officers and superintendents, and 1,634 male clerks, not to mention 368 female clerks barred from Tech admission. Of course, other self-described "business colleges" operated, though the state of Georgia and accrediting agencies refused them recognition. Tech's first daytime and evening commerce classes on campus attracted forty-four students, half of them irregular enrollees. When evening classes began meeting downtown in the Walton building, the combined total was eighty-six. Such remarkable growth "bids fair" to making the School of Commerce one of Tech's "most popular and important departments," President Matheson informed the trustees. Enrollment the next fall—seventy-three downtown and presumably that many students on campus—confirmed this prediction. The downtown student

Downtown Evening School classes began in the Walton Building in 1914.
Courtesy of GSU Archives.

body constituted a whole new collegiate constituency.[14] Younger
working Atlantans had given the Tech Evening School an enthusiastic welcome.

In fall 1916, downtown enrollment leaped to 114. The typical
fare included the popular commercial law as well as economics,
labor problems, banking, cost accounting, and finance. Gone was
most of the soft pedagogy. Only advertising had five local lecturers. In 1915, Tech graduated its first class, all seven carrying
full-time jobs. With the introduction of the four-year B.S.C.
degree in fall 1916, which required biology, chemistry, mathematics, engineering, machine shop, and a foreign language,
downtown students generally were relegated to the three-year
B.C.S. degree. While the downtown Evening School shortly
began offering French and Spanish, expensive laboratory work
was out of the question.[15]

As Dean Wayne Kell guided the embryonic campus commerce program and organized the downtown Evening School, campus students as well as downtown working youths flocked into the classes. Many who could qualify for campus admission nevertheless performed poorly in engineering, particularly Tech's famous athlete, D. I. "Red" Barron and a majority of the 1917 football team. Before leaving in 1917, Kell also admitted the first women into the Evening School. There, the student body soon outgrew the Walton building, and Kell's successor, John Madison Watters, leased four rooms in the modern Peachtree Arcade for fall 1918.[16]

In moving to the Peachtree, or City, Arcade, the Evening School acquired a location "in the heart of things," more convenient for the "men and women" who worked downtown, the *Technique* reported, noting the significant gender change taking place. The Arcade, a new, three-story structure, faced Peachtree Street and nestled among several "skyscrapers." The Evening School remained there for three years, sharing the second floor with at least fifteen shops and other businesses. Accompanying this activity, railroad engines puffed smoke and soot and whistled nearby at the main station, but the school's next move in 1921 resulted from overcrowding, not noise and congestion. With enrollment up to 364, Dean Watters went to the Murphy building three blocks away at 18 Auburn Avenue and stayed until 1926.[17]

Like all institutions, the Evening School and Tech felt the influence of World War I, described by one scholar as a watershed in American higher education. It brought curricular innovations and staffing problems. But as students and faculty departed and enrollments declined during wartime, the Evening School remained stable primarily because of the concurrent gender upheaval. In Georgia, women's groups since the 1890s had been pressing for admittance to the Athens campus. Georgia women achieved partial success in 1916 when the legislature

7

opened UGA's graduate programs. The bar to female undergraduates collapsed during the war.[18]

Women began attending the Evening School in fall 1917. Despite declining male participation, total enrollment increased that year by forty percent, from 114 to 158. About thirty coeds could be counted, over twenty-six percent of the freshman class. By fall 1919, the Evening School's postwar student body virtually exploded, doubling to 310. About 190 others attended commerce classes on the Tech campus, putting the total enrollment at nearly 500. At the same time, only 101 took business classes in Athens, where wartime attendance dropped to sixty-six. President Matheson informed the trustees that the Evening School was "supplying a very real need" to Atlanta's working students. At the 1919 commencement, Annie Teitelbaum Wise, the fifty-five-year-old principal of Commercial High, became Tech's first woman graduate.[19] Now gender-integrated and recognized for its service, the Tech Evening School could face the postwar period with confidence and enthusiasm.

2

ESTABLISHING ROOTS: THE 1920s

Atlanta grew and prospered during the Roaring Twenties and so did the Evening School. At the beginning of the next decade, it found its first permanent home. When this unusual period in American history ended in Depression and despair, the Evening School, partly through the deft maneuvers of its director, George M. Sparks, managed to survive even without Tech's guidance and support. But as Sparks's ambitions collided with reality, and as the Evening School seemed to threaten the state's pre-eminent institution, the University of Georgia (UGA), new hostility arose more dangerous than earlier challenges.

As the Evening School prospered, Atlanta expanded both vertically and horizontally. Its fifteen railroad trunk lines handled local and regional raw materials, not to mention farm products. Three-fourths of America's textile output lay within an estimated twenty-four-hour radius. The railroads served local warehouses and industries manufacturing over 1,500 products while the city, lacking a large industrial sector, also began offering industrial services. Some twenty banks made Atlanta the nation's sixteenth largest financial center.[20]

Over 600 out-of-town businesses kept offices in Atlanta, and the Associated Press located its southern "crossroads center" there for news dissemination to major deep-South cities east of the Mississippi. Besides state and county governments, federal establishments—a penitentiary, veterans' hospital, Fort McPherson and a Federal Reserve branch—employed over 5,000. Migrants flocked in, many of them rural refugees from the boll weevil. Within ten years, the population increased three-and-a-half percent, to over 270,000. New structures valued at $27,081,541 paced the population growth, ranking Atlanta nineteenth in construction, but few edifices in an age of skyscrapers could be described as either tall or distinctive. One of the least attractive, the Bolling Jones garage, became the permanent home of the Evening School in 1946. With such an economic base, Atlanta business leaders shortly began moving toward a service economy.[21]

The urban environment also received improvement. By the end of the decade, new viaducts concealed the railroads, creating a downtown on two levels. At the top, a "skyway" for automobiles, with plazas, walkways, trees, and other plantings, hid commercial ugliness. Underneath, the tracks, original streets, storage areas, and storefronts carried on in a dim and semi-isolated world. Two blocks south, a new art deco city hall went up adjacent to more stately churches and the state Capitol. Atlanta boosters in the business community remained active. Spearheading a Forward Atlanta Movement (FAM) in 1925, the Chamber set out to promote growth. After spending nearly a million dollars on promotion, FAM four years later claimed 679 new businesses with payrolls above $30,000,000, new jobs for over 17,000, and a national profile for the Gate City.[22]

Meanwhile, the Junior Chamber secured a southern airmail route over Birmingham's fierce competition. Atlanta's Candler Field opened in 1929. With the central business district rising vertically, other forces—technology, electricity, highways, and trucks—stimulated horizontal spread as light industries sought cheaper land. This outward momentum included low-density housing with people moving beyond the city to new bungalow neighborhoods. Economic development and demographic

10

change inevitably boosted urban higher education. In the nation, youths began associating college with social and occupational mobility. Urban colleges located in cities with over 100,000 people enrolled over a third of the full-time undergraduates in 1924, and additional part-time students took night and extension courses. Nationally, commerce degrees increased from 1,397 in 1920 to 5,474 eight years later. In business administration, Tech's School of Commerce and the Evening School seemed to have a rosy future.[23]

In 1921 Tech's commerce school reached the academic mainstream by joining the fifteen already affiliated with the American Association of Collegiate Schools of Business (AACSB). Athens gained admittance five years later. The downtown Evening School benefited from Tech's umbrella of respectability, although its student body probably came less well prepared. In tandem, the city's public schools with few exceptions remained neglected and under-funded. With Atlanta per-capita wealth at least nine percent above the national average, its businesses continued to oppose tax increases even as accreditation was threatened. The state was stingier with its public colleges. Higher education often languished in a revenue system based on low property taxes, sales taxes on fuel oil, and auto license fees. Agricultural decline made matters worse. Private donations financed the several new Tech buildings.[24]

Despite such neglect, Tech attracted a diverse student body, while the Evening School primarily served local working high school graduates. Emory University's extension program, begun in 1919, focused mostly on teachers and others unable to attend campus classes. Its tuition, at $105 plus fees, surely dampened Emory's appeal to most Evening School clientele. As the Evening School's popularity in the postwar period grew, Georgia legislators made sure its recently enrolled coeds did not contaminate the Tech campus. A 1920 law legalized coeducation only at the downtown facility, though Tech continued to confer the degrees. Engineering may not have appealed to most women at the time,

11

but the law barred them from the four-year commerce program and, more significantly, from doing work in mathematics and the sciences. Thereafter, all references to coeds disappeared from official Tech publications, although the student yearbook, *Blue Print*; carried the names and pictures of most of the Evening School's graduating seniors. Women comprised twenty-six percent of the wartime Evening School freshman classes. Afterward, their proportion declined to seventeen percent until the Great Depression, when their numbers again equaled wartime proportions. Elsewhere in the Southeast, women comprised only ten percent of the commerce undergraduates.[25]

Evening School enrollment fluctuated in the 1920s but nearly doubled by 1932.

Evening School Enrollment (Selected Years, 1920–1932)

1920	364	1921	298	1923	452
1924	323	1926	480	1928	525
1929	614	1931	696	1932	716

The steady increase from 1926 to 1932 during prosperity and Depression defies analysis. Only a few Evening College coeds finished the bachelor of commercial science (B.C.S.) degree, although Atlanta led the South in providing female work opportunities. In an era relegating meaningful female activity to the home, job openings for college businesswomen at the supervisory or professional levels ordinarily did not exist except, perhaps, within a family business or through self-employment, nursing, or teaching. Businesses, of course, welcomed female clerks and typists, and so did commerce school males. The *Blue Print* noted that Lily Frieda Groble, the only woman in the 1925 senior class, served continuously as class secretary, held no higher office, and obligingly recorded the minutes of the Commerce Club.[26]

Only three women graduated between 1919, when Annie Teitelbaum Wise broke the gender barrier, and 1925. Elizabeth Baker, a B.C.S. in 1923, previously had attended three respected institutions. Baker, whose chief ambition, the yearbook reported, was "to keep someone's home budget," seemed to have a good understanding of her society and the job market. The three women graduating in 1926 comprised thirteen percent of that year's senior class. From then until 1934, when Tech ceased conferring Evening School degrees, an average of four women per year took the B.C.S. degree. All together, twenty-eight (eighteen percent) went through Tech's graduation ceremonies.[27]

Tech's and the Evening School's commerce seniors probably took considerable pride in their degrees, yet critics faulted the quality of the nation's commerce schools. By 1926, only thirty-eight of the nearly 200 institutions belonged to the AACSB, with nine from the Southeast. In this context, Tech's membership represented a significant accomplishment even though only four, usually combined, fields of specialization were available. The University of North Carolina offered thirteen. The discipline ranked below accepted arts and sciences standards. Even practitioners believed that too many courses in advertising watered down the curricula.[28] From this perspective, Tech's bachelor of science in commerce (B.S.C.) and the Evening School's bachelor of commercial science (B.C.S.), both accredited, seemed to provide their students with good preparation.

13

Of course, some students were interested in commerce for other reasons. Guided by their deans and coaches, young athletes flocked into the courses, causing Dean Watters to devote some time to sports. A baseball player was rejected twice by the Tech Executive Committee for unexplained and unexcused absences from the eligibility examinations. As Watters complained, barring this student from baseball angered "the friends of the School down town as well [as] in the night school body." The existence of downtown "friends" seemed to signal growing Evening School boosterism. Shortly thereafter, two friendly companies, Stone Baking and Retail Credit, established one-hundred-dollar, nonathletic scholarships.[29]

Atlanta businesses found additional reasons to support Tech's commerce schools. In 1921, the Tech faculty, on request of the Underwriters' Association and other downtown groups, authorized a course in life insurance salesmanship provided it remained self-sustaining. Dean Watters taught real estate in cooperation with Frank Adair, a prominent local realtor. The information came largely from the company's comprehensive files, the *Technique* reported, and company executives assisted in teaching the course. Watters reported that fifteen leading colleges considered using the course as a model, the first in the nation. Under Watters's direction, the commerce school also conducted marketing surveys for area businesses.[30] Such community service already had the flavor of an urban college.

John M. Watters, Dean 1918–1925.
Courtesy of GSU Archives.

Watters carried on a vigorous promotion campaign. Employers could reduce the costs of letter writing if their stenographers learned business English in class. For ladies who may "inherit financial responsibility," the Evening School offered a course in finance. A message to young men referred to "Atlanta's Greatest Product: TRAINED MANHOOD 'Made at Georgia Tech.'" In 1923, Watters placed the downtown curriculum "more directly under the supervision and control of the [campus] school." In action apparently aimed at nonmatriculating students, the Evening School began requiring four years of work. Watters may have toughened standards anticipating a four-year B.S.C. degree downtown, but his sudden departure ended that ambition. By one account, he fell victim to a 1925 coup partially engineered by a new faculty member, George M. Sparks. He also lacked a terminal degree. Watters left with many accomplishments, including enhanced academic standards that assured Tech's admittance to the American Association of Collegiate Schools of Business (AACSB) and national recognition of the real estate program. Coeducation, begun by Dean Wayne

Kell, went forward smoothly under Watters's stewardship. In addition, the downtown program operated profitably without Tech's financial support.[31]

An administrative reorganization placed Frederick B. Wenn as director of the Evening School. Other School of Commerce faculty shortly would assume leadership roles. Leonard R. Siebert, a 1921 UGA law graduate, joined the commerce school as instructor and taught at the Evening School until 1934, when he became secretary to the Board of Regents of the University System of Georgia. George M. Sparks, Tech's publicity director in 1924, soon was teaching downtown courses in news writing and journalism. Both men exerted significant influence over the Evening School and higher education in Georgia for over three decades. The 1925 reorganization gave the Evening School some financial independence and introduced profit sharing, with twenty percent going to the director and the rest to instructors based on teaching load. The reason for this arrangement remained unclear, although declining enrollments in the 1924 recession as well as Dean Watters's tougher academic standards may have alarmed Tech administrators.[32]

Director Wenn responded with a major recruiting campaign. Competition from Emory University's new downtown evening extension school also had to be considered until its 1932 closing. In August 1925, Wenn solicited students through school superintendents who might know of "one or more bright, energetic boys" unable to get a college education because of finances. His office could find good daytime jobs in downtown businesses with earnings above living expenses. Such recruitment became extremely important in establishing an increasingly wide-ranging and loyal constituency among students and their families. His successor, George Sparks, extended this network of contacts to the entire state. As enrollment leaped to 480 in 1926, this flood of new students strained the Auburn Avenue facilities. The next year the Evening School rented six rooms on the second

15

and third floors of a Forsyth building over space previously used by an undertaker.[33]

Meanwhile, a glowing *Technique* editorial signaled the rise and commanding presence of Associate Professor George M. Sparks. Described by a former colleague as younger looking than his thirty-nine years, "about six feet tall and a little slouchy, [with] rather a dark complexion, pudgy face and grey eyes," Sparks was a "delightful man, full of jokes," who projected "a nice, warm cordial look, very approachable." Less impressive, although acceptable during that era, were Sparks's academic credentials. Besides a Mercer University journalism degree, he listed graduate courses at Emory, Tech, and Oxford, England. Before joining Tech, he directed publicity and taught journalism at Mercer, and headed the journalism department at the small, denominational Tift College northwest of Macon. In 1926, he went on the Evening School's advisory committee and shortly replaced Fred Wenn as Evening School director.[34]

Sparks took an active interest in the students, sponsoring their publications and numerous organizations. Although the Tech campus offered a variety of activities, the Evening School, with limited physical facilities, had few amenities. Its commuting and mostly working students, who converged downtown to spend a few hours of their busy lives each week, came from a different kind of world, but some participated in the school's limited social outlets. The junior class organized the Banquet of the Year for the seniors, the freshman class had weekly luncheons, and the Owl Honorary Society sponsored various events.[35]

Evening School students also could participate in extracurricular activities at Tech, including the Commerce Club, which sponsored banquets with guest speakers. After one such event, the freshmen engaged in a balloon-blowing contest. The faculty's annual and jocular possum hunts, with hot dogs and Brunswick stew, included students. Evening School students also could join Tech's Ku Klux Klan, unwelcome to the administration, which was active during the late teens and twenties. Of course, growing Atlanta also offered numerous recreational outlets.[36]

If Dean Watters sought the four-year B.S.C. degree for downtown students, director Sparks promoted the liberal arts. "[I]mmediately we increased the number of courses from twenty-four to thirty for a degree," and the next year "from thirty to forty courses, the same as the other colleges." But his first report in 1929 focused mostly on finances. Net profits more than doubled, a bank surplus existed, and a faculty dividend was paid. Of course, delayed tuition payments and uncertain enrollment sometimes necessitated borrowing to pay rent and salaries. The fall 1928 student body, at 525, increased that winter to 614 despite a lack of advertising. Sparks thus saved $2,000 besides turning a bookstore deficit into a profit of $659 by keeping a close check on the bills payable to publishers. But he fretted over the $4,000 needed annually for rent and other expenses, which a move to the Tech campus would eliminate. When the school's lease next expired, Sparks decided to purchase downtown property.[37]

17

Although pleased with the students and the financial situation, Sparks confessed to having problems "[w]hile at Georgia Tech." "I was in constant conflict with the authorities" over advocating "general subjects for commerce students instead of higher mathematics and more accounting." Consequently, "several Georgia Tech faculty members put me down as being against higher standards" and "I was thought an academic outcast." While his reference to "general subjects" undoubtedly meant arts and sciences courses not required of engineers, his approach to education, according to a former colleague, contained other beliefs less typical of academia. In teaching, he stressed "arousement," meaning professors who could charm and impress the students. Having little interest in excellence or curriculum, he mainly wanted to find "what students took, what they wanted to take, and provide the need." In short, "he had no coherent philosophy of education" and "he rather detested faculty," particularly "[f]ull-time faculty."[38]

Sparks began displaying these attitudes shortly after becoming director. His "arousement" criteria found many Tech day school faculty as "not worthy teachers." Their ineptness "not only injures the Evening School but is a reflection on the name" of Georgia Tech, he wrote President Brittain. He wanted "all [Evening School] teachers selected because of their ability and not for their connection with the campus school." Nevertheless, Tech's commerce faculty was "far superior, on the average, to the part-time teachers" that Sparks "brought in rather large numbers." Sparks also was inconsistent. He "cut out" the "very popular" Fred Wenn, who preceded him as director.[39]

Such attitudes could have unfortunate implications. For one thing, Sparks failed to recognize that Georgia Tech's status as a fully accredited institution, with a reputable faculty, reflected positively on the Evening School. In fact, to Sparks's apparent chagrin, eighty percent of the downtown instructors continued to come from the Tech day school. The president, apparently unimpressed with Sparks's negative evaluations, later mandated the use of campus faculty.[40] Nevertheless, despite pedagogical and academic shortcomings, Sparks's popularity, business acumen, and political instincts rendered him well prepared for the economic hard times that arrived at the end of the 1920s.

18

3

ATLANTA AND THE EVENING SCHOOL FACE THE DEPRESSION

he days of glowing reports and optimism at the Evening School ended with the arrival of hard times. Plagued by miserly state support, Tech, by early 1930, felt the financial strain and warned against any future deficits. Yet the state auditor that June found the downtown Evening School profitable, with $1,500 available for distribution to the faculty. The downturn had not yet seriously damaged the nation's economy. Forecasters expected a recovery by summer. In this still-hopeful economic climate, director George Sparks began looking for a permanent Evening School home. Its rooms at 106 Forsyth Street were inadequate and the floors almost too rough to mop. Loose paper hung from the walls in "the most dingy circumstances any institution ever operated," one student remembered.[41]

In his search, Sparks got support from a coal merchant, Robert R. Johnson, and a realtor, Robin Adair. Johnson, described as

George M. Sparks, Director 1926–1955. Courtesy of GSU Archives.

(Right) Walton Building, or Sheltering Arms foundling home, Luckie and Walton Streets (1931). Courtesy of GSU Archives.

"the only businessman" ever to "step in and provide encouragement," found the school's quarters overcrowded, "unsanitary," and a serious fire hazard. The "wall board partitions" separating the classrooms rendered teaching "almost a physical impossibility." Indeed, "lives were in danger." The two men located a Walton Street building, once a foundling home called the Sheltering Arms. This large, thirty-year-old brick structure, once remodeled, contained adequate space. While appearing to be "of little value," it was well constructed with mostly "Long Leaf Yellow Pine" timber. The Marietta Street car line ran nearby. In May 1930, Adair personally took up a thirty-day option at a cash price $17,500 and pronounced it "a good buy."[42]

Johnson, as building committee chair, sought Tech President Marion Brittain's permission to solicit donations. He stressed the property's more central location for better student access and the high cost of rental property at $300 a month. Renovation was estimated at $10,000. Johnson expected local firms and individuals to provide free services and donate building materials.

Brittain quickly consented. The property "would give us the best Night School quarters we have ever had." Tech would control the project and direct the work. Solicitors could seek monetary donations, but he ruled out a newspaper campaign, preferring personal calls and correspondence for corporations, firms, and individuals.[43]

Throughout the hot summer of 1930, Sparks, his administrative assistant, Pearle Hartley, Johnson, and many others vigorously sought donations, but the deepening Depression made the task difficult. Other efforts, particularly for the needy, already had started, and penurious Atlantans that year ranked last in donating to social welfare. Johnson and Hartley went out almost daily "until late summer." Luncheons and special meetings targeted important individuals, especially those with student employees. Sparks also put students to work soliciting donations. One quit his employer who had huge hardware inventories but "gave not one thing." On the other hand, four employers created scholarships for "loyal" fundraising service.[44]

The renovation revealed a building well constructed and laid out for educational purposes. All floors had three thicknesses of wood with a hardwood top and heavy deadening felt in between. With ample classroom space, extra rooms could be leased by the entrepreneurial Sparks to produce more income. Johnson's participation continued indefinitely. In upcoming months, he became unofficial purchasing agent and bursar as solicitations continued. By May 1931, the building fund had $33,528 in pledges and donations in kind, although lagging pledge payments left a $6,500 debt. The Evening School's obligations amounted to $26,500, including the $17,500 original mortgage and an $8,500-note signed by Johnson to cover unpaid invoices. When completed, the nineteen-room property had an appraised replacement cost of $58,112 on a lot valued at $20,000, with school and coffee shop equipment worth $3,000, a total estimated value of $81,112.[45]

21

In a relatively modest community effort, few contributed large sums. Coca-Cola and Retail Credit were the only major corporate sponsors. Although individuals in banking, insurance, and law offices helped out, their firms donated nothing. Two people gave $2,000 and $1,000 each, but R. R. Johnson's pledge of $10,000 outmatched all others. Five years later, he paid off the School's $14,000 mortgage. Johnson estimated his total participation in money, services, and kind at about $40,000, contributions duly recognized at the building's dedication in May 1931. Its 1,000-person capacity should accommodate Atlanta's working students for several years, the *Constitution* predicted.[46]

The Depression tightened its grip. Construction, real estate, and retail businesses went into unprecedented bankruptcies. Many Atlantans defaulted on their taxes. The city itself ran out of money, and inevitable pay cuts followed. Atlanta, like Detroit, reimbursed its employees and teachers with scrip to avoid bankruptcy, but nearly every business either refused such "money" or discounted it. Yet the wealthy elite and the Chamber remained optimistic. After all, in 1930 the department stores made a profit. The next year, 131 new firms arrived, while retail sales and employment increased. Partly through mergers and acquisitions, all city banks survived even as some forty-eight statewide went under. The Chamber tried to fight unemployment with a back-to-the-farm movement, and a few hundred whites *did* leave before the funds ran out on this largely futile effort. Meanwhile, prohibitionists, religious groups, and elements of organized labor who opposed ending the ban on alcoholic beverages waged a failed campaign to remove Atlanta's "wet" mayor, James L. Key, a misguided effort that undoubtedly diverted attention and energy from the city's real problems.[47]

Seeking scapegoats, some targeted gender and race. The legislature tried to ban females from night textile jobs. A board of education proposal to hire only men and prevent female teachers from marrying found little support. The American Black Shirts, with ties to the Ku Klux Klan, conducted noisy demonstrations for "white" jobs. They undoubtedly frightened off some black hotel workers, but business recoiled at the negative image. The organization collapsed in fall 1930. The sizeable gap between the numerous poor and the affluent few drastically widened. The 12,000 jobless registered in February 1932 was expected to number 20,000 within two months, with an estimated twenty-five to thirty percent of white Atlantans unemployed. Yet these numbers paled beside black joblessness, with three-quarters out of work. Private charities could not deal with such need. An alarming increase in crime marked Atlanta as the nation's murder and robbery capital.[48]

By fall 1930, director Sparks grew increasingly alarmed as conditions deteriorated. After paying the first quarter bills, he came up $600 short, partly because hard-pressed students had been slow to pay off their notes. Then the faculty corporate board increased instructor salaries about fifteen percent while the school made a $500 advance for the building campaign. "[T]he faculty—acting in the capacity of a democracy—does the expending," Sparks fumed. This ill-conceived action probably soured him permanently on faculty governance, and he asked President Brittain to appoint "an advisory committee of four" to study finances and "Evening School affairs."[49]

23

Brittain dissolved the corporate faculty and established a written structure specifically regulating the downtown branch. Academic activity would be guided by the Council of the General Faculty, which oversaw all Tech departments. As Sparks requested, an advisory committee of four faculty members would make policy recommendations. Other restrictions were more sweeping. The Southern Association of Colleges and American Association of Collegiate Schools of Business admission require-ments, prescribed courses, class sizes, and standards became mandatory, and campus regulations guided downtown examina-tions, credits, absences, and standing. Sparks surely bristled at such oversight and the pressure to utilize the regular day school faculty "with necessary aid by outsiders." But the plan kept the

Evening School securely under Tech's umbrella of academic respectability, which included SAC accreditation, AACSB membership, and Tech's affiliation with the prestigious American Association of Universities.[50]

The new faculty advisory committee immediately trimmed the 1931 winter quarter budget, and its members accepted extra compensated duties, such as building supervision, bookstore and coffee shop management, and enforcement of class attendance. Students arrived in larger numbers despite the Depression, undoubtedly stimulated by Atlanta's continuing growth, making it the South's third largest city after New Orleans and Louisville. In fall 1930, 652 took courses, only slightly below the previous year. That winter the Evening School offered twelve new courses, including radio advertising and Sparks's Writing for Profit. Only New York University offered work in radio, the *Technique* reported, while Writing for Profit was said to be unique in the nation. With the Evening School settled in the Luckie Walton building, fall enrollment reached nearly 700, the largest ever. Such expansion apparently convinced Tech's trustees that the Evening School's supervision had become a full-time job, and they relieved the director of all campus duties.[51]

The year 1931 ended with the School's finances in good shape despite the Depression. In the two-year period that had just ended, with annual tuition income exceeding $24,000, a small surplus existed even after office staff raises. Sparks particularly liked having the faculty excluded from budget making, and he urged Brittain to continue with the present plan of organization. But the badly needed academic discipline the president's plan imposed shortly disappeared. The creation of the University System of Georgia (USG) in 1931 ended Tech's tutelage and put the Evening School directly under a chancellor and the Board of Regents. Sparks's spring annual report expressed great optimism. The books balanced, the teaching program and curriculum would be enlarged, and the Evening School had been "standardized" to place it "on the same hour basis of other [system]

24

institutions." Intensified recruitment raised spring enrollment to 716, while "[c]areful buying" brought savings. But a new theme appeared that Sparks thrice reiterated: the Evening School operated "without cost to the state."[52] True at that time, it undoubtedly reassured budget-conscious regents and legislators.

Of course, survival also depended upon the Atlanta community. The fundraising drive had generated publicity and aroused support among business leaders. The acquisition of the Walton Street domicile planted deeper roots. Praise also came from local higher education leaders. "This Evening School is doing an excellent service among the under-privileged young men and women of Atlanta who have not been able to attend the regular institutions," wrote Agnes Scott College President John McCain to the Carnegie Corporation in support of a grant application. "It has the esteem and confidence of the business people of the city, and also of the colleges and universities."[53]

Some students might have taken exception to the patronizing tone, but Emory officials also took Evening School seriously after closing its own downtown campus. The registrar requested "an exact statement" and description of Evening School courses "in order that I may determine their acceptability toward a degree at Emory University." A number of Emory applicants wished to enroll there and transfer later.[54] Such confidence should have spurred Sparks, once removed from Tech's oversight, to stress standards and quality. That a different outcome ultimately occurred resulted from complex developments that followed the Evening School's semi-independent existence in the new university system.

4

ATLANTA, THE EVENING SCHOOL, AND THE UNIVERSITY SYSTEM OF GEORGIA

Despite the Depression, Evening School enrollment increased in 1932, and the school's financial situation eased. With the new building, paying rent ended. Significantly, the Evening School shared Georgia Tech's academic assets, including regional and national accreditation, a respectable faculty, and an adequate campus library. Had this arrangement continued, Tech conceivably could have become a multipurpose university despite its original narrower focus on engineering and science. In the teens and twenties, it had developed important ties with Atlanta's business community through the Evening and Commerce schools. In wartime and peacetime, Tech even had adjusted to coeducation downtown.

But the Evening School's prospects changed in 1932 after the state created the University System of Georgia (USG) to save money and streamline higher education, placing the public colleges under a twelve-member board of regents. In organizing the new system, the regents called on the General Education Board (GEB), which donated $20,000 for a statewide study. The GEB, funded in 1902 with a million dollars from John D. Rockefeller, earlier had made small matching grants to Tech ($50,000) and the University of Georgia ($100,000), paltry sums compared with some $60,000,000 bestowed mostly on elite, private institutions. This largesse gave the GEB considerable leverage in shaping higher education policy.[55]

The GEB viewed the plethora of inherited nineteenth century colleges as burdensome. Weaker ones should be eliminated so that the fittest survivors could achieve the "highest quality." Over the years the GEB encouraged this sorting-out process through carefully directed philanthropy. GEB goals surely were familiar to the experts chosen to study the new Georgia system. To direct the survey, Chancellor Charles M. Snelling tapped the University of Chicago's George A. Works perhaps because of his earlier, GEB-financed survey in North Carolina. His team included two education deans from Chicago and New York universities along with the presidents of three Midwestern public institutions.[56]

Works vowed to "look at the situation from the viewpoint of the state as a whole," because "at times the ambitions of communities have superseded the broader interests of the state" and change must take place. The team also would "look into the future" for achievable goals while remaining mindful of "the presence of privately supported institutions." In this context, the system should avoid "unnecessary duplication of specialized forms of education for which the need is limited." When the team began the task in May 1932, Georgia's population, at 2,908,506, was over thirty percent urbanized, but the cities harbored few of the twenty-five public colleges. Athens, a small city, laid claim to three: the University of Georgia (UGA), a state teachers college, and the College of Agriculture, whose access to federal funding bestowed unusual prestige. Scattered among Georgia's towns and communities were agricultural and mechanical schools, experiment stations, and teachers and junior colleges. A few ran local high schools at state expense.[57]

Although Savannah and Albany each had a state college, only African Americans attended, illustrating how racial segregation penalized whites as well as blacks. Columbus and Macon lacked any public colleges. Augusta had the medical school. Atlanta's Georgia Tech offered engineering, the sciences, and mathematics along with a commerce school.[58] The system displayed the kind of wasteful proliferation the GEB opposed. At the same time, Atlanta's Caucasian high school graduates and younger working adults, when lacking affluence, had no local access to state-supported liberal arts, education, and nursing, and for women, mathematics, the sciences, and engineering offered at Tech.

Before 1932 the public colleges theoretically operated as UGA branches, a fiction since separate trustees and administrators actually governed them. The act of 1931 centralized the system under regents appointed by the governor for staggered terms with senate confirmation. Works criticized that arrangement for having only one at-large regent. The others resided in congressional districts, and the governor served ex-officio. Districted regents might develop biases, and the governor's presence was undesirable and unprecedented, Works scolded. Nevertheless, that set-up prevailed and even survived later gubernatorial interference that threatened the system's accreditation. Works *did* succeed in persuading the legislature to surrender its veto over college closings and cease appropriating for individual institutions.[59]

29

The Works *Report*, released in late 1932, called for drastic retrenchment and consolidation, weeding out weaker institutions. Works would terminate advanced undergraduate programs in four of the seven senior colleges, turn over eight state junior colleges to local officials, discontinue Augusta's medical college and Athens's veterinary school, consolidate Tech's school of commerce in Athens, phase out Athens's engineering department, and place Tech's Evening School under the chancellor along with the Division of Adult Education-General Extension, to be moved from Athens to Atlanta.[60]

Probably the most difficult decision involved the disposition of Tech's commerce program and its Evening School, complicated by fierce Tech and UGA rivalry. Georgia's population neither needed nor could it support two schools of commerce at that stage of industrial development, New York University's Dean W. H. Spencer concluded. Yet the decision bothered Spencer because "no perfect solution" existed. Nevertheless, he selected Athens as the best location and then seemingly contrived justifications, the foremost being the symbiotic relationship between a commerce school and an economics department. Commerce at Tech, without economics and the other social sciences, might "develop into a narrowly vocational trade school." Spencer acknowledged a large city's importance to a commerce school, yet many business schools, unidentified, successfully operated in small cities.[61]

Spencer found ready, if simplistic, solutions for Tech's abandoned commerce students. The engineers could pick up business courses at the Evening School, "which should, of course, remain in Atlanta," and downtown students could take technical courses on the Tech campus, although few had done so. While mentioning daytime classes as an Evening School possibility for "the large number of" Atlanta students, "more and more of these…will go to Athens, which after all is not very far away." Then, too, "Emory University now provides training in business…for students who cannot leave the city." Perhaps influenced by Sparks, Spencer still envisioned the future Evening School as "the nucleus" for "a real center of adult education" offering many fields besides business. In fact, masters work "would be entirely appropriate."[62] Significantly, while cutting the Tech umbilical cord, none of the experts apparently foresaw accreditation problems for the Evening School. Spencer's contribution to the Works *Report* compromised its credibility. That the Works team, all of whom functioned in urban environments, embraced all of Works's findings was astounding. The *Report* influenced public higher education in Atlanta in a negative way

30

for over two decades. Nor did it fulfill its promise to serve all the citizens and the "broader interests of the state."

While Works's focus on Athens surely pleased the regents and the GEB, numerous conditions supported Tech's claims to commerce. It was centrally located in a major urban area that needed more business proprietors, officials, executives, and managers. Between 1919 and 1935, attendance at Southeastern commerce schools increased over 500 percent. During the same period, business colleges in the Southeast, with twenty percent of the nation's population, granted fewer than ten percent of the degrees.[63] Atlanta's growth outran the Depression, generating jobs and attracting regional migrants. Hundreds of state employees worked in the capital, with thousands more at federal installations, local governments, and the businesses continuously attracted to Atlanta. Besides new high school graduates, the hundreds of others needing degrees and specialized college training could not travel to Athens, and Atlanta's two elite private colleges posed both entrance and tuition barriers. Of the system's three surviving senior colleges, two were specialized: Tech in engineering and the Georgia State College for Women (GSCW) in teacher training. Young people of both genders faced barriers in the arts and sciences, commerce, and education except in Athens. Living there involved additional costs, and commuting was impractical despite Spencer's belief that UGA was "not very far away." The vast majority of white Atlantans and Georgians were left out.

Despite the *Reports*'s shortcomings, George Sparks could not have been more pleased, because it freed him from Tech's supervision. In fact, the engaging and persuasive director, who met Works team members as they visited the Evening School, interviewed the staff, and attended class sessions, probably influenced the outcome. He later boasted of "having furnished the study group with much information which others wished to cover up." Sparks told Dean Spencer about his own plans to turn the Evening School into a four-year institution offering graduate

31

degrees. Later, as Sparks launched an ambitious program of expansion, he repeatedly cited Spencer's seemingly mimicking recommendations as the authority for "enlarging the field of education for the Evening School."[64]

The regents concurred with most of Works's advice. Indeed, the *Report* affirmed changes some of them already contemplated. They reduced the number of public colleges from twenty-five to fifteen with only three surviving senior institutions, but intense political pressure saved the medical college in Augusta. In April 1933, the regents transferred Tech's commerce school to Athens and assigned the Evening School to the Adult Education Center, placed it under the chancellor, and named it the University System of Georgia Evening School (USGES). At the same time, UGA received assurance of its pre-eminence when regent Sandy Beaver, chair of the education committee, announced that junior colleges would feed students into the senior institutions. Of course, "Athens should supply everything in the liberal arts beyond the high school." Beaver's pronouncement became system policy. Two years later, regent Marion Smith warned system units to stay "within their appropriate field of activity," although UGA's field "is the whole state."[65]

Closing Tech's commerce school did not go unchallenged. Protests came from the Atlanta community, including an Atlanta Advertising Club resolution informing the regents that Atlanta's citizens as well as the state's taxpayers sustained the commerce school with money and effort. Its removal handicapped hundreds of "young men" in Atlanta and Georgia. President Brittain rejected the regents' financial arguments and publicly objected to Tech's increasing subservience to the Athens university. For a while, Tech's commerce program continued while grandfathered students finished their degrees, but the loss was serious. Commerce's 447 students made up nearly fifteen percent of the 1933 campus enrollment, not to mention the 716 at the Evening School, together nearly a third of the total student body. Considering commerce's popularity among the athletes, the damage to Tech's sports program surely compounded the bitterness.[66]

Protesters formed a students justice committee and distributed a flyer entitled "Ten Reasons Why the Board of Regents Should Not Abolish the School of Commerce at Georgia Tech." The tract concentrated on Atlanta as the "logical place for a Commerce School." This "commercial center of the South," with "well-equipped libraries," offered "a fertile field for business research." Because of Atlanta's size, "Many boys pay their way through by securing work," and fifty-three percent of them (238 students) "are Atlanta boys." Such opportunities were unavailable "in a smaller city." At "great cost" these students would "be forced to leave home" or "attend Emory," where tuition doubled Tech's. Not only that, Emory operated without American Association of Collegiate Schools of Business (AACSB) accreditation. Certain that both the regents and Works lacked all of the facts, the committee asked for reconsideration.[67] On this matter, the students in many ways provided better arguments and more realism than did the experts. Their request went unheeded, but the president bided his time. The following year, after the Southern Association of Colleges challenged the Evening School's accreditation, Brittain made a final bid to take it back.

The significance of these events may have escaped the notice of most Atlantans mired in Depression and economic despair. Henceforth, Georgia Tech kept its focus narrowly on engineering and the sciences. At the same time, the ambitious George Sparks pursued his dream of immediately expanding the now academically isolated and unaccredited Evening School into a four-year state college with graduate programs.

33

5

WHITHER THE SYSTEM EVENING SCHOOL?

Before the University System of Georgia (USG) organized in 1932, and months ahead of the Works Report, director George Sparks took steps to expand the Evening School. In December 1931, he asked Tech President Marion Brittain to approve downtown graduate work in commerce. Considering the absence of that degree at Tech and the Evening School's own lack of a four-year undergraduate program, Brittain probably ignored this bold and unrealistic proposal. Nevertheless, with the university system functioning, Sparks got Chancellor Charles M. Snelling's blessing. The director also "constantly contacted [University of Georgia commerce Dean] R. P. Brooks" to work out a cooperative plan "toward giving graduate work." Brooks expressed great interest "from the beginning," Sparks claimed, especially since Atlanta provided better opportunities "for business research" than Athens's "limited library facilities."[68]

Chancellor Snelling shortly arranged for Brooks and the Evening School's advisory committee to meet in Atlanta. They "went into all particulars as to hours, schedules and general content of courses," satisfying Brooks that "the work was on a par with" the University of Georgia (UGA) and "transferable." The group approved three four-year Evening School degrees, the A.B. and B.S. in arts and sciences and the bachelor of science in commerce (B.S.C.). Working through Chancellor Snelling, and apparently without regents' participation, Sparks engineered a major educational coup. Although the Tech faculty shortly vetoed the downtown B.S.C. degree, Sparks got this decision reversed.[69]

The aging chancellor, previously the UGA president, retired in 1933 to become director of the General Extension Division recently transferred from Athens. In this new assignment, Snelling took office space in the Walton building. Before stepping down, Snelling conferred with "the then-to-be-Chancellor Philip Weltner" and regents secretary-treasurer Earle M. Cooke. The three assured Sparks that the Evening School, though severed from Tech, would "continue to give degrees." In this way the chancellor-designate became apprized of Sparks's expansion activities but seemed to be unaware as to details.[70]

The university system immediately faced difficulties. By spring 1933, with state finances in desperate shape, regents chairman Hughes Spalding could give no assurance on faculty retention or salary payments. Although the self-sustaining Evening School expected no funding, Spalding's order barred the director from paying his teachers unless "the money is available." Nevertheless, Sparks optimistically believed money would come "from slow-moving notes the students have signed" or through "some adjustment in the matter of commodities paid" by them. For a time, most taught without compensation. In the meantime, the director, by one account, borrowed on his life insurance to cover "out-of-pocket expenses like heat and light."[71]

Despite money shortages, the director continued his expansion plans. Upon learning that Works had recommended separating the Evening School from Tech, Sparks persuaded his new colleague, former Chancellor Snelling, to convene still another meeting with Dean Brooks that fall at Snelling's Athens home where they discussed curriculum changes and graduate work, Sparks reported. Dean Brooks previously "had a schedule of courses for the Evening School approved" by the UGA faculty. Before adjourning, they endorsed the overall proposal to enlarge the Evening School. In the face of regents financial restrictions, Sparks still increased the teaching staff "from two Doctors of Philosophy to six." All other faculty had master's degrees except three in the advertising field, he reported, although most must have been part-timers. According to the *Evening Signal*, Sparks also persuaded Brooks to teach a senior and graduate course in higher economics in Atlanta.[72]

By fall 1933, Chancellor Weltner, apparently harboring doubts about the new program, appointed a study committee headed by UGA professor G. H. Bogg. Obviously alarmed, director Sparks on October 1 made an astonishing press announcement, seemingly to pre-empt the Bogg group. In the system reorganization the Evening School became a fully accredited "separate institution" offering courses during four quarters. Sparks enrolled students that very fall and confidently told the *Atlanta Constitution* to expect the largest enrollment in the school's history. The only authority for such expansion apparently was the approval of an aging former chancellor, the concurrence of an ad hoc committee of Sparks's own choosing, and the earlier verbal assent of a designated chancellor. Nevertheless, that December, Sparks repeated similar claims to the Associated Press despite a Bogg committee report recommending much more restricted University System of Georgia Evening School (USGES) functions.[73]

In mid-October, the Bogg committee expressed grave reservations and suggested a much more restricted graduate program. Atlanta should offer only three courses for credit, just one-third of the program, to be approved by the Athens graduate council. A thesis written in Atlanta counted as a course. Acceptance into the program did not include admittance to candidacy for the degree. Permitting such work at the USGES would be "a new departure in education," the committee warned. Experimenting could be costly to the whole system "if a mistake is made." That the USGES had too few students for a regular college division would weaken graduate programs at UGA and Tech. Standards

37

and quality also were a concern. While promising to study the situation, the committee rejected the USGES's bid for graduate degrees.[74] Nevertheless, by announcing and boldly launching his own program, Sparks already seemed to have carried the day.

The Southern Association of Colleges (SAC), alerted to possible problems in the system's General Extension Division by Agnes Scott President John McCain, became exceedingly "disturbed" about the whole Atlanta operation. The extension division remained "entirely independent" and was "not attached to any institution in your system." No unit "feels any responsibility for keeping up its standards." Its lack of a faculty to stand "behind the quality of the credits offered" placed in doubt the transfer of its degree credits. In effect, the accreditation of the university system, itself, could be threatened. SAC suggested attaching the unit either to UGA or Tech "so as to have supervision and responsibility."[75]

In increasingly contentious correspondence with SAC executive secretary M. L. Huntley, Chancellor Weltner expressed shock, and his "first inclination was to 'fly off the handle.'" Certain that Huntley had "no thought of forcing our extension into an academic straightjacket," he solicited suggestions for improvement. But Huntley's reply requesting "as much information as possible" and his inquiry about the chancellor's attitude on the matter further irritated Weltner. The new setup was not "something blowing in the wind." It had been organized by a former chancellor who now oversaw its operations. The Evening School's longtime director supervised the "resident instruction" with "practically the same [Tech] faculty." Weltner urged SAC officials to visit the extension center and find out for themselves.[76]

SAC's skepticism may have surprised director Sparks, inexperienced both as an academician and academic administrator but enthusiastic about educating young people. Realistically, transforming his small off-campus Evening School, staffed primarily by part-time faculty, without library, laboratories, and state funding, into a fully accredited, four-year and graduate state college was virtually impossible. Yet seizing on vague statements in the Works *Report*, encouraged unduly by an Athens commerce dean, and unrestrained by two chancellors, Sparks hastily enrolled students in the Bachelor of Science in Commerce (B.S.C.), previously given only on the Tech campus, and the Master of Science in Commerce. In spring 1934, the USGES had 650 undergraduates, twenty-five others seeking the Masters, and seventy-five graduates of other colleges. Seniors graduated in June 1935 without challenges, but when a master's candidate completed the requirements, the USGES still lacked authority to grant the degree. In seeking the chancellor's permission, USGES authorities weakly cited their belief that the school had degree-granting power when the student registered. Reluctantly, the chancellor concluded "that less [sic] complications will arise by letting the Evening School confer the degree." That Athens's powerful and independent agricultural college also had been granting UGA diplomas may have suggested leniency.[77] Despite concerns over standards and oversight, the whole USGES program still was a startling achievement. Certainly Sparks, an avid educational entrepreneur, at least recognized Atlanta's higher education needs better than the experts, and the enrollment figures seemed to prove it.

Once challenged, director Sparks began seeking examples and preparing arguments to justify his actions. Foremost was the University of Oregon's Portland General Extension, with twenty-four departments offering about 100 classes late afternoons, evenings, and Saturdays for "bread winning, home making" persons who "cannot attend college." Both undergraduate and graduate students earned "residence credit" at the other state colleges. At the private Northwestern University Center in downtown Chicago, students received "full residence for the University proper, which is at Evanston. This seems to clear the way for our project." He held that students taking all their

39

courses in Atlanta should graduate there as if they had attended UGA, Tech, or the Georgia State College for Women (GSCW).[78]

As the controversy over the USGES's legitimacy continued, Chancellor Weltner appointed a degree advisory council chaired by UGA's Dean Brooks. The group rendered a "Unanimous— NO" to separate USGES degrees. At the same time, they sought to bolster the USGES's academic status by setting up an outside advisory council appointed from the faculties of the senior colleges. It would approve faculty, courses, student workloads, teaching loads, textbooks, and standardized examinations. With course uniformity seemingly assured, the Brooks committee recommended that students taking USGES courses of comparable quality receive diplomas issued by UGA, Tech, or GSCW. Sparks surely favored granting the diplomas but disdained the outside supervision. The *Evening Signal* shortly reported that "you may do your college work at the Evening College and receive a degree" from any of Georgia's four-year colleges.[79]

That these recommendations received immediate approval from the senior colleges illustrated the general confusion about accreditation standards. Tech president Brittain thought the proposal resolved a "difficult situation very well." The University of Georgia's S. V. Sanford concurred while mentioning "further details to be worked out" confidentially. If our faculties "had more confidence" in the Evening College leadership, he wrote the chancellor, "your problems would" be easier to solve. The USGES "seems to be conducted for money" rather than "collegiate standards," a belief also held at Emory and Agnes Scott. Sanford suggested fixing executive staff salaries "independent of fees" to "remove the stigma that students" passed so that faculty could be paid.[80]

In late June, when the Brooks advisory council met to oversee the USGES's operations, they approved the director's faculty appointments and course offerings, and reviewed student coarse loads. Satisfied that standards had been maintained, they authorized, pending later SAC approval, the USGES's own bachelor of science in commerce (B.S.C.) diploma for four years of work. That students transferring to the USGES with nine courses in residence credit from any system or non-system colleges could receive their diplomas from the original institution received a SAC veto.[81]

With USGES status now in doubt, Tech launched a determined campaign that summer to regain control, with the chancellor's strong support. Director Sparks moved vigorously to stop it, but he shortly discovered that "getting Tech out of the way was not as hard as trying to get by Weltner." Thus he carefully operated surreptitiously. "Personally, I would like to be an unknown in this controversy," he wrote former regent Hughes Spalding, because of "severe attacks" over his contacts with the Works "survey group." That July Sparks hastily visited several Midwestern urban colleges seeking "expert advice...in favor of the downtown location." On his return, he prepared a six-page polemic, "Academic and Economic Reasons Why the University System Evening School Should be Located in Downtown Atlanta," and circulated it cautiously. It lauded Works for separating Tech and the Evening School, whose "fine financial reports" justified the decision.[82]

41

Although Sparks earlier had favored moving to the Tech campus to save rental money, he now stressed the downtown location. The University of Chicago, only fifteen minutes, and Northwestern, twenty minutes away, both placed their evening schools in "the center of the big city," as did the state of Wisconsin in Milwaukee. The USGES also had working students with "little time to get" to their classes with the "big financial burden" involving "two car-fares." A move to Tech might lower enrollment, now up by sixty percent to 853. The extension division's 350 students also would suffer by perhaps a fifty percent decline. Furthermore, the Walton building was "on the way from the employment address of more than 80% of the students" and a two-block walk to Atlanta's Carnegie Library, better "than any [system] library."[83]

In a meaner spirit, Sparks suggested ethical lapses and even corruption in Tech's administration of the Evening School. President Brittain permitted "faculty members to 'divide the spoils'" from tuition payments, with individual bonuses "as much as $600," instead of using the funds to benefit the school. For ten years they remained downtown and annually paid out $5,000 when Tech classrooms were available "without cost." At the same time, Sparks claimed wholehearted faculty support at the USGES, UGA, and Tech, because the declining enrollments would adversely affect their salaries and the "additional money" earned from "Adult Education."[84] Sparks seemed unaware that tarring the Tech administration with corruption undermined the logic of his position, while his previous personal participation in the so-called "spoils" and his gross exaggeration of the downtown rental costs opened up questions of his own integrity and veracity.

Working behind the chancellor's back, Sparks set out to influence the regents, detailed in his letters to Charles Snelling. Regent Sandy Beaver was one of his first contacts. Arriving unannounced at Beaver's Gainesville home some fifty miles northeast of Atlanta, Sparks found him "in the bath tub." Receiving a cordial welcome thirty minutes later, Sparks persuaded Beaver, who expected the USGES would "go to the Tech campus," to change his mind. "After a few pleasantries, about…seeing him years ago [at UGA] as the best first baseman in college baseball," Sparks "got in my story about keeping" the Evening School "down town."[85]

President Brittain, a worthy opponent, justly proud of Tech's accomplishments and still smarting over the loss of commerce to Athens, feared that other departments, such as architecture, might also be taken. Had a "just share" of Tech graduates served as regents, he told the 1933 alumni homecoming, the commerce school's transfer never would have occurred. Politically astute on several governmental levels, Brittain during years of service in the Georgia educational establishment could count large

42

numbers of influential friends. He believed that the commerce school would be brought back.[86]

But Sparks kept busy. Besides regent Beaver, he could count on strong support from Spalding, who also was showered with flattery. Spalding already agreed with Sparks and penned his own reasons for opposing the move in a letter to the chancellor. For one thing, he feared the USGES's large enrollment of women would bring coeducation "which is not appropriate at a technological school." In addition, an evening school located there would soon overshadow technology.[87] Spalding totally missed the point his argument unwittingly made. If increasing enrollments in a Tech Evening School could substantially alter the institute's orientation, a huge demand for a public-supported, general college in Atlanta surely existed.

The regents would decide the issue following an education committee hearing. Meanwhile, Sparks and Beaver made sure that various influential people contacted the regents for support. A regents office insider even let Sparks see Brittain's and Tech Dean Cherry Emerson's "letters of recommendation," which left Sparks unimpressed. "With such slim arguments," he told Snelling, "it is no wonder we won." During the hearing, Beaver "did everything he should have done," even prompting Sparks to "bring out all the points" during his presentation. But Beaver unwittingly revealed that he and Sparks had met prior to the committee meeting. "I don't know how Weltner is going to feel about this point," Sparks confessed. Of course, Sparks and his allies had totally undermined the chancellor. "In some way," Sparks related, "Beaver got hold of" Spalding's letter to Weltner strongly opposing Tech's claims and embarrassed the chancellor by insisting it be read "aloud to the committee."[88]

The victory came so easily that it made the director uncomfortable, but there was little need to worry. A satisfied Spalding later informed Snelling that "a definite and final decision" had been made locating the Evening School downtown. As an afterthought, Spalding mentioned that "I am going to Athens with

43

Jack [his son], and am entering him at the University, where I wish him to complete his Arts course." Spalding, a prominent and certainly public-spirited citizen, probably would not have grasped the irony. Other talented but working young people, lacking family backing and resources, and unable to leave their jobs, could not take advantage of such opportunities.[89]

Sparks's victory had significant consequences for higher education both in Atlanta and the state. Although it served Sparks's personal ambitions and also his mission to make higher education available to working young people and provide a service to Atlanta businesses, the USGES went under a cloud of academic uncertainty when SAC shortly threatened to decertify the entire university system.[90]

6

GEORGIA POLITICS, THE NEW DEAL, ATLANTA, AND THE USGES

While director George Sparks expanded the University System of Georgia Evening School (USGES) and fought off Tech, Atlanta began a slow economic revival stimulated by several New Deal programs. In May 1933, the Federal Emergency Relief Administration (FERA) began providing work for the unskilled and direct relief for the needy. By fall, the Civil Works Administration (CWA) had created 10,000 more jobs mostly repairing and restoring buildings, including $11,000 for Georgia Tech. City planners, encouraged by the Public Works Administration (PWA), prepared a "dream list" of new construction projects, including sewers, a jail, and an auditorium. By 1934, the Atlanta sewer system was the largest project in the state.[91]

Although Atlanta's economy did not "bottom out" until 1935, the New Deal stimulus in some sectors seemed to bring immediate change. In spring 1933, retail and wholesale trade increased. Two years later the Works Progress Administration (WPA) took over unfinished federal projects and started new ones, including school improvements and highway, airport, and stadium construction. Atlanta's public schools still remained under-funded, but tuition aid for needy college students was available through the National Youth Administration (NYA).[92]

By spring 1936, Atlanta had recovered from the worst of the Depression as retail sales and bank clearings returned to pre-Depression levels. The effects of the airplane and the automobile were particularly noticeable. Air traffic made the city a point of transfer between Miami and New York and assured its place as the economic capital of the Southeast. Stimulated by government airmail contracts, Candler Field developed as a major hub for Delta Airline's east-west routes and for Eastern's north-south connections, advancing Atlanta to third place behind New York and Chicago. Increasing vehicular registrations stimulated the development of neighborhood shopping centers.[93]

On the down side, private real estate and construction remained weak. Owners concentrated on renovations and additions rather than new projects. Investors who poured millions into Atlanta's 1920s-era skyscrapers built only the two-story art deco Olympia building on Peachtree Street. But manufacturing went through significant change. Coca-Cola began replacing cotton textiles even as Georgia's and the South's massive textile strike in 1934 dramatized that industry's decline. Atlanta moved out of the Depression with an increasingly diversified economy and as the Southeast's financial center and transportation hub.[94]

The New Deal's emphasis on construction and renovation boded well for the university system. With the Evening School's Walton building barely adequate, larger quarters had to be found. The chancellor and regents also wanted office space there. Months before the regents endorsed the Works recommendations in spring 1933, director Sparks with the chancellor's blessings began searching for more space. He hoped to trade the Walton property or sell it to pay off "the [$17,000] loan," and avoid upkeep and "probable renovation for new tenants." In a budget justifying the move, he projected $15,000 in University System of Georgia Evening School (USGES) income, the bulk being $9,000 from tuition. Bookstore profits of $2,000 and the coffee shop's $1,500 would be supplemented by rent of the building's extra space: $1,000 for the garage underneath, $800 from the Southern School of Pharmacy lease, and $600 for use of the assembly hall for dances.[95] The plan illustrated the director's extraordinary talent in handling the school's finances.

By November 1933, federal help seemed within reach. System officials learned they could apply to the PWA for $3,200,000. If approved, the Evening School could expect $15,000 for repairs and eligibility for a $358,435 loan to finance a new building. Considering the $882,400 earmarked for the University of Georgia (UGA) and $677,000 for Tech, the allocation seemed generous. Easy approval came from local federal officials, and regents committees made three trips to Washington. Telegram notification in December confirmed the approval of $3,570,000 in PWA funds. Sparks quickly produced a new budget showing that the USGES could meet the estimated $17,165 in annual payments on a $358,435 loan and still end up with a surplus of over $4,600. By May, the *Signal* cited an Associated Press release that the school would be centrally located one block from the Henry Grady Hotel. Work could begin when the regents approved the contract, although the total PWA system loan had been trimmed. That December, the school paper announced the signing of the architect's contract.[96] .

Serious problems were on the horizon, however. The PWA needed a nationally recognized bond counsel's assurance that the regents had the power to borrow money and issue bonds as security for the federal loan. Affirmation by the Georgia Supreme Court late in 1934 led the regents to approve the PWA contract. The loan and grant would give "new life to the University System," they announced. But a political minefield lay ahead. Governor Eugene Talmadge, denied federal patronage appointments and control of the funds, became an implacable New Deal foe. Unable to dissuade the regents, many of them his own appointees, from applying for PWA money, Talmadge in January 1935 turned to a compliant legislature. Shortly thereafter a bill appeared curtailing regents' power and declaring system

47

"properties and various incomes including fees and other revenues" to be property of the state.[97]

Attacked as "ill-considered" and "dangerous" by the *Atlanta Constitution*, the bill would nullify the PWA loan, already reduced to $2,600,000. It also placed the system "on the same plane as other departments" and jeopardized regents control of several thousand acres of land and various gifts made over the years. If the regents lost title, the *Constitution* warned, such properties would revert to "the descendants of the original donors." The progeny of Civil War Governor Joseph E. Brown, who had bequeathed $300,000, reportedly would challenge the legislation in court. Talmadge threatened to veto all system appropriations if the bill failed. Less certain of the outcome in the Senate, his supporters moved quickly to avoid debate. On January 19, a rump meeting of the Senate university committee, summoned hurriedly by its vice-chairman, voted the bill's unanimous endorsement and abruptly adjourned three hours before scheduled regents testimony. Meanwhile, a Talmadge-controlled House committee agreed to hear them, reportedly so the regents could "release their steam."[98]

System spokesmen put up a spirited but hopeless fight. Calling the bill a breach of faith, chairman Marion Smith predicted a court fight if it passed. Worse, it would "make the university system" a political football "disastrous" to building a great educational establishment. Unimpressed by Smith or the chancellor, the House passed an even more stringent bill which also mandated the surrender of all matriculation, lab, and other fees, and athletic gate receipts to the state treasury before their reallocation. When the Senate later concurred, thirty-two to six, state control of the athletic fees, at least, had been removed.[99]

But the regents already had capitulated by accepting the role of officers of the state. Certain amendments, they understood, would clearly state that "any donations, gifts and bequests to the System" remained unaffected. With Talmadge's promise of a million-dollar appropriation for system buildings, they endorsed

48

his actions. The governor had provided "a reasonable building program essential for the proper progress of the System." Yet the million dollars covered a three-year period with only a third available in 1935. Furthermore, Talmadge likely financed this special appropriation by subsequently reducing regular system funding. The following year, Georgia's $280,000 higher education expenditure was one of the region's lowest.[100]

Despite the turmoil, the system ultimately received money, materials, and labor from the PWA. The legislative struggle scarcely had ended when the chancellor received regents instructions to apply for federal matching funds. Georgia's annual appropriation of $333,333 for three years was matched by the PWA's $270,000 on the same basis. Of course, Talmadge seriously harmed the USGES and delayed its move at least by three years. Instead of the shiny, new downtown facility that Sparks envisioned, he obtained an old, run-down structure as far from the city center as the Walton building. The struggle over the PWA loan also disrupted the system's leadership. Chairman Hughes Spalding resigned amidst speculation that regent Smith would do likewise. Chancellor Weltner, undermined by the regents as well as the governor, departed a few months after the PWA loan conflict.[101]

7

DOWNSIZING DEGREE PROGRAMS

During the threatened Tech takeover and the uncertainty over federal funding, director George Sparks kept pushing to expand the University System of Georgia Evening School (USGES). His new degrees spurred enrollment, above 800 by spring 1934, with every room nearly filled to capacity. During the next year, 1,274 came despite the space shortage. Fretting about the Southern Association of Colleges (SAC) occupied much of the director's time that summer. In Sparks's defense, accrediting agencies had been criticized for inflexibility, particularly in the enforcement of standards. Indeed, their concern about uniformity brought charges that they penalized experimentation.[102]

Inconceivably, Sparks somehow failed to grasp SAC standards or their application, evidenced by the scattered pieces of irrelevant information he assembled justifying the Evening School's situation. He repeatedly reminded the chancellor of Dean W. H. Spencer's praise two years earlier. Eight faculty, instead of three, now had doctoral degrees, although most taught only part-time. *Who's Who in America* listed three USGES faculty, including himself, more than any other Atlanta institution. How that recognition enhanced their teaching qualifications was unclear. Sparks mentioned the close curricular alignment to the University of Georgia (UGA) and touted the USGES's improved financial situation.[103] Yet he remained in denial over the key SAC issues, academic supervision and mandatory state funding.

A visit by SAC executive secretary M. C. Huntley, accompanied by Agnes Scott President John McCain, brought devastating criticism. While checking the system's extension work, which they pronounced "very satisfactory," they "learned of the present plans for operating the Evening School." Both men concluded that SAC would find it "wholly unsatisfactory." McCain, earlier a strong supporter of the Tech Evening School, expressed great concern over any "large investment of money on the basis of student fees." Such funds were for salaries and "other current expenses," not "loans for development plans," which the state should fund. Georgia provided its university system with "only two-fifths of the minimum [SAC] requirement." Without more state "income per student," the whole system was "in serious danger."[104]

In November, Sparks responded with the familiar generalities. He mentioned the USGES's "greatly strengthened" association with Atlanta's Carnegie Library, and the use of Tech's laboratories "until our new $275,000 building is completed." By December, SAC's Huntley, perhaps weary of dealing with a redundant Sparks and a prickly chancellor, warned the university system through UGA President S. V. Sanford. Huntley viewed the Atlanta situation "with astonishment." That the three senior colleges would "grant degrees for work done in the Evening School" violated a "fundamental [SAC] standard" that degrees "be of equal quality." Ordinarily, the University of Georgia would suffer a year's probation followed by termination. Out of sympathy for "the Chancellor's idea of doing adult education," SAC would "wait a year before taking any drastic action in order that there may be adjustments."[105] Granted the USGES's shortcomings, "doing adult education" placed SAC, itself, in unfamiliar territory. Dealing with an urban college appeared to be a novel

52

experience. Throughout its existence, SAC membership comprised traditional institutions usually located in small-town environments with young middle- and upper-class constituents. Even so-called Southern urban colleges, such as Vanderbilt, Tulane, Emory, and Rice, chose suburban, not downtown urban environments.

Chancellor Weltner, by-passed by SAC, displayed additional anger. Its findings were "an arrogant bit of stupid Bourbonism," he wrote Sanford. Initially, the chancellor considered "withdrawing from" SAC, Sparks reported. Although the director had engineered the USGES's expansion, fought returning to Tech, and deserved most of the blame for the current accreditation difficulties, he avoided all responsibility. Posing as an obedient public servant, Sparks had "carried out every instruction" from the chancellor and "the [system] committee from the senior units." Instead, he focused on "our great responsibility...to the students" and feared the "lash of" their "indignation" should any change be made "in our present program."[106]

A major SAC complaint was the absence of supervision from a system senior school. Sparks thought the USGES already had plenty of outside participation. UGA officials would vouch "that we are in touch with them" as much as "their own campus faculty," he told the chancellor. Then he suggested revolving "as many as six to ten faculty members" from the three senior schools "to the Evening School each year[.]" It would provide "much of the modern contact so many of them need and...also relieve the sameness every year." Such transfers would "try out new teachers in the System," although "Evening School students would not receive as good instruction as under the plan we are now operating." This rambling discourse and bizarre proposal seemed to reveal the director's ignorance of academic practices, teaching, scholarship, accreditation, and the type of administration necessary to carry them out. At the same time, Sparks strongly opposed a plan that would resolve the accreditation crisis: "[C]reate a department at Georgia Tech in conjunction

53

with the Co-Operative courses there." Besides limiting enrollments, it was "inadvisable with the present [Tech]
administration," and it reversed the Works "Survey Group in
their direction of divorcing the Evening School from Georgia
Tech."[107]

The chancellor, in dealing with SAC, first had to decide
whether to risk expulsion by authorizing the USGES to grant
system degrees printed in the catalog. Weltner was determined
to award them at June graduation, he wrote Sanford. The president agreed, and the threat to accreditation ended when SAC
accepted Weltner's statement that "we cannot in fairness...go
back on our published announcement." Thereafter, diplomas
would be issued "in the name of the institution" the students
had attended.[108]

Weltner's departure in spring 1935 left S. V. Sanford, his successor, with the USGES's unsolved problems. He also had to deal
with Sparks's determination to salvage all of the degrees, out-
lined in a detailed, four-page "Policy to Govern the Work in the
Evening School." Basically a polemic rehashing old arguments,
the document, signed by Sparks and Charles Snelling, dismissed
the accreditation problem as irrelevant, because SAC's "jurisdiction over the Evening School will not come up until...application
for membership" is made. It was another accreditation fantasy,
because the university system could not sanction mixed accredited and nonaccredited units and maintain its SAC standing.
Nevertheless, these encounters with SAC left Sparks embittered
and hostile. By one account, he "absolutely detested them." The
director also deeply distrusted the new chancellor, believing he
would use SAC "as the instrument of shutting us down." At the
same time, he feared that applying for accreditation would produce the same result, because the state lacked the funds to meet
SAC standards.[109]

Having visited the Northeast and Midwest during previous
summers to study evening schools, Sparks bombarded the new
chancellor with catalogs and other literature along with his

54

interpretation of their meaning. Sanford read Sparks's material "very carefully" and professed great disappointment. "You did not give a single quotation," stating that "any Evening School awarded degrees," he wrote Sparks. "All the excerpts merely stated that credit was given for courses taken in the Evening School." Even the Portland Center in Oregon "can not award degrees." Instead, "one year's residence is required" at one of Oregon's senior colleges.[110]

Sanford thought the Georgia System had "gone a long way." A USGES student "can do real college work at little or no expense," and senior institutions agreed "to give them credit for three years." Although Portland ultimately confirmed that students in a few fields "like history, English, education and sociology" sometimes could complete "a master's degree," few succeeded because of the very limited course offerings. While the Portland Center and its faculty enjoyed high "academic respect" among Oregon's senior colleges, the USGES had no such esteem in Georgia.[111]

Meanwhile, the chancellor could not solve this "perplexing problem," he told the regents, because he found no evening schools that gave degrees. Furthermore, awarding USGES degrees would set a "dangerous precedent," he wrote regent Sandy Beaver. How could that power then be denied to similar centers "established in Macon, Augusta, and Rome or elsewhere?" The regents sought to decrease, not increase, the number of system units. Yet "in opposition to all I have said" and contrary to his "best judgment," Sanford made an exception for Atlanta, ostensibly because "of my respect for chancellor Snelling" whose presence guaranteed the USGES's academic standing. It could grant the three-year bachelor of commercial science (B.C.S.) degree previously given by Tech when they had been "one and the same institution." But within a fortnight the chancellor changed his mind again. If the Atlanta Evening School granted degrees, he wrote regent Beaver, substantial increases "in our appropriations" were possible "in the years to

55

come." More to the point, recent catalogues from state universities with "large evening schools" indicated "a tendency" for their becoming "additional universities." Sanford knew "the Regents are not interested in building another university in Atlanta."[112]

While the chancellor opposed USGES degrees, he *did* favor a junior college and a year of additional work "to prepare boys and girls of maturity for college." The regents agreed, but they again overruled the chancellor and authorized the three-year B.C.S. degree at the newly named "Atlanta Extension Center of the University System of Georgia," also called the "System Center" and the "Atlanta Center." Sparks's four-year (B.S.C.) and masters (M.S.C.) programs were terminated. Nevertheless, the Atlanta Center still had won an important victory by keeping the B.C.S. degree without the Tech affiliation. The regents adopted all of Sanford's other recommendations, increasing the faculty to six full-time instructors and ordering a library upgrade "as rapidly as possible." To avoid competing with local colleges, the Center operated only "in the late afternoon" after two, "evenings, and on Saturdays."[113]

Typically, Sparks's initial concern involved public relations, because junior college status projected "very bad publicity," he told Snelling. He wanted the regents to "just keep it out of the press." The Center had "nothing in common with other schools." If left alone, Sparks was "perfectly satisfied" having salvaged this much for "adult education." Above all, the director wanted to protect students who had been promised baccalaureate and master's degrees. Atlanta employers would make a spirited fight for these young people, he warned Sanford early in August. SAC reluctantly agreed. Students grandfathered under the USGES catalog should be given a chance to graduate provided the program ended by June 1938.[114]

The large 1936 class, with ninety-eight graduates, revealed the startling extent Sparks in 1933 had expanded the program and the variety of degrees: Masters of Science in Commerce (six), Bachelor of Arts (fourteen), Bachelor of Arts in Education (eleven), Bachelor of Arts in Commerce (forty-four), Bachelor of Science in Education (twenty-two), and Bachelor of Science (one). Among the undergraduates, a majority was nonbusiness majors. None took the three-year B.C.S. Despite his losses, director Sparks had let the degree genie out of the bottle, and Chancellor Sanford soon felt the wrath of unhappy Atlantans.[115]

The expansion of the USGES by 1936 and the growth of urban higher education elsewhere foretold significant new national trends. Many states began responding to the educational needs of their expanding cities as young working people migrated to the Milwaukees, Portlands, and Atlantas demanding better educational opportunities even as the state universities operated in the more distant and isolated Madisons, Eugenes, and Athenses. State education officials usually turned the problem over to experts in the state universities, and urban extension centers began to appear. But achieving a four-year, liberal arts degree in Atlanta, if not in Portland, still required a residency only at UGA.

57

The process, understandable in maintaining standards and containing costs, had a perverse side. It preserved the universities' customary hold on academic prestige, programs, and particularly, state funding. During the early 1930s, with the Depression, high unemployment, and undervalued human resources, states avoided doing better. In this context, the university system's services for young, urban, working Caucasians seemed in the mainstream. Later, demands for new urban colleges threatened the older academic establishments as they would the University of Georgia.

From this perspective, George Sparks exhibited foresight far ahead of his Georgia contemporaries despite the negative effect of his personal ambition and the weakness of the educational edifice he created in the early 1930s. Given the troubling economic conditions and loss of academic prestige after the Tech separation, the USGES continued against great odds. To one contemporary, three things stood out: "First, was Dr. Sparks's holding power." The Center would not "have survived without it." In addition, "a large proportion of gifted faculty," teaching "for almost nothing" made it substantively worthwhile. Finally, "the important thing" was the need of hundreds of Atlantans "who wanted an education and saw opportunities" at the Atlanta Center. They "flocked in, any door you opened they were coming through."[116]

8

PROSPERITY AND WAR

By 1935, with economic recovery and increasing enrollment, the Atlanta Center needed more space. For three years, director George Sparks devoted considerable time and energy to this formidable chore. With that task barely completed, the onset of military preparedness and then war transformed and invigorated Atlanta's economy. These events presented the Atlanta Center with unparalleled opportunities as prosperity and war replaced the Depression and economic stagnation. Despite the academic downsizing that the regents ordered, the Center's senior and graduate work in the short run survived. Students grandfathered into these programs received degrees as late as 1939. Meanwhile, the Atlanta Junior College expanded rapidly, from only seventy students at its 1935 opening to nearly 500 five years later. The grandfathered programs occasionally brought protests from Athens. The director should stop announcing "courses in journalism" which clearly duplicated "the work done here," the dean complained to UGA President Harmon Caldwell, who thought the violations were "rather serious." This issue and several others signaled Athens's acute awareness of the Atlanta Center's activities. By the war's end, Athens's anxiety was evolving into real fear of the Atlanta Center as a potential rival.[117]

Even before the senior and graduate programs faded away, the director found ways to preserve the Atlanta Center's image as a senior institution. As the *Evening Signal* announced in fall 1935, the three-year B.C.S. degree would be greatly liberalized. Sparks permitted third-year undergraduates to major in practically any field, including English and the social sciences. He also provided a broad curriculum with large numbers of course electives to provide depth. In the words of one administrator, "We really were a school of arts and sciences masquerading behind a B.C.S. degree."[118] Although the Atlanta Center lacked accreditation and at times sound pedagogy, hundreds from Atlanta and Georgia received Sparks's creative bachelor of commercial science degrees that undoubtedly changed their lives when the state had neither the funds nor the political will to provide better.

In a less salutary way, Sparks's liberal policies often permitted academic standards to suffer. The small, full-time faculty carried heavy teaching loads with many new course preparations out of their fields and sometimes beyond their competencies. Numerous part-time teachers filled in the gaps. One student complaint cited a "science" teacher who also taught Spanish. Actually, he was a nondegreed mathematician who confessed his lack of interest in Spanish, failed to "answer our questions," often "admits he just doesn't know," assigned difficult readings "before teaching grammar," and refused to let the students keep their papers.[119]

On the other hand, competent nonacademic professionals from Atlanta's banks, business offices, government agencies, and hospitals often made excellent part-time teachers. During the war years, two trained economists, a Duke Ph.D. at the federal reserve and a North Carolina doctoral candidate at the national housing agency, filled in. Tech professors and area psychologists and sociologists also served. Occasionally, high school teachers supplemented their incomes at the Center, and Sparks, who "evaluated faculty in terms of their capability of attracting students," hired these as well as local preachers.[120]

By fall 1935, the Atlanta Center had a combined enrollment of 1,278, crowding the Walton building beyond capacity. In

October, disgruntled students, to the delight of director Sparks, held two protest meetings. Both Sparks and Charles Snelling addressed them. As registrations climbed, Sparks predicted 1,600 students in the 1936–1937 academic year. Seeking more space, he turned the cafeteria and library into classrooms while describing the Atlanta Center's situation as "dangerous." In fact, some of the nearby structures leased by the Center apparently merited that label, including two former auto tire stores and an abandoned tea room over a plumbing shop. Sparks stopped publicizing the opening date for registration and school activities because applicants would only be turned away.[121]

Certainly, the director, who had been seeking new quarters for over three years, bore no blame for the crowded conditions. When Governor Eugene Talmadge sabotaged the system's Public Works Administration (PWA) loan and replaced it with only a million dollars, the regents cut the Atlanta Center out of the allocation and even denied it PWA matching funds. Months passed before a newly appointed regents committee took any action, but Sparks had his own resources. Through regent Miller Bell, a Talmadge ally, the director got the attention and support of the governor who had been the source of much of the Center's grief. Talmadge "has been our best friend in getting this building," Charles Snelling later told the faculty. "Sixty thousand dollars was given us. I want to give the devil his due."[122]

The building mentioned was the old Baptist Hospital, or Nassau Hotel, on Luckie Street around the corner from the Center's Walton building. Owned by the Southern Baptist Convention, it once carried a $200,000 appraisal. The church trustees reluctantly accepted the regents' $60,000 and turned over possession in October 1936. Sparks found the old building in "pretty good shape," and the governor promised $25,000 for improvements. But the director's expectation that renovation would begin immediately after the regents dispossessed the renters left him disappointed. The system engineer had been

61

Old Baptist Hospital, or Nassau Hotel, Luckie Street (1938).
Courtesy of GSU Archives.

overworked and ill, and the academic year ended the following May with nothing done.[123]

By fall, Sparks again poured out his dismay to regent Miller Bell. In dispossessing the renters, whose leases brought in $400 a month, the regents had lost $4,000. In his frustration, Sparks proposed to renovate the building himself using regents-approved Works Progress Administration (WPA) money. Impatient, Sparks wanted the Center's problems brought up for action at the next regents meeting. The WPA renovation still did not begin until January 1938. Although the old hotel's three floors and basement had less space than anticipated, it still was well over twice the Walton building's capacity. A U-shaped structure with 55,000 square feet, partially fireproofed, it provided a campuslike court the size of a small city lot. But the structure needed extensive basic repairs involving wiring, plumbing, and heating. The completed building cost $143,990, including some

$31,000 in federal matching funds. Its completion came in the nick of time. During the previous academic year, the Center had registered over 1,500 students, and the numbers increased to 1,748 in 1938–1939.[124]

Of course, the Atlanta Center's physical expansion and astounding growth in enrollments seemed to flout the mandatory academic downsizing that began three years earlier. And as Sparks warned, Atlanta citizens would demand more. The Georgia League of Nursing Education's displeasure with Athens's two-year, pre-nursing program brought demands for an alternative in Atlanta "so that students" could keep their "positions at home and still continue their studies." An angry University of Georgia alumna, apparently confusing the Atlanta Center with UGA, wondered why she and others "who come to Atlanta to work, CANNOT GET OUR MASTERS DEGREES FROM THE U. OF GEORGIA?" Numbers of area teachers went "*to Oglethorpe or Emory*...simply because the Evening School" lacked authorization, she fumed at the chancellor. "*WHO FAILED TO AUTHORIZE THEM? YOU.*" Using a pseudonym, the writer did "not need any complaint coming to my Supt. [superintendent]."[125]

Grandfathered D. D. Joiner had been working on a B.A. degree since 1933 and his job did "not permit a summer vacation" to fulfill the mandatory nine courses required in residence in Athens. He wanted permission to complete his noncommerce work and graduate from the Atlanta Center. Receiving no reply from the chancellor, he wrote the governor and regent Sandy Beaver, and personally repeated his request at the June regents meeting. The chancellor, in his belated reply, gave a brief history of the university system along with a refrain that the regents and system administrators would repeat endlessly for nearly two decades: Giving the Atlanta Center degree-granting status would encourage every town and city in Georgia to demand similar facilities. But the dissatisfaction continued. In summer 1939, the Fulton County Teachers Association, whose members in summers traveled to Athens, wanted training programs in Atlanta.[126]

63

Unable to claim accreditation or offer academic degrees, the director endlessly promoted the Center by other means. His annual reports, correspondence, and press releases cited increasing enrollments and depicted the Center as outstanding and different from other institutions. Its 1,748 students in 1938–1939 made the Center the largest school of commerce in the South, fifth in the nation, and third in female participation. Of course, the majority were arts and sciences majors. While meaningless in the context of quality higher education, the claims undoubtedly projected a special identity for local and statewide consumption. Sparks grasped at evidence that accreditation did not matter. Center graduates readily transferred course credits and were universally accepted. Emory and other colleges recommended the Center to students who later would finish in one of their professional departments, he told the chancellor in 1940. Athens officials strongly disagreed. "We have been embarrassed on several occasions by having to decline to admit [Atlanta Center] students" with the B.C.S. degree "to full graduate standing," the administrative council complained.[127]

In truth, some Center students *had* been accepted at prestigious institutions. Rogers Hammond received an honors day key for the highest men's junior college average, but he went immediately to Harvard without seeking the B.C.S. degree. Of course, the salutary experiences of a few could not validate Sparks's overblown claims. Perhaps the director had not heard that George Manners, class valedictorian in 1935, was denied admittance two years later to the University of Georgia's graduate program except "on probation." Manners had not known until then that the Atlanta Center "was unaccredited." In dealing with others even less informed about such matters, Sparks sometimes dissembled. The Atlanta Center "is the only accredited unit in the University system, which is practically self-supporting," he wrote the Joseph B. Whitehead Foundation.[128]

As the 1930s drew to a close, the nation's preparedness program transformed Atlanta's economy. By then, the city proper comprised an area of approximately eighteen square miles, with a two-square-mile central business district. The metropolitan area's population that decade registered a nineteen percent increase, from 370,920 to 442,294. The city expanded its robust, diversified manufacturing sector, which produced food products, textiles, wearing apparel, machinery, lumber, furniture, and paper products. Even more important was the development of industrial services that assembled automobiles; sold, warehoused, financed, and distributed services; accommodated conventioneers; transported automobiles, trucks, and airplanes through its networks; and educated and serviced the growing population.[129]

By 1940, lucrative defense contracts began changing many textile firms from civilian to military output, while heavier industries converted to arms and munitions. By the end of 1942, about 140 federal departments and agencies, over half with regional jurisdiction, employed over 20,000. The most dramatic development came with the Bell Aircraft Corporation's new plant in nearby Marietta. By early 1943, over $342,000,000 in government contracts had created nearly 26,000 jobs by the war's end. As the metropolitan area grew, the reach of its labor market area extended beyond the original three metropolitan counties to include five more, with a total population by 1943 of well over half a million.[130]

65

As defense preparations placed demands on the nation's colleges, director Sparks quickly got involved, although some system administrators may have questioned his extravagant claims about the Atlanta Center's contributions. At the end of 1941, Sparks reported, the Center "led the way of all [Southern] colleges," offering numerous "emergency courses." Furthermore, it became "the only Evening College in the United States having students deferred until June according to the American Association of Urban Colleges [AAUC]," a national organization that disseminated as fact unverified accounts reported by its members on their own activities. A full two years before Pearl

Harbor, Sparks told the regents, the Center had introduced war emergency subjects to the university system.[131]

National education leaders by 1942 predicted record postwar enrollments. A "real boom" would go on "for several years after the war" as veterans returned to finish their education. Director Sparks picked up on this theme. "With a vast rehabilitation program in the offing," he told the regents, "the sound, established evening college will be one of the most logical and accessible of educational programs open to young adults whose education will be curtailed by war demands." The Atlanta Center must begin planning programs, developing facilities, and organizing resources.[132]

66

The Atlanta Center also established an army-enlisted reserve corps. Again, citing an AAUC report, Sparks labeled it "the *only* evening college program in America to be accepted and given a quota [of 305] in the enlisted reserve corps." By the end of January, the refectory had been turned into a modern rifle range and a rifle team formed, but Captain William P. Layton could requisition only four Winchester target rifles. Although records of the Center's Army and Navy contracts could not be located, such programs often were very lucrative. By 1945, some colleges for males only were receiving up to fifty percent of their incomes therefrom.[133]

The director expressed justifiable pride in the Atlanta Center's chemical warfare course introduced early in the emergency. Organized by chemistry Professor Joseph LeConte, it was so well received that Chancellor Sanford allegedly ordered other system units to adopt it. When the chemical warfare service accepted much of the plan, the Army commissioned LeConte and put him to work on the program. Meanwhile, the Center's laboratories, aided by the U.S. public health department, had been equipped to serve premedical, predental, nursing, and clinical service students. Five Atlanta hospitals by fall 1943 had 150 students taking basic training with federal support.[134]

The Atlanta Center also introduced other, more peripheral courses for the war effort. While classes in Spanish had been available since the 1920s, French, German and Russian, taught by existing faculty, were added in 1943. The *Junior Collegiate* announced that Chinese, Portuguese, and possibly Japanese also would be available. These last offerings must have strained the Center's teaching resources, and only one full-time faculty, V. V. Lavroff, a Russian émigré who spent time in east Asia, seemed even remotely qualified for the task. At the same time, the wartime scarcity of clerical workers in Atlanta businesses brought courses and certificates of proficiency in junior and senior clerking, typing, and stenography.[135]

As expected, the number of regular students declined during the war. Pessimists even predicted civilian attendance at only twenty-five percent of the prewar level. While the total September 1943 system enrollment of 13,939 proved this dire forecast wrong, the armed forces' 7,443 men and women cushioned losses in most system units. The Atlanta Center experienced similar fluctuations. Enrollment in 1941, at 1,602, dropped only slightly from the previous year. Even so, the Center's student body had become the system's third largest, replacing the Georgia State College for Women. Nevertheless, the war took its toll. Center enrollment declined to 1,306 in 1942 and 1,227 the following year. By spring 1943, some 1,500 Center students had entered the armed services, and a year later over 2,700 departed. Cumulative enrollments, which included those in the well-attended summer school sessions, told a different story. During 1941–1942, for example, the Center's total student body numbered nearly 2,682, and two years later, 2,541. Of these, 1,998 were women and 543 men.[136]

By the end of 1944, with the war winding down, the Atlanta Center shifted toward a peacetime curriculum, abandoning war-related sciences and mathematics. But the director had larger matters on his mind. "Evening Colleges all over the country are making preparations to care for their biggest enrollment after the

67

war," he informed the regents. Regulations in the recently passed "GI Bill" permitted discharged soldiers and sailors to attend college part-time and still receive benefits. Another provision favorable to evening colleges permitted training in industry and business as well as academic pursuits. Returning servicemen could get jobs and "learn while they earn," placing additional strain on the Atlanta Center as it prepared to offer veterans refresher courses. "If we are properly to serve the thousands of Georgia men and women…coming to us year after year," Sparks wrote, "an additional school building" was essential. Perhaps as many as 50,000 service people would be living within an hour's drive of the Atlanta Center, and the present space could not accommodate them. Returning veterans alone would raise enrollees by 5,000 in the next four to six years, Sparks believed. The immediate postwar enrollment confirmed the director's predictions. In 1945, it reached 2,174.[137]

68

The wartime experience set the Center and public higher education in Atlanta on an entirely new course, although its future role, scope, and dimensions remained unclear, even unimaginable. In addition to the war, the director's active participation in the American Association of Urban Colleges (AAUC) and his ceaseless promotion brought the Center unprecedented national recognition. In 1945, Sparks reported that the United States Office of Education (USOE) had selected the Atlanta Center, along with Western Reserve's downtown Cleveland College and the Minneapolis Center of the University of Minnesota, for a study of metropolitan centers. A USOE representative spent three days in Atlanta gathering information for use in Mississippi and Alabama, where Jacksonville and Birmingham planned new educational facilities. "So national in scope has grown the reputation of the Georgia Evening College," Sparks told the regents, that he was outlining programs for similar centers in Milwaukee, Buffalo, Omaha, and other large cities.[138] It was an impressive achievement for an educational entrepreneur whose institution lacked accreditation.

Meanwhile, during the previous decade, student and faculty life, although routine and generally unremarkable, still assumed importance. In the 1930s, school loyalty developed. It radiated from the students' social and academic activities, the enthusiasm of its graduates, the sterling qualities of the small permanent faculty, and, of course, the promotional activities and popularity of the director.

9

STUDENT AND FACULTY ACTIVITIES
BEFORE WORLD WAR II

As director George Sparks expanded programs and degrees, he still found time to oversee student activities. At Georgia Tech, he had demonstrated a deep interest in their affairs. The *Technique* in the late 1920s virtually lionized him. Of course, the Evening School, lacking both campus and residences, presented an entirely different environment, and its older matriculates, who came to class at odd hours from offices, jobs, and homes, had different priorities and responsibilities. Yet Sparks wanted the Evening School to have at least a veneer of college social life. Inevitably, at the downtown facility with its mostly part-time faculty, he became an even more commanding figure and apparently enjoyed a genuine rapport with students. In spring 1933, he must have viewed as particularly galling a petition criticizing his leadership and requesting a regents investigation.[139]

Signed by leaders of eighteen organizations, the document aired complaints both serious and trivial. Three involved academics: the "lowering of the scholastic standards," "inefficient and inexperienced instructors," and shortened class recitation periods. Other charges cited the lack of "management" cooperation in granting a charter to the scholastic fraternity Delta Mu Delta, building a stage for the dramatic club, and correcting coffee shop inefficiencies. Administrators also failed to follow student body recommendations. Finally, the director "participated" in and "aggravated disputes," and he neglected to cooperate with the new building's fundraising efforts. Having just separated from Tech, the Evening School faced internal administrative friction. By one account, two disgruntled faculty, previously Sparks's superiors, encouraged the revolt to embarrass the director and regain control. The student council's president-elect promoted the petition, but perhaps sensing lagging support he refrained from circulating it.[140]

As Delta Sigma Pi fraternity members rallied behind Sparks, the senior class and the speaker's club boycotted the "secret petition." One student leader disagreed with "the charges it contains," he wrote regent Hughes Spalding, "AND THIS IS NOT A MINORITY OPINION." The signatures "do not represent the actions and opinions of the organizations named," and the "majority of the students resent the petition very much." Though the writer warned that "removing the present director" would be "a serious mistake," no evidence suggests such a drastic move or any other regents action as a remote possibility. The controversy revealed the existence of at least eighteen student organizations in the school's cramped quarters, and that working students found time to get involved in school affairs. Besides the student council, the speaker's club, Delta Mu Delta, and the five classes, the petition listed the Commerce Club, the Venetian Society, the Owls Club, Delta Sigma Pi, Alpha Kappa Psi, Phi Chi Theta, Hilarian Club, Inter-Fraternity Council, Tech Night Players, and the Progressive Club. The petition's mention of the delay in granting a charter to Delta Mu Delta referred to a dispute between Sparks and Professor Fred Wenn, who as faculty sponsor attempted to install that organization without consulting with the director, although Sparks usually warmed to such student activities. Later, Sparks organized the campus leaders into men's (Intramural Key) and women's (Crimson

Key) groups. In addition, students went "to city clubs and lunches and debate[d] issues of the day."[141]

Other clubs, fraternities, and organizations undoubtedly existed besides the eighteen on the petition. The committee on student activities granted de facto recognition pending the submission of their bylaws and charters. At the same time, the committee warned of limits to their tenure: "[A]ll extra curricula activities...should be coordinated with and subordinate to the regular academic work" and administration policies. Considering the hard times and financial needs, the involvement of so many working students with campus organizations seemed to indicate a healthy school spirit. According to one graduate, "They were highly motivated." Although "a good many adults" participated, the "tone was set primarily by the younger students." The typical undergraduates "were a few years older" than traditional students. Perhaps because of the realities of the Depression, they were "dedicated" and "decent people" who "worked hard" and learned how to "maximize the use of our time."[142]

73

Students and their organizations engaged in public activities. Alpha Kappa Psi surveyed local businesses to find out if the course offerings covered the cultural and educational subjects needed in present day commerce. "In the public utility field," Atlanta Gas Light responded, "perhaps the most important subject would be the training of students to intelligently converse with the public." Retail Credit had a similar reaction. "So many men come into business with fine technical training but are unable to adapt themselves to working with other people." Its spokesman suggested "a course in personal relationship" as a remedy. Individual students also kept busy. Howard "Swede" Johnson from Tallapoosa in west Georgia came to the city in 1929 to take a job at Atlanta Gas Light and continue his education. A senior by fall 1933, Johnson still had the job and served two scholastic organizations as president besides sponsoring the speaker's club. Later, he headed the Atlantic Steel Company.[143]

Important to student life was the campus newspaper. The Evening School's *Technite* appeared briefly in 1926 and regularly between 1930 and 1932. Until the separation, the campus *Technique* carried news about the downtown Evening School. Shortly thereafter, the monthly *Evening Signal* appeared in October 1933 sponsored by the student council. Money became a continuing problem for the paper. Initially offering free subscriptions, it depended entirely upon advertising income. One assistant business manager "sold ads, Rich's [department store] and theaters were my clients at that time." Each student had a duty to patronize them, the editors warned, so "take notice of those firms that are helping us." Still short of funds after the next edition, the *Signal* charged five cents per copy. An upbeat staff hoped that it would be one of the best college papers in the South and sought topics of interest. One editorial, "Women's Stake," may have attracted attention by stoutly maintaining their right to be equal to men.[144]

The *Signal's* funding problems were serious enough to send the student advisory committee to the faculty seeking donations. One dollar per capita would support two issues. The administration financed a May issue to get 1,000 additional copies for distribution to high school graduates. In May 1938, the staff again warned of a major crisis. Issues came out irregularly, the editorial and business departments lacked adequate personnel, and printing bills lay unpaid, although large accounts, if collected, would have created a surplus. Despite such uncertainties, the *Signal* somehow made it through several lean years, sometimes with only a single page issue, paper-sized, front and back. The senior class Annual also suffered financial strains. Hoping to fare better than the *Signal*, it risked taking voluntary subscriptions.[145]

The appearance of other student publications also helped establish a college atmosphere, such as the student council's yearbook, the *Nocturn*, and the literary magazine *Flambo*. Looking for money, officials in 1933 authorized two student referendums on charging a uniform fee to all students. Two votes, one taken at a mass meeting and the other by mail, won majorities, but a two-thirds vote was needed. The student activities committee rejected a proposal for a third election as "contrary to all principles of fairness, justice," and "democracy." In fact, repeated efforts to pass a student activity fee failed throughout this period. Nevertheless, the *Evening Signal*, the *Junior Collegiate*, the *Flambo*, the *Nocturne*, and later the yearbook *Gateway* somehow functioned. Supported solely by advertising solicited by students, they operated free of debt in 1941, according to comments in the *Signal*.[146]

Social activity remained unsupported. When the *Signal* in November 1933 announced the participation of over 600 students in a turkey dinner and dance between seven and twelve midnight at Davison's Tearoom, it labeled the occasion the school's largest social event of the year. With a well-known local orchestra providing entertainment amplified over loudspeakers, radio station WSB carried fifteen minutes of the festivities. Director Sparks assured the attendance of local educational luminaries, including Chancellor Weltner, President Brittain, Dr. Snelling, and Evening School benefactor R. R. Johnson. Two days before this fiesta, the students chose the official colors, red from the University of Georgia and white from Tech, but the decision was not unanimous. Blue and white was the runner-up. This affinity for the bland white seemed to indicate the students' surviving affection for their erstwhile alma mater.[147]

The 1933 season ended with the December presentation of two one-act plays, the drama group's first. Considering the absence of classes in diction, voice culture, acting, and stage technique until 1937, the players seemed both star-struck and exceedingly courageous. The event may have been well attended and a cultural contribution worthy of acclaim, but the *Atlanta Constitution*, which announced it, carried no review. More theater was on the way. The following May the School's thespians presented "A Scrap of Paper" at the roof garden atop the Walton

75

building. As time passed, the drama group read a play each week and did a public performance "once per quarter."[148]

Other student activities flourished, which, according to one participant, had a citywide "social impact." The Venetian Club's annual Buttermilk Ball featured costumes and a dance, which "made the society columns." Alerted by "a bottle of buttermilk" on their doorsteps "early Sunday morning," young women knew they had been tapped. Others could attend "the dance by invitation." Although the director seldom participated, he insisted on the observance of one cardinal rule: "*[N]o drinking at any function*," and he enforced it "with an iron hand."[149]

The 1935 opening of the Atlanta Junior College (AJC) brought another newspaper, the *Junior Collegiate,* a second campus government, and new daytime organizations. Later the AJC held its own homecoming. School officials made a special effort to keep track of AJC women, keeping a register of their participation in student activities. English Professor Merle Walker held personal conferences and had a list of each coed's commitments to determine which girls were uninvolved but also to find social overachievers. Some eighteen coeds in 1936 were nonparticipants. Supplementing Walker's efforts, history Professor Carl Mauelshagen worked with the sophomores "to arouse more spirit" by holding dances and games. Chemist Joseph LeConte advocated athletic competition for arousing class spirit, especially basketball and tennis, with prizes for winners. Of course, AJC males were not neglected, and all students were required to attend assemblies. To oversee this activity, the faculty chose fifteen student monitors described as young people "who stand out as representative of the finest students in the college."[150]

Besides fostering campus activities, the administration also addressed students' financial problems. Most had to work and needed all the help they could get. Although Sparks once referred to payments in kind, most student aid involved promises to pay either within sixty days of enrollment or by monthly installments. By 1938, with so many accounts in arrears, the college engaged a private collection agency. Despite student indebtedness, Sparks the previous year organized a student credit union. Its first quarter of operation in summer 1937 produced over fifty loans. Up to sixty percent of the twenty-five-dollar tuition could be borrowed and paid back monthly.[151]

Other help came through the National Youth Administration (NYA), whose scholarships, available to those recommended by faculty or a high school principal, covered fifteen dollars of the tuition. By system standards, the amount was so generous that the Center could use a single scholarship for two applicants. Recipients signed affidavits affirming their need. While they performed tasks, some in the library and others for administrators or faculty, none could replace the regular staff, although some Georgia colleges violated this rule. NYA students working in the dormitories and kitchens at the Georgia State College for Women, for example, took the jobs of black women.[152]

In fall 1935, Sparks described the Center's NYA contingent as a "wonderful group." But so much care had been taken in selecting them, "too careful" in his opinion, that about $1,500 had accumulated. Fortunately, the money could be applied to the next quarter permitting about fifty to sixty more to enroll. Nationally, some 600,000 got NYA support. In 1938, 203 Atlanta Center students received $11,475, and the twenty-one in the AJC, $3,570. In 1941, shortly before its abolishment, the NYA provided over $4,000 to forty-six AJC enrollees. Others received aid under the Federal Emergency Relief Administration (FERA) although they did less well academically. "We did not have time to select our students for this plan," Sparks explained to the faculty, "and they fell out pretty badly." Among the regular Evening School student body, fifty or sixty dropped out the first month "because they find out there is work to it," and others departed when "it is too hard for them." FERA student failures and attrition rates were as high as twenty-five percent.[153]

Despite its focus on students, the Center, surprisingly, did not inaugurate a formal honors day program until spring 1939, although giving special recognition to individuals began four years earlier. The first honors day primarily recognized scholastic achievement. The faculty chose to award the most cooperative senior, and the Hilarian club recognized an outstanding woman for leadership, activity, and personality in addition to scholarship. The W. S. Kell award went to the senior coed with the highest average. Other seniors competed for the gold scholarship key sponsored by Delta Sigma Pi, and juniors for the Alpha Kappa Psi honor, both awards for the highest average in commerce. The top junior in liberal arts received the R. R. Johnson key. Even the lowliest class member commerce major could get recognition by winning the Delta Mu Delta key. By 1939, the Center began offering scholarships to honor graduates of eight area high schools.[154]

While more conventional colleges had placement bureaus for their graduates, the Center concentrated on finding employment in the Atlanta business community for incoming freshmen and other undergraduates. In 1937, the director reported finding 200 jobs and the next year, over 600. Many were junior college recipients, although a few transferred from the University of Georgia (UGA) and the GSCW. Sometimes money earned in Atlanta enabled them to return and graduate from the original colleges. Significantly, by 1940 this Center activity was attracting statewide attention. A Waycross attorney could not afford further education for a nineteen-year-old son finishing two years at the Gordon Military Academy and also send his daughter, a high school senior, to college. Can a young man "find work in the City of Atlanta which would enable him to make his own living while continuing his college studies," he asked Sparks.[155]

The Atlanta Center took special pains to maintain contacts with local businesses. Retail Credit, sponsor of a scholarship, wanted performance reports on all of its twenty-two student employees, including the dates attended, courses taken, grades, and faculty comments. These student affiliations with the business community could be very important. The 1939 winner of the Retail Credit scholarship, a Tech High graduate named William Lee Burge, later became the chief executive of that expanding company and a system regent.[156]

As the 1930s progressed, the Atlanta Center's new activities seemed to range, figuratively, from the sublime to the ridiculous. Instructor William Layton in 1939 organized a junior college orchestra, apparently in some haste. His notice in the *Junior Collegiate* beckoned interested "students with musical talent to report to his office immediately." Conductor Layton's talents also included supervising physical education and coaching the basketball team. That sport became so all consuming that personal conferences with male students were discontinued during the season. As for athletics and health programs, the Evening School's location only a block or so from the downtown, "white" YMCA facilitated a physical education program that had a ninety-hour requirement, although students could also get credit for participation in sports. In 1936, the Atlanta Center's Redbirds played basketball against Commercial High and also competed with the YMCA league's several local corporate teams. In 1937, they took the metro title with thirty wins.[157]

The *Signal* made no mention of women's sports throughout the 1930s. The director *did* attempt to interest a few coeds in tennis and arranged matches with sister colleges, usually only for two players. By March 1938, the variety of male sports prompted the *Signal* for the first time to begin carrying a separate section with regular reporting on basketball, swimming, bowling, and tennis. With the coming of wartime labor shortages, the Atlanta Center paid more attention to the academic needs of women. It offered new courses at more convenient morning hours particularly for housewives available for clerical positions in local businesses. As the armed services thinned the male ranks, women often filled the void. Early in the war, Jean

79

Johnson became the first female student body president elected by a comfortable margin of 217 to 150.[158]

The absence of a campus led the Center to seek student recreational opportunities elsewhere. In 1936, it leased for two years an eight-acre property some ten miles east of the city near Stone Mountain at Indian Creek, known as the old Venable home. Although the *Signal's* description, a "country club for the student body," greatly exaggerated its amenities, the property did contain an old, fourteen-room house on a wooded lot, tennis courts, and a swimming pool. It was for all the students, not any one group, such as fraternities, the *Signal* announced pointedly. The Center's subsequent purchase of the property, ultimately called the Indian Creek Lodge, provided students, faculty, and staff with a recreational asset of inestimable value then and indefinitely into the future.[159]

Although the Evening School held annual homecoming banquets, its alumni did not organize formally until March 1938 when four graduates met with registrar T. M. McClellan and formed an alumni association. After drafting a constitution, they prepared a circular letter that went out to 414 graduates. When the alumni association first met in March at the Center's roof garden, 125 attended. After a buffet supper, they elected a president and listened to a talk by the director. The following fall, the alumni homecoming banquet attracted seventy-five.[160]

In the 1930s, the faculty went through change. Although the Depression eased by the middle of the decade, college positions still remained scarce. At the same time, the appeal of an increasingly vibrant Atlanta could overcome some of the disadvantages of teaching in the undistinguished Evening School. In this buyer's market, Sparks picked up some promising, permanent faculty, two of them research scholars and all with doctoral degrees from reputable universities. To head the physical science department, Joseph H. LeConte arrived from the University of North Carolina in 1935. Having done research for five years on forest products, LeConte had an article accepted by the *Journal of*

Indian Creek Lodge. Courtesy of GSU Archives.

the American Chemical Society. Emory recognized his scholarly reputation by providing the use a laboratory for his research.[161]

The next year Merle Walker, with a Harvard degree in English, joined the faculty and became an unofficial dean of junior college women. Carl Mauelshagen came from the University of Minnesota, his history of American Lutheranism just issued by UGA's division of publications. Later he headed the social sciences. Mauelshagen devoted considerable time to the college's small library, which started up in 1931 with a handful of books provided by Sparks. Several hundred more, donated by founder W. S. Kell's widow, enlarged the collection in 1935. By one account, Mauelshagen persuaded Sparks to set aside a room and contributed many of his own books. With the "little bit of money" Sparks provided, Mauelshagen augmented the collection through used-book purchases from catalogs. A plaque commemorating Mauelshagen's role as "founder of the library," since lost, once adorned the Sparks Hall library entrance. Although George E. Manners did not yet have a doctoral degree, he joined the part-time faculty in 1937 to teach introductory accounting. A 1935 Evening School graduate, Manners had passed the state certified public accountant's examination while a sophomore. This part-time appointment was the beginning of a long association with the college, eventually as an upper-level administrator. In 1937, the year Mauelshagen arrived, Sparks reported other Ph.D.s as department heads with degrees from Chicago and Johns Hopkins. Elmer Campbell, a biologist and botanist, wrote feature stories in the *Atlanta Georgian* and later turned out a textbook in human biology. James Routh headed the English department. *Who's Who in America* listed both men, along with Sparks. Routh, who sported a Phi Beta Kappa key, listed writing, lecturing, radio broadcasting, and editing among his accomplishments.[162]

As a regents mandate, system faculties held monthly meetings. Compounding the requirement, the junior and evening college faculties met separately. In the early 1930s, the small faculty performed such tasks as approving the catalog and settling student problems, duties in later times handled by faculty committees or administrators. They dealt with requests to defer finals, excuse absences, and grant course substitutions, among other business. As the years passed and meetings proliferated, the director and his staff still proved up to the task of providing ample announcements for the faculty to absorb. The February 1935 meeting opened with introduction of every member. Besides information about the new conference rooms, personnel policies, and student absences, the thirty-one faculty received advice on ventilating the classrooms, assurances that the new Electrolux sweeper reduced the number of colds, an announcement of a fraternity candy sale, a request to help arrange student rides home, and a reminder that the "Office force is helpful and sympathetic." More appropriate, perhaps, was the registrar's parting request: "Be certain to require the Evening School students to do the same amount of work as the campus students must do."[163]

Although the director by the mid-1930s had appointed nominal department heads, the faculty's anemic committee system often left heavy burdens on individuals who apparently received neither released time nor extra compensation. Besides Merle Walker's AJC counseling, Elmer Campbell wrote sympathy notes to parents or students in cases of sickness or death. The messages, consciously informal and spontaneous, presumably were hand-written. In this busy setting, office space for department heads, if it even existed, had to be shared. Fortunately, anticipating the move to the Luckie Street building in 1938, Sparks reported that the "eleven full-time faculty members now have private offices so as to more easily carry on their heavy consignment of teaching."[164]

83

Joseph LeConte helped students find jobs. Fortunately, he could use form letters to contact those with applications on file. Even so, "Most of his time out of class has been taken up lately with interviews with these students," the faculty minutes reported. James Routh headed the committee on absences, whose three members monthly telephoned or wrote seventy-five to 100 students accumulating three or more absences. The dearth of replies undoubtedly compounded the task. Finally, Carl Mauelshagen worked up statistics from the placement exams.[165]

Some faculty got involved in Atlanta community and neighborhood activities. Of particular note were Mauelshagen's weekly lectures at the federal penitentiary, attended by about 100. Mauelshagen's wartime teaching duties at the Atlanta Center also took more time as he prepared new courses in Latin America, the United States and the Far East, the Americas, and American diplomacy. Sparks during the war years served as supervisor of the state merit system in the Bureau of Unemployment Compensation. He also held the rank of lieutenant commander as a member of the Naval Aviation Cadet Selection Board.[166]

The director expected faculty understanding of the students and their problems. Consult with them "and offer a word here and there," he urged. "So many things have been discovered by consultation. So many troubles have been ironed out." One quarter, when "winter weather and sickness...interfered with the smooth running of the school," Sparks "asked the teachers to help the students to complete their work for this term.... Those who have been ill need a little help to catch up now."[167]

Toward the end of the 1930s, the student body seemed to go through a change and so did faculty attitudes. By spring 1938, lagging student attendance became so widespread that the faculty voted to exclude from final exams those with more than six absences. In addition, registrar McClellan asked the teachers to try to stop the cheating. He also reported some vandalism, although probably "our own [Atlanta] Junior College boys" were not responsible for writing on the walls.[168] Then, as the new decade began, the faculty, at a meeting decidedly different in tone, seethed over student behavior.

The meeting began with complaints of noise in the lobby. Few faculty believed that getting the students into the library where they would make better use of their time would solve the problem. They made noise even when studying. Some faculty blamed the National Youth Administration scholarship students for setting "a bad example." A proposal to turn the auditorium into a study hall with a supervisor brought the director's intervention. Sparks believed "that there are many things worse than noise." The students "are in the age of 'shrieks,' and cannot be curbed too much." Indeed, "if they are kept quiet in the library they will be noisier in the lobby, and vice versa." Responding to Sparks, another teacher found not only the noise in the lobby "offensive" but "the petting carried on by the students." After noting an extended discussion, the minutes stated "that what there is of it [petting] would not go any farther and will not influence the other students or outsiders for the worse."[169] The faculty next focused on individual students making trouble and

84

annoying teachers, some by misbehaving in class. Surprisingly, the accusers mentioned names as well as offenses. One coed, a "very clever" girl who made "A" grades despite cutting classes, had become a nuisance "by capitalizing on her cuteness" to "attract attention." Another was "A material" and likable, but combined extra-curricular interests and classwork had over-loaded her. She seemed "to be attending college for its activities." Another used "chemistry as an excuse for failing sociology and to another teacher, slights chemistry in the same way." The only male singled out for criticism "just doesn't bother about taking tests" and is "absent when home work is to be given." Although a member of an honorary group, his grade had "fallen from A to F." By one professor's logic, the cause of these seemingly new student attitudes, particularly the unruly behavior and noise, grew out of claustrophobia in the absence of a campus.[170] Yet by this time, the Center had moved to better quarters on Luckie Street. Perhaps release from the blighting effects of the Depression affected them as it did the population as a whole. The beginning of the European phase of World War II in 1939 may have contributed psychological factors impossible to identify or measure.

85

Early in 1940, professor Mauelshagen's analysis of test per-centiles from national placement examinations introduced another equation. Atlanta Junior College students performed very well. The percentile, at sixty-three, compared favorably with Georgia Tech's seventy, Emory's and Agnes Scott's sixty-two, UGA's sixty, and the GSCW's forty-two.[171] Would any of the Atlanta Center's faculty even dare to surmise that this crop of brighter students might be bored and under-challenged? Director Sparks continued to picture them as mostly poorer, working stu-dents, although their test scores, grades, and interests seemed to indicate otherwise. By manipulating the curriculum, adding courses, and offering undergraduate majors in forbidden fields, Sparks had enlarged the Atlanta Center into a business *and* lib-eral arts college. These new opportunities may well have explained the popularity of the junior college among the area's brighter high school graduates who wanted to attend college but simply would not or could not leave home.

10

ACCREDITING THE ATLANTA CENTER: UGA TO THE RESCUE

While the war emergency introduced new challenges at the Atlanta Center, the accreditation problem still haunted the institution. The Center's tenuous position became clearer when the university system's standing with the Southern Association of Colleges (SAC) was threatened from another quarter. In 1941, Governor Eugene Talmadge launched a vicious attack on so-called "radical" professors. His meddling led SAC to suspend the "white" colleges, effective September 1942. Despite the seriousness of this action, director George Sparks remained a Talmadge loyalist. Citing a radio news report as his source, the director told the faculty that SAC's censure did not affect the system's professional schools, such as law, medicine, or agriculture. Since he placed the Atlanta Center in that category, "we do not belong to the Southern Association."[172]

Repeating a familiar and wishful refrain, Sparks held that accreditation did not matter. Transfer credits from the Evening School, although occasionally challenged, had "never been refused in any part of the United States." In fact, the Evening School was "fully accredited" by West Point and the United States Naval Academy. With the state's Democrat primary scheduled in September, one week before the SAC decertification order became effective, Sparks advised the faculty to wait for the results. As the only system unit head not supporting Attorney General Ellis Arnall for governor, Sparks surely believed that the incumbent Talmadge would prevail and the accreditation crisis somehow would disappear. After Talmadge's decisive defeat, the director quickly got the message. Georgia voters really cared about the system's credibility, and the unaccredited Atlanta Center could be in serious trouble. By January, Sparks had prepared for the chancellor a twenty-page report listing SAC standards and a rather casual assessment of the Center's qualifications.[173]

Sparks gave a passing grade to the admission and graduation requirements because they followed the University of Georgia (UGA) "to the letter." He rated the quality of instruction as "good in general." Admitting that no study had been undertaken, he would appoint a faculty committee to work on it. "What we do know is that hundreds of our transfer students every year make good in their work at other colleges," including Emory and UGA. While the Center's fifteen-hour teaching load per quarter was normal, the twenty-six to one average student ratio exceeded SAC's required twenty to one, and the Center probably needed three more full-time faculty. Low salaries, particularly for professors, also failed to pass muster. Twelve-month faculty incomes barely equated to SAC's standard for nine months. The Center's lack of adequate faculty governance necessitated the creation of at least eight departments, the minimum, and the appointment of faculty committees.[174]

The director also faced unpleasant financial realities. Having touted for over a decade the Atlanta Center's independence of state funding, he now recognized its absolute necessity. The Center needed a minimum annual state contribution of $150 per student for senior colleges and somewhat less at the two-year level. Although the state provided $21,000 the previous year, SAC mandated $58,000 more. Even the Center's in-house expenditure of $109 per student for instruction fell short. Reliance primarily on tuition payments and excessive numbers of low-cost, part-

88

time faculty would have to end. Regarding other matters, the director remained upbeat. The library "will pass," he stated flatly. Extra curricular activities had been properly supervised, alumni records kept, and contacts maintained. As to the administration, "surely under the University system we meet this standard." Overall, Sparks concluded, SAC standards had been met.[175] Although outside experts shortly refuted this unrealistic assessment, at least Sparks officially had acknowledged the problem.

Searching for a remedy, the regents once again turned to George A. Works for an evaluation both of the Atlanta Center and the General Extension Division. Works's 1932 *Report* on the university system, financed by the General Education Board, had pleased the regents. Two years later, at the behest of Emory, Agnes Scott, and Georgia Tech, he returned to study Atlanta higher education for the Rosenwald Fund. In both cases, he advised against duplication and institutional proliferation. If this philosophy still guided his thinking, his 1943 reappearance did not bode well for the Atlanta Center.[176]

Not surprisingly, Works assumed the Center would function solely as a commerce school. In this context, he severely criticized the wide selection of fields (seven) and courses (119) supporting Sparks's three-year bachelor of commercial science (B.C.S.) degree. A commerce degree for a social science concentration was "not at all appropriate." Although the Atlanta Center obviously had a liberal arts curriculum in place, Works refrained from recommending four-year degrees. He found the Atlanta Center relying "largely on part-time instructors," some forty-three out of the fifty-four teaching staff. Of the eleven regular faculty, the five Ph.D.s, one M.A., and five B.A.s, all seemed to have good academic preparation, but with teaching loads of twenty hours per quarter, they were overworked, and too many taught during summers. The part-time teachers also carried excessive loads. In addition, each instructor had too wide a range of subject matter, a practice "certain to endanger the maintenance of educational standards."[177]

89

Works reported the freshman attrition rate at thirty-three percent and even higher for advanced students. Although he drew no conclusions, excessive dropouts could signal respectable academic standards amidst the low admission requirements. Class sizes were too large, ranging from three to eighty-five, with senior division classes even larger. Of course, the Atlanta Center must be accredited, Works warned, or "the status of the entire system" would be threatened. The Atlanta Center's finances also had serious weaknesses, particularly "the inadequacy of its income from sources other than student fees." Regents support ranged from three percent ($2,000) to eight percent ($7,952) of the Center's budget between 1936–1941, finally rising to twenty percent ($20,040) in 1941–1942. Works's conclusions appeared almost perfunctory. The Atlanta Center needed more state funding, lighter teaching loads, additional full-time instructors, and a faculty in charge of curriculum and instruction.[178] His findings left little doubt that Sparks by himself was not up to appraising the Center's accreditation and academic standards.

Despite Works's sound judgments on faculty, financing, and accreditation, he continued to ignore the needs of the rising metropolis. The Atlanta Center "will serve the community more effectively" by developing "strong programs in the field of business." It should "offer no senior division liberal arts courses other than the few needed as service courses" in commerce. It was outdated advice ultimately to be rejected by accrediting bodies, such as the American Association of Collegiate Schools of Business (AACSB) and the Southern Association of Colleges. His conclusions seriously compromised the college careers of the Center's hundreds of majority "liberal arts" students. He assumed that only in-service teachers took social science courses, which could be provided by the private colleges. Despite high student enrollments, Works found only a limited constituency for the Center's eleven courses in art, seventeen in English, twenty-six in history and political science, five in journalism, two in music, six in philosophy, and eight in sociology, all in the senior division.[179]

Such conclusions ignored the Center's background and development and the large number of students with arts and sciences (A&S) majors, which included education. In 1933, when the Evening School began offering three senior-level degrees, a large A&S constituency developed almost overnight. Although the original enrollment figures could not be located, ninety-two undergraduates took degrees in 1936. A majority of forty-eight were A&S majors; a minority of forty-four commerce students graduated. Fourteen (thirty percent) of the A&S graduates received B.A.s, and four became teachers; eleven took the B.A. in Education, although only five took teaching jobs. Of the twenty-one B.S. in Education graduates, all but three pursued teaching careers. Also, one B.S. in the sciences graduated. Thus, of the forty-eight noncommerce majors, twenty-seven (fifty-six percent) were teachers, and twenty-one of that majority (forty-four percent) went into other occupations. A&S students at the Atlanta Center entering after the 1935 downsizing still could major in arts and sciences fields under Sparks's liberal bachelor of commercial science program. That the balance of enrollees shifted toward commerce by 1943, when Works did his study, was possible but by contemporary observation, generally improbable.[180] As Works evaluated the Atlanta Center, the Chicago educator, already a disciple of the General Education Board philosophy of elitism, surely was aware of the regents' determination to concentrate the liberal arts in Athens.

Once again, at a crucial point in the development of Georgia's public higher education, George Works rendered the dubious judgment that the state's resources should be concentrated at one higher education center. As economist Allan Cartter later pointed out, the Southern states had a choice between "expanding educational opportunities or improving the quality of the higher educational establishment." Georgia opted for quality, which affirmed its affection for UGA, but for decades the

91

state could achieve neither goal because of a tax system that impeded the procurement and allocation of financial resources. Works's belief that Atlanta's private white colleges offered a viable alternative also lacked realism. High tuition and selective admissions raised formidable barriers to young working Atlantans, in-service teachers, and white-collar professionals. Works's recommendations undoubtedly pleased the chancellor, regents and UGA. For the regents, the 1943 study became a system blueprint for nearly two decades. At the same time, they rejected Works's suggestion that the Atlanta Center "be continued as a separate unit...with a director responsible to the chancellor."[181] One important message got through, however. The Atlanta Center's problems with SAC threatened the university system, yet neither regents funds nor legislative will existed to finance an accredited Atlanta Center.

92

In the meantime, Athens came to the rescue with a plan already under study there. Authored anonymously, the document concluded that the "Evening College" could get accreditation as part of the university in a merger beneficial to both. In summer 1944, Chancellor S. V. Sanford began reviewing the plan. It revealed Athens's uneasiness with the "Evening College's" growth and other higher education developments in Atlanta. Of particular concern was the Atlanta University Center (AUC), a proposed amalgamation of Emory, Tech, and Agnes Scott supported by the Julius Rosenwald Fund, which chose Atlanta as one of five proposed Southern university centers. Atlanta's institutions should specialize in quality training as an inducement for outstanding teachers and graduate students to remain in the region. In 1934, after a study led by George Works, the Atlanta University Center received a $200,000 grant. In addition, Emory would get $2,000,000 on a double matching basis, and Agnes Scott, $500,000.[182] Chancellor Sanford pledged Tech's cooperation and also UGA's, even as Athens viewed these developments as threatening.

As Athens plotted to take over Atlanta's "Evening College and Junior College," concern over the AUC surely inspired that action. After the merger, "We should be in a stronger position to safeguard the University's interests...and remedy unsatisfactory aspects" of the AUC proposals. The merger also would aid in "the competition" for students who "cannot spend four years in Athens" or who "prefer to live" part of their college careers "in a metropolitan center." In this respect, an "Atlanta branch would" be a feeder to Athens's "professional and graduate schools" and help the University of Georgia compete "in certain professional and vocational fields," particularly "business administration, pharmacy, journalism, [and] education," all of which "could, and possibly should be taught in Atlanta." Of course, "we of the University should retain the right to specify subjects, teachers, credits, etc." From time to time, "duplicate sections of various subjects could be offered in Atlanta without disturbing the work or the mental security of [Athens's] faculty and students."[183]

93

Athens's interest in Georgia's major urban area was understandable. An urban setting generated levels of civilization and culture, as well as competitive advantages unattainable in semi-rural environments. A large city, with its court system, health facilities, financial institutions, industrial plants, and research and social centers, was like a social laboratory. There, professionals in these various fields could be more adequately trained. Indeed, many state universities already had established professional schools in the larger cities. But Athens's obviously calculating motives complicate appraisal. Basically, this audacious master plan for UGA expansion projected self-aggrandizement rather than service and "responsibility to society," a founding principle of the original extension movement. Of course, Chancellor Sanford saw it as a noble service. In unseemly haste, he sent it to the regents without the knowledge of UGA's administrative council.[184]

The Atlanta Center had "an excellent" facility, whose entrance requirements fulfilled SAC standards and whose degrees matched the rules of four-year colleges, Sanford told the regents. In the absence of SAC "machinery" for accrediting it, he recommended that the Atlanta school be made part of the University of Georgia. All faculty would be included in the Athens budget and selected by the heads of its various divisions. The regents' unanimous approval displayed their ignorance of accreditation and the serious issues involved. Contrary to Sanford's superficial analysis, the Center, in several areas already enunciated by George Works, clearly failed to meet SAC standards. Surely the chancellor knew that SAC "machinery" *did* exist to get the Center accredited. While accepting the general proposal, the regents referred it to the education committee for further study. But the decision, taken without UGA faculty consultation, seemed to be final. When the regents education committee met a week later, it recommended favorable action. In the meantime, it belatedly welcomed "any suggestions which the [UGA] Administrative Council…would care to make with reference to the proposal."[185]

The merger plan had circulated for months among Athens and system administrators, but the administrative council learned about it on October 11 when President Caldwell announced the regents approval. With little time to study this important matter, the council gave its endorsement provided the implementation be delayed until July 1945 when the new fiscal year began. The administration's secrecy inevitably aroused consternation and "grave doubts about the advisability of such a merger," and the council requested the appointment of "a subcommittee" to "prepare recommendations." The regents three weeks later backed off when its education committee inexplicably recommended that the "present status" of the Atlanta Center "remain unchanged."[186]

With the proposal under challenge, the chancellor prepared a detailed justification citing several universities that pursued urban adult education in order to extend "the benefits of higher education" to the "humbler citizens" who might desire learning.

94

He implied that UGA had similar lofty goals. At the same time, "certain schools" in Athens, such as nursing, social work, business administration, and graduate education, needed "a large area in which to operate," code words for "a large [urban] area [like Atlanta]." Indeed, the chancellor admitted, "metropolitan areas are essential for certain phases of university education. Atlanta provides the slum area, the clinics, the field work, etc." In summation, Sanford told the regents that "the state university of the future" must have "a social vision...dedicated to the making of a better world to live in."[187] While the chancellor's rhetoric soared, UGA's merger proposal remained decidedly earth-bound. As the original UGA document clearly revealed, the real object was to make a "better world" for Athens.

The administrative council's sub-committee wrestled with the merger issue for nearly three months. After a meeting with the chancellor "removed some of the doubts," the committee recommended approval provided UGA could take whatever steps "might be necessary to raise the academic standards[,]...reorganize the work," and appoint and change Atlanta Center personnel. At the same time, it made clear that the council "was in no sense an advocate" of the merger and vigorously disapproved "any action which would make the" Atlanta "Center, as it now stands, a part of the University." In the absence of adequate regents funding, there should be no "encroachment whatever upon funds" otherwise "provided for the University." The council pleaded for "more adequate support" so that UGA programs would not be jeopardized.[188]

Apparently in deference to the administrative council, the regents for a time held the final merger decision in abeyance. Meanwhile, chairman Marion Smith directed Sparks to state in a written memorandum what the Atlanta Center must do to qualify for full accreditation. "Of all the twenty [SAC] standards," Sparks replied in a statement that reflected Works's recent study, "those which this school cannot meet...relate to the allotment from the Board of Regents." At "$150 per year" for

95

each of the Center's 530 full-time students, $79,500 was needed. In addition, "a single, one-time allotment of $15,000 would probably be required...to meet immediate needs in additional library books and equipment." Over a two-year period, such an allocation would permit the employment of additional faculty, the enlargement of the library, the purchase of "necessary laboratory equipment," and the improvement of the physical plant. But there would be future needs. According to Veterans Administration estimates, 5,000 or more servicemen "will enroll with us," not to mention some "1,200 part-time students" presently attending "on any school day." Surely, the Southern Association of Colleges would require the acquisition of "a better and more adequate building."[189]

Ultimately, neither Sparks's optimism nor the University of Georgia's administrative council's doubts prevailed. The council, a purely advisory body, lacked the power to do anything but accept the *fait accompli* that its own administration, the chancellor, and the regents favored. The merger would take place in July 1947. But the Athens mindset, revealed in the documents both of the Athens expansionists and the UGA administrative council, foretold a difficult and adversarial relationship with Atlanta. Despite their differences, both Athens groups wanted to build programs and power in Athens, not Atlanta, and they had the full support of a board of regents dominated by UGA alumni. Nevertheless, in the upcoming merger, the Athens establishment faced some equally determined educational promoters at the Atlanta Center with expansionist dreams of their own, significant community support, important business contacts, and political allies in the capital city.

11

A PERMANENT HOME: ACQUISITION OF THE IVY STREET GARAGE

As Athens administrators and the chancellor plotted the University of Georgia's expansion to Atlanta, other developments propelled the Atlanta Center into an exciting postwar role. In summer 1942, President Franklin D. Roosevelt created the American Council on Education (ACE) to study postwar readjustment problems of civilian and military personnel. FDR wanted people whose educational pursuits the war interrupted to have an opportunity to renew their schooling, particularly with the draft age's lowering to eighteen. Under ACE leadership, the government, the higher education community, and veterans groups began intensive planning to accommodate armed services people. The Servicemen's' Readjustment Act of 1944, popularly known as the GI Bill, sealed FDR's commitment. The Veterans Administration (VA) estimated that 700,000 returning service personnel would enter college annually, while others put the figure at only 150,000. By February 1946, over a million had enrolled.[190]

Aware of these developments, director George Sparks and other adult education administrators also predicted large postwar enrollments, particularly of veterans. By 1945, the VA's Atlanta office estimated "that not less than one thousand, and possibly as many as five thousand returning veterans, will desire educational instruction" at the Atlanta Center. Clearly, more space must be provided.[191] It took the entrepreneurial and promotional skills of Sparks to make it happen, and, initially, he approached politicians rather than education officials.

The director first made the case for expansion to a legislative committee as it toured the Center in spring 1945. The committee rendered a favorable report widely endorsed in the press. Three thousand students attended, with 5,000 expected and 10,000 predicted in the postwar period, half of them veterans. The Center's Luckie Street home, overcrowded with one wing badly deteriorated, also was a fire hazard. The state would have to spend $400,000 for better facilities, particularly to keep "in this state at least $3,000,000 a year under the G.I. Bill." The regents should give the Center's building program an emergency classification.[192]

Aware that postwar shortages could cause endless delays for new construction, director Sparks searched the downtown area for space convertible to a teaching facility. In late spring, the large, six-story Bolling Jones building, or Ivy Street Garage, became available. Located two blocks from Peachtree Street and Atlanta's downtown "Five Points," this unlovely edifice combined office space and a parking garage, with elevators and driving ramps. Its 180,000 square feet of reinforced concrete construction dwarfed Luckie Street's 40,000-square-foot area of brick veneer.

A mid-1920's project costing $600,000, the building's disappointing Depression returns continued because of wartime parking and rent controls. The stockholders offered it for $296,000, a price below the appraised value. The Surplus Property Act of 1944 made available the kind of federal supplies and equipment, free or heavily discounted, needed to prepare the building for educational use. After an initial refurbishing, other renovations could be undertaken piecemeal as the school expanded. Besides lacking visual appeal, the Garage had another drawback. Although situated across from the stately, turn-of-the-

Bolling-Jones Building, or Ivy Street Garage (c. 1946).
Courtesy of GSU Archives.

century Hurt building, to the south it shared a city block with
several dilapidated structures and saloons in a Decatur Street
red-light district.[193] Although in the past Sparks had fought to
keep businesses of pleasure away from the school, his determination to possess the Ivy Street Garage overcame such reservations.

Sparks boldly acquired the property without official authorization, although by one account he had financial backers in the
business community. Having undertaken the purchase on his
personal signature, he had to persuade the regents to come up
with the $296,000. But this substantial sum represented only
part of the cost. Renovations could require over $100,000 more,
which had to be raised by selling the Luckie Street property. By
the end of May, a professional engineer estimated the Luckie
building's fair market value at $150,000, an unusually optimistic
figure.[194]

Armed with evidence of the Atlanta Center's potential financial viability, Sparks procured a letter from the state education

department predicting the enrollment of hundreds of veterans. Thus persuaded, the regents in June asked the governor to approve "the deal" and also provide the funding. While these negotiations proceeded, another obstacle appeared. Sparks had to inform the regents that the Luckie building's sale at $150,000 was unlikely. But Sparks knew he could raise additional money because the Veterans Administration, in a move to help colleges and universities prepare for the vast influx of postwar students, had agreed to pay out-of-state tuition for all veterans, including state residents. By fall 1945, the Atlanta Center already had over 150 registered.[195]

During the weeks immediately after the regents' approval, the negotiations became so tortuous and complicated that "we all but lost the fight for this building six times" when Governor Arnall refused to help, Sparks wrote. Ironically, money to purchase the Garage eventually came from three unrestricted trust funds established decades earlier by private donors for the University of Georgia (UGA) and Tech. The assets consisted of low-interest, federal, state, and railroad bonds maturing in 1945. Athens officials had been reticent and, in Sparks's view, "misleading," in discussing these assets with the regents. The director learned of their existence through his friend, state auditor B. E. (Ed) Thrasher, who "actually pointed the way on our first visit to him." With these funds, the regents authorized a $296,000 loan to the Atlanta Center at four-and-one-half percent interest. The principal would be amortized annually at $20,000 from the Center's rental income. This use of UGA money introduced another irony. Interest therefrom had been dedicated to loans for "deserving [UGA] students."[196]

Income from the Garage's tenants was vital. The highest monthly rents came from the Railway Express Agency ($750), the Southern Bell Telephone and Telegraph Company ($550), and the cotton brokerage firm, Anderson, Clayton and Company ($534), which since 1931 had occupied 25,000 square feet on the top floor. But that business's dust and congestion led the director to seek its removal months before the school moved in. With only a third of the building needed for the Center's immediate operations, Sparks expected the remaining rentals to yield over $30,000 annually, an amount that eventually doubled. As the renovation progressed, the regents fixed the rent at one dollar per square foot and moved their offices there, along with the teachers' retirement system. The regents' consulting engineer unsuccessfully tried to get over 1,800 square feet of office space free.[197]

The rental income and the veterans' out-of-state tuition placed the Center in good financial shape, and the fortuitous sale of the Luckie property to the Tabernacle Baptist Church that July cleared $85,000 for the Garage's renovation. Then, an unforeseen financial windfall turned up. According to a contemporary, the registrar's mistake in the Center's catalog cited the out-of-state tuition at twenty-five dollars per hour instead of twenty-five dollars per course. A later 1947–1948 Bulletin stated the matriculation and tuition fees for nonresident students at $50 per course, compared with $10 for resident students. With these funds, Sparks by June 1947 had retired the building's indebtedness and garnered an additional $91,000, with other large VA payments forthcoming. An official statement of estimated income for the year ending in June 1948 projected total nonresident tuition for the regular session at $310,000, and for June 1949, $447,200. For every thousand veterans, Sparks reported, "we shall receive $100,000 more than our present students pay, and you know enough about the finances of our program to know that we live very well on the tuition we receive from regular students."[198]

As Sparks and the regents negotiated the Garage's purchase, its renovation was turned over to the regents' resident engineer. When the architect he selected submitted cost estimates as high as $216,000, an alarmed regents chairman emphatically declared the purchase to be impossible. Within a week, the director found architect G. Lloyd Preacher, Jr., who agreed to perform the task

101

within the $85,000 budget, including his fee. Sparks also began contacting "nearly everybody in Atlanta" for leads "concerning surplus [federal] property." James "Jimmy" Carmichael at Bell Aircraft and "about a dozen other[s]" watched for the government order "to get rid of building material."[199]

The director's "ripest contact" was "the old Fisher Body plant where Firestone" made "wings for PBY planes." Its "movable partition material" when disassembled "could be used in our building." There also were "thousands of electrical fixtures," but Sparks knew "we are just one of many who will be in the general scramble." Help also came from politicians, including Mayor William B. Hartsfield, Atlanta's congressman, and the two U.S. senators. In his letters the director repeatedly mentioned "many of these returning soldiers [who] are coming back with the loss of legs." The new "fire-proof building" had "ramps and elevators." "[O]ur dreams for them would be a reality."[200]

By October, a University System Surplus Property Committee had established guidelines, ordering each unit to appoint a surplus property representative. Regents secretary Leonard Siebert urged immediate action because of the fierce competition. The first problem involved finding the federal locations where the material was available. In this quest, alumni might provide valuable information. Within six months, the system's procurement program appeared to have succeeded brilliantly. Other schools "have flooded congressmen" with protests, claiming favoritism, so that the Army was now reluctant to honor additional system requests. No publicity should be given out on the system's successes, Siebert warned, because public announcements only made it more difficult to secure additional property in the future.[201]

To procure materials, Sparks appointed physicist Newton S. Herod as administrative dean. On wartime leave from Georgia Tech, he worked at the Tennessee Oak Ridge nuclear facility. When Joseph LeConte, then a captain in the chemical warfare division, tipped off Sparks about surplus laboratory equipment at "two big chemical war plants in Columbia, Tennessee," Herod left immediately by plane "to select this material, which is to be given us and the freight prepaid to Atlanta." The continued search for surplus government property during that fall produced a windfall, and Sparks took everything he could get, selling or trading unneeded items. For weeks the Atlanta Center's truck, itself a surplus army vehicle "from Fort McPherson," busily hauled goods from government installations nearby and more far-flung places. The Bell Bomber plant at Marietta had lumber, electrical and plumbing fixtures, and "acoustical ceiling Celotex." Tennessee's Oak Ridge provided "47 tons of iron pipe," while the army base in Huntsville, Alabama, offered chemistry and physics equipment. With construction materials pouring in, the work proceeded so rapidly that all of the classes could move in from Luckie Street by March for the spring quarter.[202]

103

During the renovation, unforeseeable problems arose. One involved the unexpected flood of veterans, 1,300 by spring 1946 quarter. The Atlanta Center would have "to greatly enlarge our classroom and laboratory facilities" and run classes "from 9:00 in the morning to 9:00 at night." More renters would have to be terminated. The "run-down" condition of the property posed another problem and "added much expense." The "outside of the building" needed cleaning, "especially old wall-painted" advertisements on the side and back. To meet these costs, Sparks got an "additional $30,000" from the regents, because the GI money would not arrive until the end of the fiscal year in June.[203]

Sparks placed the value of the donated government property at over $200,000, and the release in August of heavy air conditioning equipment by the Bell Bomber plant may have boosted that figure to $300,000. In the collegiate rush for materials, the Atlanta Center did very well. It and the other 152 participating colleges and universities, by one estimate, received at least $43,000,000 in materials for less than $1,500,000, while another writer placed their value as high as $66,000,000. The flow of federal largesse would continue in summer 1946 with the Mead

Act's appropriation of $75,000,000. Sparks applied for $250,000 to the United States Office of Education (USOE) to make improvements, including a temporary gym annex at a reported value of $100,000. In addition to the building, the Atlanta Center received thousands of dollars more in equipment for classrooms, science laboratories, and the physical education department. Looking back on the project in fall 1947, dean Newton Herod believed that the use of war surplus materials shortened by a year the conversion of the Ivy Street Garage.[204]

The gymnasium, a surplus airplane hanger, measured 100 by 200 feet, enough space for two basketball courts that together could accommodate the entire student body. Over 5,000 such buildings were transferred to various colleges by the federal government, which usually paid the costs of dismantling and re-erecting them. The gym was in place behind the Ivy Street Garage by August 1947.[205]

The director took every opportunity to acquire land, particularly the vital parking lot to the north along three major streets near the Garage, including Courtland Street, where frontage was absolutely essential. Sparks "watched for several days the patronage of this property" involving "about 100 cars...at any one time," each bringing in ten cents per day. Having learned that the lot's purchase price earlier that year was $32,000, he concluded that under the Center's ownership even more could be made, because unknown to the lot's owner, "[t]he very day we close down [parking in] the garage...twice that many cars" would be paying rentals, and the property would "increase in value." Stressing the importance of "immediacy," the director shortly received regents authorization to purchase the lot for $51,700 with money derived from enrollments and a $28,000 advance from the state on the Center's 1946–1947 allocation. With this acquisition, the outlines of a downtown campus took shape that over the years involved picking up numerous small lots whose prices continuously escalated.[206]

By the end of May 1947, on the eve of the merger with the University of Georgia, the director reported the Atlanta Center's

104

total value at over $2,000,000. Engineers appraised the Ivy Street Garage at $928,000 "based on present cost of construction." The building material came to $300,000 and lab equipment at $160,000, all from the army, navy, and government agencies. The Center also received furniture and fixtures from several closed sites of the Office of Price Administration (OPA) in Atlanta and six other Georgia cities. Finally, the shortly-to-be-completed gymnasium-auditorium was valued at $250,000. Director Sparks's role in purchasing, renovating, and shaping up the Ivy Street Garage and contiguous properties probably constituted one of his most solid accomplishments. Even the Center's bitter enemies in Athens appreciated this feat. "I always knew that Dr. Sparks was a genius," dean of faculties Alvin Biscoe later wrote, "and I am glad to have the summary of the miracle he has accomplished."[207]

These had been heady times for the Atlanta Center and its director. Nevertheless, despite the receipt of hundreds of thousands of dollars in federal largesse, Sparks in his exuberance revived the myth that the Center could pay its own way and that the state could have a public college in Atlanta at little expense. All of these assets have "cost the taxpayer nothing," Sparks told the regents chairman, even as he reported the use of $71,000 in tuition income as building expenditures, a practice forbidden by SAC. The phrase "without cost to the state" appeared three times in Sparks's annual report for 1945–1946.[208]

While tight-fisted regents and legislators applauded Sparks's financial acumen and good luck, they ignored SAC admonitions that the state's contributions still remained inadequate and that the Atlanta Center's use of tuition money for capital expenditures could not continue. Although Sparks *did* recognize the "moral obligation" to repay "tuition payments from students," the practice continued.[209] In the ensuing years, these issues, along with accreditation, cast doubts on the Center's credibility and threatened its future.

12

POSTWAR EXPANSION: ATLANTA, THE CENTER, AND UGA

A s the Atlanta Center acquired the Ivy Street Garage, the city around it virtually leaped into a postwar decade of expansion. The Garage's startling increase in market value reflected these developments. While part of Atlanta's industrial base still included low-wage, nondurable industries like textiles, the future lay with the region's natural resources, particularly food processing and the manufacture of durable goods. Although state-of-the-art manufacturing lay in the future, Atlanta excelled as a distribution center, with twenty-eight percent of the labor force in wholesale and retail pursuits. In this setting, the railroads, joined by air, truck, and auto transportation, continued to provide the basis for growth. As early as 1944, a blueprint of the city's transportation needs included expressways as well as street improvements. The city's freeway system was well underway before large-scale federal funding became available in the mid-1950s.[210]

Atlanta also used surplus war material to upgrade its airport and construct a new passenger terminal, and by 1949 it ranked seventh nationally in traffic volume. In nearby Marietta, the huge Bell Aircraft complex, which during the war assembled B-29 bombers and employed over 27,000, came back to life. In 1950, the Lockheed Aircraft Corporation reopened the plant and shortly began assembling B-47 bombers for the Korean War. Within a short time, some 10,000 workers occupied the once-abandoned facility. In a region of hot, humid summers, air conditioning already had begun to enhance the quality of life, and other amenities followed. In 1950, the Army Corps of Engineers began constructing the first of two dams that assured an abundant supply of water as well as recreational opportunities. By 1972, the Lake Lanier-Chattahoochee River recreation area attracted fifteen million visitors, more than the combined patronage of four great national parks. Atlanta began World War II with some 300,000 inhabitants. Ten years later, 330,000 lived just within the city limits, with over half a million in the larger urban area.[211] Such postwar expansion put extra demands on the still unaccredited Atlanta Center, which the upcoming merger with the University of Georgia (UGA) in July 1947 sought to repair.

While director George Sparks oversaw the Ivy Street Garage's renovation, the Atlanta Center's administrative and academic affairs suffered serious neglect. Reorganization was required before the merger and as a prerequisite for the March 1946 filing of the Southern Association of Colleges (SAC) application for accreditation. Except for the executive council, the institution always had been run very much out of the director's hat. With Sparks preoccupied, the executive council in January 1946 addressed reorganization by authorizing a new administrative council, faculty advisory council, and several faculty committees. It also designated departments and approved the appointment of their chairs. Yet it is unclear if or when this new organizational structure began functioning, or how much independence Sparks permitted. In a May meeting, Dean Newton Herod gave the department chairs orders that violated the Catalog: mature students need not observe the required prerequisites when registering for advanced courses. Faculty committees ordinarily handled such matters. The appeal to SAC went unmentioned.[212]

By mid-February 1946, the regents office began expressing considerable concern. Secretary L. R. Siebert could not get Sparks's response to his urgent letters about accreditation and the Center's allocation of regents funds. With the system, itself, in danger, Siebert strongly urged Sparks to seek help from unit presidents and administrators when preparing and presenting the Center's SAC application. Sparks heeded this advice, but his attention to other matters continued until April when Siebert again admonished him. In order to strengthen the Center's SAC bid, the regents twice came up with special allocations for administrative positions and new department chairs. They believed any new administrators should be "persons of real stature" to facilitate accreditation. Yet none of the appointments had been made, nor had the money earmarked for the full- and part-time faculty, extra staff and equipment, and purchasing library books been properly allocated. Siebert asked for "an immediate complete report" which Sparks should make "your number one concern."[213]

109

Sparks responded six days later, justified the delays, and offered no apologies. When the regents' first allocation had been made, most faculty "were easy to employ." Since the war ended, "every college in the nation also has growing pains." Nevertheless, the Atlanta Center had hired three men of real merit, including the scientist Joseph LeConte, retained at considerable cost "when he returned from service." Delays also had occurred because the chancellor held the Center up while reviewing the UGA merger. Other problems surfaced because the regents' appropriation in September 1945 had come too late for recruiting; "colleges over the country had already opened. But Sparks had "several other Ph.D.'s" in mind. One from Iowa would interview that very week, "a southerner...[who] wants to come back home." Another under consideration was a Ph.D. from Yale.[214]

As for SAC, Sparks had sent certain materials to executive secretary Huntley at the end of March, probably without immediately informing Siebert. The director also personally had stated the Atlanta Center's case for accreditation to President John McCain of Agnes Scott College, who chaired SAC's admissions committee. Sparks speculated optimistically about the Center's prospects, although these ruminations were no more acute than his earlier comments on that subject. SAC's reply contained specific procedures to be followed. "[T]he purposes and work of the school...[were] not entirely in line with the other" SAC institutions, Huntley wrote. Consequently, "Before serious consideration can be given to an application for admission," a special study must be made. He assured Sparks that SAC "would certainly deal with the subject from a service standpoint and would not be concerned with meeting Southern Association standards." Having a "considerable waiting list for such studies," Huntley proposed an "informal appraisal by some out-of-Georgia people" and suggested four Southern college presidents, including Tulane University's Rufus C. Harris.[215]

Shortly, SAC officials advised the director to begin an immediate increase in the Atlanta Center's full-time faculty for the upcoming academic year, which required an additional $27,650 in state funding. Considering his past reluctance to request *any* money from the state, Sparks apparently pondered such a move with apprehension and even sought the advice of Tulane's Rufus Harris by long-distance telephone. He also consulted a confidante, state Treasurer W. Wilson Noyes, before deciding to make the request. "[L]ow appropriations" made it difficult to find faculty, Sparks noted, and "other colleges, by necessity of big enrollments, [were] out offering everyone who can teach a big salary to come with them."[216]

Meanwhile, Sparks began contacting the "out-of-Georgia people" for the Atlanta Center's preliminary SAC appraisal. He rejoiced that Rufus Harris would be one of the visitors. Sparks telephoned Harris, a native Georgian who still kept a home in the town of Madison east of Atlanta, to express his pleasure. He "seems to be the one man they all listen to," Sparks enthusiasti-

110

cally told Siebert. After his inspection, "we will know what to do."[217] Sparks's unwillingness to confront the basics of accreditation had been a longstanding problem for over a decade and a half. After countless SAC communications over the years, and after detailed studies by outside experts and his own staff, Sparks still seemed very much at sea as to what had to be done. Undoubtedly, he deeply feared having to apply for additional state funding. Perhaps he confused the academic scene with the world of politics. His belief that Rufus Harris would be listened to and "know what to do" suggested that perhaps an academic politician or influential friend in the Southern Association of Colleges could cut corners and get the Atlanta Center past the requirements. In reality, the procedure would be frustrating and time consuming, to which the chancellor's office, if not Sparks, apparently had become reconciled. But as the proceedings dragged on, SAC would not meet again until December.

111

With accreditation in temporary limbo and with the Ivy Street Garage renovation nearly completed, the Atlanta Center began preparing for the upcoming merger with UGA in July 1947. Initially, the Center's two top administrators favored such a union. Director Sparks wanted it primarily to receive the university's mantle of accreditation, while the newly named Atlanta Division, he believed, would continue to operate independently. By one account, Sparks also harbored hopes that the merger would bring his appointment as a UGA vice president. The new, acting resident dean of business administration, George E. Manners, favored merging for a different reason. He hoped that the university would assist in developing "an academic program of some consequence," because the director, left on his own, would never support that kind of excellence.[218] Of course, both men expected the Atlanta Division to expand in meeting the city's academic needs. As it turned out, both miscalculated.

In spring 1947, leaders at the Atlanta Center put forward their vision of the new relationship. A policy committee appointed by the director recommended total autonomy in nonacademic areas and near independence in academic affairs. The Atlanta Division's internal business operations and the income therefrom, already mostly dedicated toward the removal of the debt, should remain independent of Athens's budgetary control. But the committee also suggested that plant operations as well as more sensitive matters, such as institutes, publicity, public relations, and promotions, among others, should also be autonomous, with faculty salaries and rank handled independently of appointments made at Athens.[219]

The Atlanta Center's curriculum for over a decade had followed the University of Georgia closely, but in some cases, business students' needs in Atlanta differed from those in Athens. Thus, the division's business faculty freely should be able to initiate new courses with the approval of its own executive committee and dean of faculties. The Atlanta unit also would have the power to propose budget amendments with copies furnished to the comptroller in Athens. The chancellor would arbitrate any disagreements with the Athens administrators. Finally, the committee requested that UGA's business college begin offering graduate work in Atlanta and investigate a four-year program in the liberal arts.[220]

The regents' demonstrated willingness to break its own rules regarding unit functions may have encouraged the Atlanta Center's planners to pursue the arts and sciences. The previous year, the small, two-year North Georgia College in Dahlonega, fifty miles north of Atlanta, received four-year status accompanied by authority to grant the B.A. and B.S. degrees and offer a full range of course concentrations, including premedical and predental programs. North Georgia's president, Jonathan C. Rogers, explained that the change had been requested by the U.S. War Department so the unit now could retain its military college status and listing with other institutions, including the Citadel and the Virginia Military Institute.[221] Of course, unlike the Atlanta Center, North Georgia College posed no threat to UGA.

Thus, in the waning days of the Atlanta Center's independ-ence, some of its leaders had high hopes that some happy, trouble-free, and nearly autonomous existence would result from a merger with the University of Georgia. Considering the many problems involved, especially accreditation and state funding, such expectations were highly unrealistic.

113

13

LOST OPPORTUNITIES:
THE FIRST MERGER PLAN FAILS

When the Atlanta Center became the Atlanta Division of the University of Georgia, Athens officials had an unprecedented opportunity to enhance public higher education statewide and provide a significant public service to Georgia's major urban area. As Atlanta's population grew, the need for extended public higher education had never been greater. When the war ended, the influx of GI Bill veterans with their government tuition and support checks enhanced the Atlanta Center's status. With the UGA merger, Athens now had the chance to provide real academic progress.

George Manners, a recent UGA master's graduate in economics and the Atlanta Center's new resident dean, made such proposals to UGA dean of faculties Alvin Biscoe shortly after the merger. "I tried to persuade him...that the president of the University would be president of Atlanta and Athens." The two institutions would be governed together with "a resident in Atlanta as well as Athens and a small core of vice presidents...to coordinate the two institutions and really make them one." Manners would "let students go back and forth whichever way they wish," with each discipline growing "in relation to its environment." Administrative and teaching responsibilities could have been shared, duplications avoided, and genuine cooperation achieved. Above all, a united entity could get accreditation from the Southern Association of Colleges (SAC).[222]

But a harmonious relationship never developed. Initially, Athens imposed rigid oversight as unrealistic as the loose relationship envisioned by director George Sparks. The plan unraveled within a year. Some Athens administrators viewed the Atlanta Division as a dangerous rival to be continuously reined in. Resentful division leaders had their own expansionist agenda. Later, as evidence mounted that the merger had failed, a determined UGA president fought relentlessly to maintain control for the sole purpose of blocking the division's expansion. After eight years of angry co-existence, in 1955 the regents, also divided, separated the two.[223]

The University of Georgia during its long existence had no previous satellite beyond the Athens campus that prepared it for administering the Atlanta Division. True, until 1932 all Georgia public colleges theoretically were branches of UGA. Even the Georgia Tech catalog paid homage to that fiction. Yet most units functioned independently. When, for financial reasons, Augusta's private medical college in 1873 became a UGA department, its trustees and faculty maintained independent operations and curriculum development, although the Athens chancellor signed the diplomas. In 1911, with a new board subordinate to UGA trustees, the medical school still remained virtually autonomous. The university's Savannah branch at Hunter Air Field, established in 1946 primarily for veterans turned away from the overcrowded Athens campus, became an administrative disaster. Rivalry with Savannah's white Armstrong Junior College, faculty unrest, and veteran protests over restricted curricula and limited expansion plans led to its closure in 1948, a year earlier than planned.[224]

In approving the UGA-Atlanta Center merger, the regents provided no guidance, giving Athens the overwhelming advantage in the ensuing dialog. That July, Dean Biscoe unveiled a plan of operation that bound the Atlanta Division to UGA like a campus department. Forwarded for director Sparks's signature, the "first plan" already had been approved by the Athens administrative council, the president, and the chancellor. It vested the selection of all Atlanta Division officers and faculty in Athens. The director, appointed by the UGA president, had vague duties "of a general administrative nature with coordinating powers." Dean Biscoe's Athens "Coordinator" kept "policies and regulations in Athens and Atlanta unified." The university's arts and sciences dean, with the director's approval, chose his own Atlanta resident dean who was "responsible to the [Athens] Coordinator."[225]

Mid-level Atlanta administrators, from dean of students to publicity officer, also were chosen by Athens to "be responsible to the appointing officer." In his titular status, director Sparks had one dean of his own choosing, the previously appointed George E. Manners. UGA deans and department heads had the same responsibilities in Atlanta as in Athens, including appointment, dismissal, promotion, and the determination of all course offerings, with division approval. Curricular additions and changes passed through various UGA departmental and college committees, each with one Atlanta representative.[226]

Besides the seventy-mile distance to Atlanta and the two or more hours of commuting time, the plan appeared unworkable for other reasons. "Coordinator" Sparks's administrators reported to different Athens superiors. If a division veto had any meaning, faculty recruits would shuttle between Athens and Atlanta for two sets of interviews. Curriculum proposals passed through two departmental and administrative structures. Administrators and committee members would be traveling more or less continuously between the two units. To Dean Biscoe, however, "This plan must be followed" in order to get accreditation. Besides its complicated execution, the plan also signaled UGA's strong distrust of the division, its administration, and the faculty. Athens assumed that the "quality of work" was inferior, undoubtedly true in some cases, although the division's

117

small faculty included some highly qualified people. Shortly, Dean Biscoe informed the director that UGA administrators "are assuming full responsibility for the operation of your offices." By early October, various Athens officials had completed their Atlanta visits and established what Dean Biscoe enthusiastically described as "working arrangements."[227]

Skirmishes over division faculty appointments became inevitable, and the first clash could not have strengthened Athens's confidence in the director's judgment. The son of a high state official close to Sparks became division librarian, despite Athens's warning of the man's incompetence, "even in a junior position," and his rejection for a position at UGA. In recruitment, Sparks needed both help and direction, but previous commitments to seven faculty candidates could not be derailed. While Athens administrators delayed their approval because insufficient data had been submitted, the offers had been made several months before the merger, and some already had resigned their previous positions. In the future, Biscoe warned, Sparks should "submit all available data...before any commitments are made." Division "chairmen can simply recommend."[228]

118

Sparks also must refrain from making public statements about division affairs. The University of Georgia publicity director journeyed to Atlanta just to make the point that Athens would handle all public relations releases. Sparks's announcement of the merger had upstaged President Harmon Caldwell's press conference, planned to follow the September meeting of the regents. The director, a deft practitioner, had used his formidable skills in promoting the Evening School for nearly twenty years with considerable success. The Athens establishment could never silence him, and separating such a popular figure from the division would have been impossible.[229]

Disagreements also developed over the future of Atlanta's business program. A key issue was the division's degree-granting power. Resident Dean Manners knew that the division's three-year, nonaccredited bachelor of commercial science (B.C.S.)

degree must be eliminated with the adoption of a four-year bachelor of business administration (B.B.A.). Yet dropping the B.C.S. would end the division's popular, three-year arts and sciences and education degrees, which Sparks and Dean Newton Herod strongly supported.[230]

Negotiations that September took place on a fairly level plane because the Atlanta program, particularly accounting, surpassed Athens's in quality. A conference of area accounting professors held at Emory University recognized this fact, expressing the "general opinion...that the offerings adequate to prepare for a CPA [certified public accountant] examination were those now offered at the Georgia Evening College." In fact, one UGA faculty member proposed installing the Atlanta program on the main campus, a suggestion emphatically vetoed by his dean. Not only did the division offer several courses unavailable at Athens, but it also followed more closely the regulations of the American Institute of Accountants, which recognized as majors only graduates passing the CPA examination. In the negotiations, Atlanta kept its advanced accounting courses but agreed to adopt Athens's freshman and sophomore requirements for the B.B.A.[231]

119

Other issues proved equally contentious. The Atlanta Division's older students often brought knowledge of the business world to the classroom. While such individuals could take special exams and receive course credit, UGA rejected such "a radical departure from our practice." A degree should represent class hours actually taken, not a level of achievement. UGA students taking such exams received only an exemption from the course. The conferees also disagreed over the length of time students needed to finish degree requirements. Athens's young, full-time students had a time limit. Numerous division students, older, often married, with jobs and families, struggled for years, a course or two at a time. Manners strongly opposed setting limits on the grounds of student health, and the subject was dropped. Another important matter involved the residency requirement, which had a direct bearing on the Atlanta Division's new bachelor of business administration degree. At the time, the residency issue provoked little discussion. It would be optional, the UGA dean pledged. Thus, the Atlanta Division would be allowed to offer the four-year B.B.A. degree.[232]

The business school conferees had aired a wide range of issues, some of limited consequence, and others, such as exemption exams, time limits, and textbooks, without resolution. Almost all of the discussion revealed differences between a powerful university serving primarily young high school graduates, many from the state's "best" families, and an emerging urban college that dealt with a different type of student. Besides the matter of power, two philosophies of education contended, each expressed with elements of moral certitude. If Athens officials believed that airing several points of disagreement and enunciating the UGA position produced a consensus, and that the division leaders and faculty obediently would fall into line, they seriously misunderstood the new relationship. Often the frustrated Atlanta conferees returned to the division and simply carried on as before. As events revealed, Athens purposely misled Manners regarding the B.B.A. degree. He shortly discovered that the residency requirement, so easily disposed of in conference, remained very much alive.

The following month, having been "advised that the University faculty" on October 17 would discuss resolutions affecting the Atlanta Division, Manners was present when the faculty fleshed out the merger plan and tightened Athens's control. But a statement about UGA's residency requirements infuriated him. A senior must take a minimum of forty-five hours of Athens credit and in the major field, one half of the courses in a campus department. At the same time, the faculty authorized the continuance of the Atlanta Division's three-year bachelor of commercial science degree (B.C.S.), signaling the death of the division's four-year bachelor of business administration. In effect, the B.B.A. required the senior year in Athens.

Except for the B.C.S. program, the Atlanta Division's status would be the same as nondegree-granting off-campus centers in Columbus, Waycross, and Gainesville.[233]

Manners immediately visited Dean Biscoe. What followed was "one of the most...shocking and somewhat vitriolic meetings I ever had." Biscoe planned to meet shortly with the Southern Association of Colleges and announce that the Atlanta Division would become an off-campus center. "Well, Dean Biscoe," Manners stated, "You're going to take away the degree programs of thousand[s] of veterans all on your own[,] talking with a few people here [at Athens. A]nd you think that's going to be the end of it?" As the first thing, "we will revoke the merger.... We're not going to commit suicide." Biscoe's action "could not survive the outrage that would come at that particular time." After three hours, the two men finally "parted with the understanding that he [Biscoe] would take no action" at that time.[234]

The Atlanta faculty two days later unanimously resolved that the quality of the division's work "deserve[d] accreditation" and requested authority to grant the B.B.A. degree. After meeting in December with the UGA president and academic deans, Biscoe signaled that Athens had given up. "The [division's] B.C.S. degree [would be] changed to the B.B.A. as soon as the class work and the personnel are satisfactorily integrated." In Atlanta, the administrative staff received the news with elation, although the faculty insisted that the B.C.S. degree "be retained for those already registered." The B.B.A.'s implementation came in fall 1948 with business students enabled to take all their required courses in the daytime program. The action was immensely significant,

George E. Manners, SBA Resident Dean, 1948–1955; Dean, 1955–1969. Courtesy of GSU Archives.

because the division now had a four-year degree with the same requirements and academic standards as UGA. Later, academic work in Atlanta received American Association of Collegiate Schools of Business (AACSB) approval.[235]

The four-year business degree became one of the turning points in that institution's short history, perhaps no less significant than the Evening School's purchase of the Sheltering Arms, expansion of the B.C.S. program to include arts and sciences majors, the passage of the GI Bill, and the acquisition of the Ivy Street Garage. Without the bachelor of business administration, the college's academic development could have been delayed for years. Manners's vigorous action involved more than bluff and bluster. Director Sparks could count on important support in Atlanta after having completed the purchase and renovation of the Ivy Street Garage, which lay just across the tracks from political power at the state capital. The director had friends and influence in the chancellor's office and with certain regents and legislators. Unhappy veterans already had made waves over UGA's sparse course offerings and limited programs at its Savannah branch, and the Atlanta Division's clientele included hundreds more of those older, more mature, and independent spirits.

Despite the friction accompanying the merger, Athens made many useful contributions. As the resident staffs merged with the University of Georgia, one Athens dean corrected inequities in division salaries, particularly the faculty's extra, uncompensated administrative work. Some division departments, overseen by their Athens superiors, recruited faculty probably for the first time, because Sparks previously hired the part-time teachers and apparently ran the outside searches. Nevertheless, one division chair was particularly amateurish: "IN ORDER TO RECOMMEND CANDIDATES INTELLIGENTLY MUST KNOW SALARY ATTACHED TO POSITION MENTIONED," stated a Columbia University telegram. One impulsive department head had to be restrained. Regardless of a candidate's strong curriculum vita,

122

"any man [sic] considered for an associate...or full professorship should be personally interviewed," Athens advised. The division's English department, having to recruit high school teachers, learned from Athens that a candidate's "long teaching experience...does not qualify for the rank of associate professor." Give him "what [money] you consider necessary to get him on your staff."[236]

On the other hand, Athens's recruitment sometimes compromised the division faculty. In 1948, when UGA transferred nine administrators and faculty from its deactivated Savannah branch to Atlanta, only one, a foreign language instructor, held the Ph.D., and few had any research interests. Acquiring the Savannah group had ramifications far into the future. Accumulating longevity as full-time faculty, at least three became department heads without terminal degrees, and one, Savannah's acting director, with only a bachelor's degree, later served as the Atlanta registrar and then academic dean. Further Athens dumping occurred on the division's mathematics department and the business school.[237]

123

Although the director had been pushed to the sidelines in faculty recruiting, he challenged some appointments. In late summer 1948, he rejected four. One philosophy candidate, opposed on moral grounds (alleged "drinking sprees"), accepted a Pennsylvania position at $5,200, a sum beyond both the division's and UGA's reach. Another, a former Center undergraduate and Emory graduate student, was too young and inexperienced for "our adult students, many of whom are years older." Sparks's ideal philosophy instructor was a friend and preacher in nearby Newnan who commuted "back and forth...to give his inspiring lectures to the day division students," Sparks wrote President Harmon Caldwell. One candidate was suspected of harboring liberal racial views. Still another, a young biologist, could not command respect, because "[m]any of our adults" were "years older," having been recruited "from the army posts and hospitals." Exasperated Athens Arts and Sciences Dean Leon P. Smith vowed to cease offering philosophy courses "at the Atlanta Division" taught by "unqualified part-time men [sic]" unless full-time faculty upheld university standards.[238]

Dean Smith also had a salutary influence on other division practices. He ordered the English department to reduce class sizes and increase the number of full-time faculty. He brought the nighttime program more in line with daytime standards and ended their separate identities. He also imposed more discipline over the division's part-time teachers and kept a constant watch for grade inflation. His comparison of division and UGA grades in spring 1949 found "only 5.5% of the [Atlanta] grades" below the "D" level, an unsatisfactory distribution in the absence of selective admissions policies. Some instructors "had no failures at all," one "gave only A's," and another "more than 50% A's." Dean Biscoe's grade analysis the following summer, like Smith's, found some grade inflation, but he seemed to delight in disparaging the division faculty. Biscoe seemingly made no allowance for the generally high attrition rate of division students, with large numbers of withdrawals early each quarter. The Works study six years earlier found no fault with the Atlanta Center's grades, and even Biscoe's statistics showed that the large majority of the division faculty exercised grade restraint, some being extremely tough taskmasters.[239]

Initially, the University of Georgia's fine arts college also made important contributions to the Atlanta Division, introducing new programs and faculty where few previously existed. UGA artist Lamar Dodd discovered the division's art program lacked both a chair and full-time teachers, persuaded Sparks to fund an art program with $10,000 over two years, and found three faculty candidates. Despite Dodd's best efforts, the project lagged in part because the program competed with work offered at Atlanta's High Museum. UGA's music department under Hugh Hodgson hoped to expand into the metropolitan area with a two-year program in preparation for senior work in Athens. Of course, Hodgson suffered from the usual Athens paranoia:

124

"Every effort must be made to avoid any impression of the transference of the Athens Department to Atlanta," he warned, but his activity there would "eventually add to the musical strength of the mother institution." By April, the division began taking faculty applications for the new fine arts department and found about 100 Atlanta high school seniors interested in enrolling. Sparks ordered six new pianos, including two Steinways and a Baldwin.[240]

That summer, Hodgson planned to make the division "the Music Center of Atlanta." On weekends, the recently formed Atlanta Symphony Orchestra practiced there, and conductor Henry Sopkin became a part-time division instructor. But as time passed, the orchestra's practice sessions, often extending from Fridays into Mondays, ran afoul of the Atlanta Division's "very profitable" institutes for businessmen. In a letter to Hodgson, direct and ungracious, Sparks's secretary, Mrs. W. B. (Laura) Cantrell, stated the case: "Atlanta business men cannot see why they should bring in a $500.00 a day expert...and then be shoved around by an orchestra practice," especially when "the orchestra gives the school no publicity—not a line." Nevertheless, the orchestra apparently continued practicing there until 1965. Besides art and music, the Athens drama department also sought to expand into the Atlanta Division.[241]

While Dodd and Hodgson planned programs and searched for staff, the UGA business school lured division faculty away. James Whitney Bunting, a promising young economist, departed to direct the UGA's bureau of business research. The Bunting case illustrated the division's ability to attract top-flight faculty and the difficulty in keeping them because of the restricted programs. When UGA Dean James Gates later recruited another division economist, resident Dean Manners strongly objected. Athens's own procedures for inter-faculty recruitment had been violated. The professor must "initiate the request" and if successful, leave with "the same salary and rank." Manners insisted that the man leave only after "a replacement can be found."[242]

125

Regardless of the University of Georgia's contributions to music, art, and drama, and despite Dean Leon Smith's attempts to introduce university standards, many at Athens treated the Atlanta Division badly, a fact which Dean James Gates readily admitted. While some conscientiously sought to build programs and faculty, others belittled the Atlanta Division and sought to restrain its development. All viewed the division as inferior, true in some respects, but they also feared its potential rivalry. Not only did conflicts over faculty appointments sour the relationship, by summer 1948 Dean Biscoe's cumbersome merger plan had caused serious budgeting delays. "[D]uplicative handling in Athens," the director complained to Dean Smith, had occurred "at the expense of getting several most competent teachers." As a result, the Atlanta Division would face "turmoil at the beginning of next Fall."[243]

Meanwhile, SAC had not been idle. In June, it warned President Caldwell that the merger threatened UGA because of the Atlanta Division's inadequate funding. In 1947–1948, the state provided only $10 per student. SAC, whose standards required $150, asked for data on appropriations and enrollment for both units. Unless the state became exceptionally generous, "the inclusion of the Atlanta Division will cause the income per student for the University as a whole to drop far below minimum requirements." Grave problems and serious decisions lay ahead. Among other things, the first plan of merger had failed.[244] In late September, UGA and division officials met again in an attempt to patch up the relationship.

14

REORGANIZATION, RECESSION, AND FINANCIAL RESCUE

When a joint committee met in Atlanta in late September to discuss the Atlanta Division's future, faculty appointments and budgeting delays headed the agenda. All agreed that the budget's late approval had hampered division recruiting. President Harmon Caldwell, seeking to calm the Atlantans, promised to change UGA practices that conflicted with division needs. The budget "was not completed and returned to us until July," Sparks later complained to regent Pope Brock, a Coca-Cola executive. By that time, all good faculty had found jobs elsewhere. Having been delayed in recruiting, "we took over fifteen [nine] faculty members from the Savannah Division, including the only Ph.D. Athens secured for us."[245]

The Atlanta conference adopted new procedures "to facilitate the inter-relations of Athens and Atlanta." The Atlanta budget process would be handled independently of Athens. "[P]repared at the Division and submitted in duplicate to" the University of Georgia (UGA), one copy would be returned to director Sparks "with approval or with suggested changes...within two weeks." Preparation of the division's academic program also would be expedited. Finally, the group dealt with division recruitment, which, under Dean Alvin Biscoe's plan, had broken down the previous July. Yet the adopted solution revealed Athens's unwillingness to yield any ground on this important function, nor perhaps should it, considering the director's faculty priorities. Dual recruitment continued, with efforts to expedite the paperwork. Meanwhile, the two business deans, George Manners and James Gates, cooperated with the Standard Oil Company in establishing a new, two-year division program on transportation and traffic movement based on a similar experiment in Chicago. Transportation in Atlanta and the South had become a business needing specialists, Sparks told the *Signal*. Full college credit and a certificate would be provided.[246]

While budgets and recruiting dominated during the first merger year, financial problems overtook the system in late 1948. For over three years after the war, the Veterans Administration (VA) had been a contented money cow for the Atlanta Center. It paid out-of-state fees for all veterans, including native Georgians, and provided undetermined reimbursements under the Center's faulty catalog. Sparks justified, and the VA granted, nonresident tuition because "[w]e do have a situation quite different from all others [in the system]." As Sparks later indicated, UGA and the extension division in separately negotiated contracts received smaller amounts. Following the 1947–1948 University of Georgia catalog, the amount collected from each out-of-state student included $100 for tuition plus the resident matriculation fee of $47.50. The Atlanta Center collected an additional fifty-dollars per quarter for each full-time veteran. At the merger, this lucrative VA arrangement as well as the division's auxiliary income motivated Sparks to insist adamantly on the separation of all division funds from the university budget.[247]

Following the merger, Sparks seemed in no hurry to notify the VA of the Atlanta Center's new affiliation. Consequently, the existing VA tuition payments continued in fall 1947. Sparks reported the school's changed status only after being so advised by J. Thomas Askew of the UGA veterans division, who became concerned over "the difference in fees." At a November 1947 meeting of university, division, and VA representatives, Atlanta's

128

nonresident tuition arrangements finally were openly aired. After careful study, Askew ascertained that the division registrar handled all veterans affairs and concluded "that this arrangement should not be disturbed." It involved a VA "official [who] spends three-fourths of his time with the Atlanta Division and one-fourth...checking on student problems," he wrote Dean Biscoe. "We feel that this is equal to the payment of a full time man for the University of Georgia." But UGA officials and the chancellor's office ignored this advice. Over the next nine months, their spokesmen traveled "to Washington on five occasions" attempting to increase UGA tuition payments. Instead, in November 1948 the VA ended all nonresident system tuition retroactive to that fall's enrollment. Efforts to save the situation proved fruitless.[248]

129

With over 1,000 veterans still enrolled at the Atlanta Division, the director was beside himself. For one thing, an anonymous letter to Washington syndicated columnist Drew Pearson claimed that educational institutions gave veterans the runaround, citing the Atlanta Division as "a local case." The school charged "a resident student twenty-five dollars per quarter for one course, [but] if the student is attending school under the 'G I Bill' the charge for the same course was one-hundred-twenty-five dollars until the past week." Of course, as resident Dean Manners replied, "the fee is charged to the Veteran's Administration," which approved that arrangement, not to the student. While concerned over the adverse publicity, Sparks was most upset over the lost funds. "A $300,000 a year loss faces this institution," he wrote a fellow Georgian in the "Farmers [sic] Home Administration," unless "we can get in touch with people in Washington" and convince them "that this institution is one different from all others in its service." The chancellor's assistant had "evidently made some of the 'big brass' angry" and used the Atlanta Division "as a 'whipping boy.'"[249]

The loss of VA funds, amounting to at least $217,000 for the rest of the system, had been particularly hard on the Atlanta Division because its needs, even survival, had the regents' lowest priority. In early 1949, a recession brought a serious decline in state revenues. Meanwhile, the Southern Association of Colleges (SAC) in December 1948 had warned that the Atlanta Division still did not qualify for accreditation. Even UGA had received only $100 per student, two-thirds of SAC's $150 requirement. The Atlanta Division, which should have been allocated over $400,000 from the state during the 1948–1949 fiscal year, actually got $75,500. Its library expenditures fell below SAC standards as did the student-teacher ratio.[250] Throughout most of 1949, as the university suffered stringent budget cuts, the Atlanta Division once again placed the entire system in jeopardy.

To deal with accreditation, Harmon Caldwell, the former UGA president recently named chancellor, in February sent Athens General Extension Division director Earnest A. Lowe to confer with SAC officials. Lowe was an unfortunate choice because his instructions placed the general extension in a conflict of interest with the Atlanta Division. The three options he presented to SAC involved difficult decisions. First, the regents would fund the Atlanta Division "at a sum of money not less than the equivalent of $150.00 for each full-time student on an equated basis." Since it took money away from the cash-strapped university, system officials surely were not serious. The second option seemed equally untenable; i.e., detach the Atlanta Division from the university, give it whatever funds were available, and cease seeking accreditation. Of course, the system's standing still would be in doubt. The final option would cut back the division to junior college status, place it under the general extension, and stress noncredit adult education.[251]

Not surprisingly, the third option had strong support from the regents and Chancellor. Lowe reported that SAC officials also responded with "an enthusiastic, 'Yes.'" The regents "must either put more money into the program or cut it back to two years and put it in the Extension Division" to satisfy SAC requirements. The Southern Association of Colleges for some time had appeared uncomfortable with the emerging trends in urban, adult higher education. Rumors floated about low academic standards at the division, but studies by outside experts made no such findings. The division's contrast with conventional colleges was striking. Lacking stately, ivy-covered buildings and spacious lawns, the Atlanta Division looked to one journalist like a "knowledge Factory on Ivy Street." It served mostly younger working adults instead of affluent young high school graduates. Students attended at night as well as during the day, with needs that warranted experimentation that traditional academics often opposed or did not understand. Nevertheless, sacrificing the degree-granting division apparently was inconsequential to remote SAC officials, as were the personal and professional aspirations of thousands of students. "[S]imilar programs are being conducted in other Southern states…in very much the same way," SAC's Huntley noted.[252]

131

During the financial stringency, Chancellor Caldwell gave UGA top priority. Responding to a faculty resolution, he increased the allocation by $357,400, making a total of $1,202,400. While citing as justification the higher costs at senior, graduate, and professional colleges, he admitted that the university's financial difficulties remained less serious than other system units except Tech. The others all suffered reductions. Director Sparks, with understandable bitterness, blamed Athens. "[S]ome of your faculty," he wrote new UGA President Jonathan C. Rogers, "wish to cause one segment of the University System to fail." Last year the Atlanta Division budgeted for "six 'big men' in Business Administration," and Dean Gates could not find them. Having accumulated "our building income surplus" that now permits the acquisition of "the best of faculties," the program was being suppressed by "a few visionless [UGA] faculty members."[253]

President Rogers demanded a unified Athens-Atlanta budget. Sparks's negative response intentionally left the impression that he had influence. One regent had praised Sparks's management of the Atlanta Division's affairs: "You have done such a good financial job for many years, your many friends on the Board of Regents do not want your budget bothered." Sparks's letter to Rogers revealed the exasperating dilemma that he constantly faced. Through the VA's past generosity and his own superb financial management, the Atlanta Division had excess funds and literally *could* function without state funding. Yet SAC requirements threatened its accreditation unless public money was provided. Given the choices, the director repeatedly had refused to request state money though advised to do so. As events unfolded, his fears that the division would be penalized hardly were groundless.[254]

132

Meanwhile, a financial rescue effort for Georgia public education was under way. The passage of a three-cent statewide sales tax for education, guided by Governor Herman Talmadge, made possible the approval of the Minimum Foundation Act, which authorized educational spending. With new funding eventually available, the regents could reconsider the role of the Atlanta Division. A resolution on March 29, 1949 simply stated that the Atlanta Division would continue to function as a branch of the University of Georgia with its financial and academic affairs subject to the general jurisdiction of the president. Once again, the Atlanta Division, which from the system's inception had been regarded as an unwanted stepchild, survived a serious crisis. With two years needed to effect the new tax system, any increase in education funding must wait until 1951. In the meantime, the regents levied an emergency fee of ten dollars per quarter on all white college registrants and five dollars in the segregated black colleges. The Atlanta Division's accreditation still remained at risk, SAC officials reminded.[255]

In the wake of Herman Talmadge's financial rescue, Georgia legislators also addressed other needs. They created the

University System Building Authority with the power to float bonds for capital improvements, including construction, maintenance, recreation, and housing. Within a year, the Atlanta Division received regents permission to plan a new building on Gilmer Street and Capital Avenue, adjacent to the Ivy Street Garage. For this effort, Sparks announced that he could raise $78,000 from the school's rentals and concessions "with little effort." This money, in turn, could be used to secure a loan from the Teacher's Retirement Fund which Sparks chaired.[256] The division's prospects had greatly improved.

LOOSENING THE TIES: THE 1950 MEMORANDUM OF UNDERSTANDING

Although the certainty of more funding and the creation of the building authority signaled a happier future for the Atlanta Division, its accreditation problems would prejudice an upcoming system study by George D. Strayer of Columbia University, director George Sparks fretted to the chancellor. The "major obstacle" was the Southern Association of College's (SAC's) $150 per student requirement that the state could not fund. "[B]ased on our present student body," it amounted to some $500,000 annually. Strayer would begin in September 1949, and the director, overcoming previous qualms about requesting state money, urged an immediate allocation. Its use for "assembling of the library, laboratory and teaching equipment, and fulltime faculty" would assure SAC approval. But Sparks, who had kept the discredited bachelor of commercial science (B.C.S.) degree, still hoped for the Center's expansion into the arts and sciences (A&S). Since SAC "accredits the liberal arts program alone," the state expenditure, besides achieving accreditation, would make "a full four-year liberal arts program" possible, he told the chancellor. In return for Athens's loss of a monopoly on the liberal arts, the director made a bizarre proposal. With "the [UGA] salary scale" at "47th among the states," he suggested using Atlanta Division funds "to supplement the salaries of outstanding Athens and Atlanta professors. The division's 1948–1949 fiscal surplus of $454,967.55 permitted such generosity.[257]

The director surely knew his bid for A&S degrees to be futile. But if Athens's hold remained unbreakable, its dominance over nursing education had become more tenuous. A UGA study found that "too few students" took "advantage of the services" in Athens, which required a campus residence "for their first two years." The group recommended that new students attend any accredited institution and take the last three quarters at the Atlanta Division "where the community provides ample hospital facilities for clinical and other professional courses." In fact, the nursing education department should operate in Atlanta, where the department head spent two-thirds of her time and "the majority of the students live." But the program's administration would remain in Athens, and, of course, the degree would be awarded by UGA's arts and sciences college. The faculty approved the report with a belittling qualification: senior level courses must be offered in close contact with the extension service, not the Atlanta Division. In fall 1949, 375 students enrolled.[258]

Nevertheless, Athens opponents persisted. The following spring, the nursing program needed several new courses in zoology and bacteriology. "[O]ffering so many senior college courses" in Atlanta had been overlooked when nursing educa-tion moved there, A&S Assistant Dean S. Walter Martin wrote. "Frankly, I think the students should be made to come back to this campus for these academic subjects," although "other administrative officers [may not] agree with me." Martin, then and later, embodied the negative Athens mindset. "We do not want to open up any avenue which might lead to the offering of A.B. or B.S. degrees in the Atlanta Division."[259]

As the system prepared for the Strayer study, the division bore little resemblance to the Atlanta Center housed in the tum-bledown old Baptist Hospital only four years earlier. Besides the capacious Ivy Street Garage, the division's physical dimensions included the 10,000-square-foot auditorium and gymnasium along with several acres of contiguous downtown property acquired for a new classroom building and library. While finding rental space in the Garage for SAC offices, the director evicted some commercial tenants as burgeoning enrollments brought expansion onto the fifth and sixth floors. The regents reported a cumulative enrollment of 7,156 and an average of 4,855 for 1948–1949, while the *Signal* made the claim that those numbers exceeded Georgia Tech's student body.[260]

The division's full-time faculty numbered 101, with salaries generally comparable to the University of Georgia's. But only seven held the Ph.D. degree, and the average student-to-teacher ratio, 33.5 to one, ranked second highest in the system. The division also scraped the bottom rung in the allocation of state funds per student, at twenty-two dollars. In contrast, UGA received $166 and Tech, $148. Figures on instructional costs vividly revealed the disparities. In 1948–1949, student fees paid nearly fifty-four percent of the Atlanta Division's costs, but some thirty-two percent at UGA. The library had around 24,000 books. Its annual circulation of five books per student also was the system's lowest. All UGA students, including upper division and graduate, checked out twenty-six per capita, and Tech students, eleven. On the positive side, the division's new classroom and library, approved at $2,000,000, held a number two priority in the system's building program.[261]

137

As the Strayer study got underway, Atlanta's continuing postwar growth brought more demands for the division's expansion. From the influential Personnel Club came a petition for a graduate level business program. It listed over sixty-five major banking, commercial, business, and governmental institutions as supporters, including the powerful Chamber of Commerce, Georgia Power, the Federal Reserve, five private banks, six major insurance companies, and Emory University. In Atlanta's environs, "thousands of college graduates" with jobs in business "are entitled to this instruction being provided with the tax payers' money." They could not leave their jobs "and devote full time to graduate work" at Athens or attend Emory University's daytime-only classes, financially prohibitive for most.[262]

As Sparks feared, the Strayer Report, issued that December, disappointed. Commissioned because of the system's critical financial problems and duplicating functions, among other reasons, the study did not take the Atlanta Division expansion goals seriously. The Strayer group flatly rejected graduate work. Athens had little to fear from Atlanta's undergraduate business program, although the division should offer only two years in the liberal arts. Strayer saw problems in achieving accreditation, including the division's under-funding, the dearth of faculty doctorates, the inadequate library, particularly in periodicals, and the poor laboratory facilities. The division needed $225,000 immediately, and $2,500,000 over the next three years for a building program.[263]

The Strayer group took a dim view of the merger. The seventy-mile distance seriously handicapped University of Georgia supervision, while "striking dissimilarities" made oversight impossible. The division should be "divorced entirely from the University" and become "an independent unit." Considering its "limited program and type of [working] students," Strayer saw little evidence of "undesirable competition" with other system units. On the other hand, as UGA pursued its various functions it should not control "all of the professional education of the Georgia System," nor should it have a monopoly of the graduate work "either directly or by remote control." Considering Athens's lack of any appreciable business activity, UGA's business school should "make arrangements in Atlanta, and in other centers, for a cooperative experience and for field laboratory work." In conclusion, the report heaped heavy criticism on the state for its dismal support for higher education, placing Georgia close to the bottom among the Southern states. Even as the Strayer group completed the study, SAC sent another warning. If the Atlanta

138

Division continued as part of UGA, the "parent must have complete control over finances and academic programs," a situation
Strayer saw as administratively impossible. In the absence of
total integration, SAC also advised separation.[264]

Not surprisingly, Strayer's advice on separation found no
support in Athens, and President Rogers responded with the
familiar negative arguments previously voiced by other Athens
promoters. While Sparks could not have been pleased with
Strayer's findings, the Atlanta Division did receive a consolation
prize. In March, the regents allocated $250,000, more than
Strayer recommended, for science apparatus and equipment,
library outlays, and normal salary increments. A serious attempt
to upgrade the Atlanta Division for SAC accreditation apparently
had begun.[265]

139

Shortly after Strayer departed, the regents appointed George
Sparks assistant chancellor in charge of plant development and
special services. The move accompanied an increase in the
University System Building Authority's funding, from
$10,000,000 to $12,000,000. As chair of the teacher retirement
fund, he also oversaw loans to the building authority. Some
system officials may have seen Sparks's promotion as advancing
the UGA merger, but regents chairman Hughes Spalding, by one
account, promised Sparks a veto of his successor. Moving with
some haste to find a replacement and apparently unaware of
Spalding's commitment to Sparks, President Rogers still was
careful to seek Sparks's recommendations. The testimonial
dinner, tributes, and accolades may have signaled the departure
of the director, but not of his influence.[266]

When Rogers's search focused on Earnest A. Lowe of the
General Extension Division, Sparks vehemently objected and
charged the man with incompetence for reasons that Rogers,
having carefully checked Lowe's Alabama background, judged as
invalid. Although Lowe's correspondence with Sparks over the
years, signed "Rastus," always had conveyed cordiality, his earlier meeting with SAC, followed by attempts to downgrade the

Atlanta Division, totally alienated Sparks. "The whole administrative procedure...breaks down when a person" in Sparks's
position "undertakes to exercise veto power," Rogers complained.
His letters to Sparks brought no reply, and twice Sparks had
refused to discuss the subject. Eventually, Sparks "turned
thumbs down" on three of his own appointees in Atlanta as well
as others. In fact, Rogers discussed fourteen candidates with
Sparks and finally decided to resubmit Lowe's name. Finally,
Sparks provided the solution by returning to the division, officially because of unhappiness with his new position, although
the *University Signal* reported that no satisfactory replacement
had been recommended.[267] Of course, the entire episode illustrated Sparks's enormous prestige and staying power as system
officials avoided challenging him. At the same time, his permanent departure conceivably could have left Athens a free hand to
control the budget and restrict the Atlanta Division's growth and
development, particularly with a compliant Athens insider as
Sparks's successor.

140

    While Sparks and Rogers sparred in spring 1950, a bitter
battle went on among the regents and at UGA that undoubtedly
affected the Atlanta Division. As various interest groups vied
over the status of the Agricultural College, a regents faction on
May 31 mustered enough votes to set up agriculture as an independent unit. That action followed A&S attempts to move all of
the sciences to the main campus. This threatened agriculture's
federal research funding, which stunned university officials. For
the Atlanta Division, this internal UGA conflict provided a welcome distraction. The whole controversy dealt a severe blow to
President Rogers's authority and prestige.[268] During this period,
serious contact between the university and the division apparently abated.

    As these troubles erupted, Sparks was preparing the Atlanta
Division for visitations by the three outside experts earlier recommended by SAC. Separately, toward the end of June, each

made short, two- or three-day visits, but none attempted an exhaustive report. By concentrating solely on the Atlanta Division, however, they submitted far more detailed findings than the Strayer group's system study. To all three, the school was familiar territory. One had taught there during the war.[269] Their findings, coinciding with system internal difficulties and the struggle among the regents, undoubtedly had some influence.

The visitors focused mainly on the merger and accreditation. On the former, two agreed with Strayer. The division should become independent from Athens, "administratively and educationally," so that it could "fulfill the demands of a large urban population." The geographical separation made the merger unsound administratively. The director and deans lacked "authority to carry out their work without receiving [Athens's] approval." Worse, the treasurer and comptroller "were responsible to more than one individual," causing "confusion and uncertainties." Separation would give the director "not only the responsibility" but the authority "to develop and operate an efficient educational program."[270]

141

All three investigators recognized the need for a well-rounded A&S program with the continuation of the bachelor of business administration (B.B.A.) degree, although graduate students should go to Athens. If the liberal arts expanded, the division's "teaching faculty" needed upgrading, particularly in the sciences. As a whole, however, the faculty "is considerably better than" junior college level work required. The part-time faculty also passed muster, particularly in the business school, some being "outstanding leaders in their fields." Their "fund of knowledge and experience" could not be secured outside a large urban community. But the business school, with seventy-three part-timers and only twelve permanent faculty, *did* need drastic improvement. The group found no grade inflation. A comparison with Athens "shows relatively fewer A's and B's and more C's in Atlanta."[271]

Atlanta's urban setting had a salutary effect on library resources. Although the division's holdings "must be strengthened in certain major fields," the public libraries provided reserve facilities far beyond those available to "the average college or university of this size, located outside of an urban area." The laboratories and classrooms proved adequate for junior college work at the present level of enrollment. The building had sufficient space that was well utilized, but the physical surroundings were "not lovely," with "little dignity or beauty" about the place. "The general impression is that of a factory or industry rather than a college." None of the administrative officers had "private offices" for "personal interviews or conferences" while "the secretaries have their typewriters in the same office with their chiefs."[272]

142

The Atlanta Division fell short of SAC standards in some areas. The teaching faculty needed more Ph.D.s who did advanced work and took leaves of absences. The faculty had not participated in program-making, and faculty committees did not function. Even the business faculty held no formal meeting until December 1950. The director made all decisions at all levels. Too-heavy teaching loads and high student-to-teacher ratios also existed. State funding, already inadequate, would face a new hurdle in 1951 when the minimum SAC requirement per student increased from $150 to $200. The library, improved with 29,000 volumes, lacked adequate seating space despite a business branch on the sixth floor. Forty thousand dollars annually would be needed for books, periodicals, bindings, and salaries. While student placement was excellent, the school should keep a record of its graduates and its transfers to other colleges "for about ten years back" to establish its standing in the educational world.[273] With these generally encouraging reports in hand, the director had expert opinions in the emerging bitter contest with President Rogers and other Athens administrators.

Sparks next took to his administrative council a typed statement in rough draft for approval. Its contents reflected the recent outside evaluations, but it also aggressively attacked the Athens administration for causing the plan of integration to fail and requested immediate separation from UGA. The petition provides insight into Sparks's angry state of mind, but the administrative council wisely rejected this rough, undiplomatic, and awkwardly worded missive. Another more conciliatory statement, "Suggestions for the Operation of the Atlanta Division of the University of Georgia," replaced it. It seemed to state the Atlanta Division's negotiating position in talks shortly to take place with the chancellor and a new UGA president. In mid-July the regents dismissed Rogers and replaced him with education Dean O. C. Aderhold. They also rescinded the earlier separation of the agricultural college. In view of that settlement, the Atlantans' "Suggestions" seemed to reflect their realization that the division's escape from UGA also was impossible. Instead, the "Suggestions" seemingly tried to contrive ways to limit UGA authority. The division director, for example, would be appointed by one official (the chancellor) but be responsible to another (the UGA president). In budgetary matters, however, the director would prepare and submit a budget for the president, who would send it forward to the chancellor "in the same manner as the budget of any independent [system] unit."[274]

143

With Athens's preoccupation over the agricultural college ended, campus administrators turned to the Atlanta Division. In August, business Dean James E. Gates confirmed with the American Association of Collegiate Schools of Business (AACSB) that the division shared Athens's accreditation. It was an important point, because SAC, which dealt only with arts and sciences programs, required AACSB approval before granting accreditation. Nevertheless, Gates learned that an independent Atlanta Division would face AACSB rejection because of its classification as an evening school. At the same time, the dean undoubtedly recognized the irresistible pressure from the growing Atlanta metropolitan area to expand the school. If the division separated, he warned President-elect Aderhold, it "will undoubtedly, within a couple of years, become a cluster of schools with" the liberal arts, law, education, pharmacy, and others "demanded in an urban environment." With that kind of setup, an independent Atlanta college ultimately would be AACSB-qualified.[275]

By September, with Athens's fears of a separation over, Gates began exploring "the ultimate needs and requirements of our Atlanta Division and the services" that could be performed there. He mentioned "graduate study in social work," because the tentative selection of the black Atlanta University by the Southern Regional Education Board "leaves high and dry the Atlanta area" for whites. Training was badly needed in "particular specialized courses" in order to get "higher paid positions, as attested to by the personnel directors of Fulton County, Atlanta, the State of Georgia, and the United States Civil Service Commission." All "urge us to install some sort of program there which will enable them to (1) upgrade existing personnel, and (2) provide some elementary training" so others could become qualified. Although Gates identified real Atlanta educational needs, he refrained from proposing that Athens "install a full-fledged graduate school of social work." Sooner or later, however, the university itself should consider "going into offering such a program," perhaps on an in-service basis.[276]

President Aderhold, Chancellor Caldwell, and director Sparks met that September to define "the working relationships of the Atlanta Division with the University." The regents' struggle over the agricultural college and the disruption in UGA leadership made a quick and amicable settlement a matter of some urgency. There had been no administrative honeymoon for the newly appointed UGA president, who later confessed to "devoting most of my time to other reorganization problems" during that period. At the same time, the reports by the visiting experts had to be addressed. Shortly, the group produced a "Memorandum of Understanding" that gave the Atlanta Division considerable autonomy to operate "as an integral part of the University," but it denied the widespread concessions sought by division leaders. Adopted on a trial basis, the Memorandum would be in effect for just one year, a limitation that Sparks inexplicably concealed from his administrators. Bachelor of business administration-level work and nursing education would continue as before, but the agreement authorized "courses at the junior level in the arts and sciences, education and journalism," work previously available only through the General Extension Division.[277]

Under the Memorandum, the "channel of administrative responsibility" passed "through the Director.... directly to the [UGA] President," a contemporary later noted. Proposals and recommendations for new faculty and courses, various catalog materials, and the budget, all originating in the Atlanta Division, would "be processed in the same manner." The direct control formerly exercised by UGA deans and department heads ended, and the division could begin independently recruiting its own faculty. Nevertheless, the Memorandum encouraged "planning and cooperation by and between officials and departments.[278]Despite these changes, the relationship still remained ambiguous between two system units dissimilar in philosophy, purpose, mode of operation, and outlook. Once again the regents rejected the advice of outside experts and continued an association in which the elder regarded the younger as a serious threat. Making such a union work after earlier failures would take compromise and generous amounts of good will.

145

16

THE FINAL PUSH FOR ACCREDITATION

As tensions increased between the University of Georgia (UGA) and the Atlanta Division in spring 1950, resident Dean George Manners again attempted personally to open up a dialog with Dean of Faculties Alvin Biscoe. The timing seemed propitious. The Strayer report a few months earlier had advised the UGA's business school to use Atlanta's resources, because Athens lacked any meaningful commercial activity. Manners noted "the tenuous thread" holding the two institutions together and hoped that "this letter" might "reopen channels of planning." The Atlanta Division "represents the only opportunity" for UGA to maintain its statewide "influence and leadership" without an enormous expenditure, he believed. Metropolitan Atlanta, with nearly one-fourth of the state's population, and one-third projected by 1960, "will provide a larger proportion of college students than other areas," possibly fifty percent. If UGA did not provide educational opportunities, "others will."[279]

The failed proposal to give graduate work in Atlanta would have used the Athens "graduate faculty" and granted UGA degrees. Since the university "did not seize this opportunity, Georgia Tech is stepping into the picture" in industrial management and accelerated "work in commerce." The University of Georgia also passed up the opportunity to train teachers.

Local school systems, aided by a private foundation, sent large numbers of teachers to Emory. Oglethorpe University, recently re-accredited, planned "an enormous expansion of its teacher training program." The new Emory law dean had been rethinking "his avowed intention to kill the evening school of law," and Emory's journalism program would be gearing up to take advantage of Atlanta's opportunities.[280]

Meanwhile, "we are both holding each other down," and "a firmer and sounder foundation" must be found. He doubted that Athens alone could "maintain any real leadership in higher education (except in Agriculture)" without dividing "its activities on some basis between Atlanta and Athens." Otherwise, "the philosophy of controlling Atlanta" would ultimately produce "a serious explosion." Manners preferred to have the two institutions "support and sustain each other in our mutual program" and urged "a special meeting of the [two] administrative councils" to discuss the UGA's statewide leadership. Surely if Atlanta refrained from building dormitories, "the competition which Athens fears can never materialize." Of one thing Manners seemed certain: "As I read events, it is time to decide if we want to stay together on a permanent and lasting basis." Having already "discussed these ideas with" UGA's Dean James Gates and the division's academic dean and registrar, Manners hoped for a meaningful response. Apparently none came, and Athens's mounting problems over the agriculture college, President Jonathan Rogers's departure, and the explosive relations with the Atlanta Division made further action pointless until the September signing of the Memorandum of Understanding.[281]

While the *Atlanta Alumnus* approvingly described the Memorandum as being like a marriage with an equal rights clause added, director George Sparks saw problems. It made his office responsible for the "elimination of administrative difficulties" while shifting that task away from the campus group. Sparks thought it opened the possibility of his censure for failing to abide by the agreement. The Southern Association of Colleges

(SAC) study, which had been called for in the Memorandum, might heap criticism on "our academic deans," who lacked "formal degrees." This "weakness at the top" also brought disdain from "our neighboring institutions." Citing his "added responsibility," Sparks asked his staff for their "real cooperation and loyalty" as the division struggled to make improvements, addressing all five administrators in writing as "Mr." instead of the customary academic titles.[282] Of course, the director himself possessed only an honorary doctorate and often tried to keep staff offbalance while harboring a distaste for firing people.

Apparently seeking to impress the new UGA president, Sparks mentioned his own personal contacts with individual regents, possibly displaying his influence. The director had paid an overnight visit to regent Cason Callaway, who "calls me down there quite often to talk about projects" of the Ida Cason Callaway Foundation. "I have for years seemed to have been on his priority list in many of his business ventures." During this sojourn, Sparks told Aderhold, "I took considerable time...to give you quite a build-up in your new job." Aderhold undoubtedly would be invited to meet with Callaway, and Sparks strongly advised him to accept.[283] Since the UGA president surely had his own influential contacts, Sparks may have surprised him with such gratuitous and patronizing comments. It seemed like an inauspicious beginning for two aggressive educational entrepreneurs with shared past antagonisms.

That a new day had dawned for the Atlanta Division seemed doubtful. President Aderhold's new arts and sciences dean, S. Walter Martin, operated as if the Memorandum of Understanding never existed. In October, he informed Sparks that Athens would choose the new permanent head of the nursing program without consultation, although that official spent two-thirds of her time in Atlanta. The division was expected to pay that portion of her salary plus all travel expenses to "our campuses." Martin insisted that the division's academic dean attend UGA committee and faculty meetings. Visitations between the

149

two institutions for advice and consultation would continue, but Martin's action strained the Memorandum's wording, and he knew it. "Do you think I am within my 'rights' to do this?" he asked Aderhold. The UGA president apparently approved. He, too, ordered the continuance of close administrative contacts, instructing Dean Biscoe to arrange a joint meeting for administrators and selected faculty.[284]

Spring 1951 brought an explosion over curriculum. "In your office...at our first organization meeting after the agreement," Sparks wrote Aderhold, Dean Biscoe wanted curriculum matters channeled through his office. "I objected," because "he was too close to the many [Athens] imperial empires" and could be "pressured by them." Sparks refrained from appealing to the Memorandum, but he probably was mindful of Biscoe's earlier handling of the division's transportation program that remained on his desk for nearly three years without action. Shortly, Biscoe rejected a division course in industrial sociology already advertised for the spring quarter, but he communicated his decision to the resident dean rather than telling Sparks directly. Twenty people had already registered for the course, Sparks complained to Aderhold in a special delivery letter. He vowed to offer the course unless telephoned to the contrary, because Biscoe's late rejection "was not our fault."[285]

Apparently the director received no call, but Aderhold's written response displayed real impatience. Sparks had surprised him "with such a large number of new course requests." In view of anticipated enrollment declines "for next year," he had instructed all schools and colleges "to make no expansion of new programs" and courses except for "specific needs." A majority of Sparks's courses involved expansion, "and many...show evidence of lack of study and careful planning." Others contained subject matter available in existing courses. Even so, of the fourteen, Aderhold had approved seven. Sparks also had "proposed three courses which seem to overlap offerings at Georgia Tech," a matter that required consultation with the chancellor.[286]

The director's reply laid out a rationale and a philosophy undoubtedly unfamiliar to the UGA president, who Sparks accused, along with his staff, of failing to understand the Atlanta Division's situation. Athens's "fixed student body" had a standard curriculum applicable "to that group," compared with the division's "adult evening students," who needed new courses designed to fit their needs. Such a curriculum brought "in new students," a fact already proven by the large enrollment figures. "[T]hey are service courses in the true sense of the word," especially in marketing and advertising, taught by instructors who were specialists "well endowed by degree." One of the rejected courses, Sparks pointed out, had been suggested by UGA's own Dean Gates. As for Georgia Tech, it had violated regents rules just by offering business courses, and the matter should not concern the Atlanta Division or, he implied, the UGA president. Finally, Sparks suggested that the two men go to the chancellor to settle their differences. After Caldwell became chancellor, he "soon acquired a metropolitan rather than a campus viewpoint."[287]

151

The president and the director also quarreled over personnel matters, an area in which Sparks's previous performance put him on shaky ground. The director wanted to create a new position, coordinator of student services, for "Dr. R. C. Young," whose "magnetic charm" could "impress the students of their own worthwhileness [sic]" whether he addressed them "en masse or individually." Sparks believed Young had "succeeded in holding" at least 500 of the present student body who otherwise would have dropped out of college. Aderhold, who apparently had counseled administrators to avoid creating new positions which required regents approval, composed an angry letter to the director with the notation, "Did not mail." In that missive, the UGA president took Sparks to task for failing to submit a job description. Especially, he expressed surprise at Sparks's statement that "pressure" had been exerted. "It is never my purpose to put pressure on an administrative officer regarding his recommendations."[288]

Following these exchanges, and lacking any hope of removing Sparks, Aderhold decided to appoint his own representative in Atlanta. "One of the difficult problems in administering that Division," he later wrote, "has been the false propaganda that gets to the press." But he agreed to continue "provided the Board would allow me to select an Academic Dean...[with] complete authority" over the program. After a regents by-laws amendment creating that position, Aderhold in April appointed Thomas Mahler, a young, talented, enthusiastic, but inexperienced, nondegreed and lower-level Athens administrator who seemingly could add little much-needed prestige to the division's top ranks. Atlanta's administrative council expressed doubts about a nominee who lacked the qualifications, background, and experience "in schools such as this" or even "on a college campus." They wanted someone with the doctoral degree, but they remained unaware that the UGA president, at least, believed that in approving this position the regents favored a new mode of operation practically repealing the Memorandum of Understanding.[289]

After Dean Mahler's arrival, one of his duties soon became apparent. "I would like to get" some information to "Tommy Mahler," Dean Martin told Aderhold. Martin had hearsay evidence that some Atlanta Division students "have been allowed to take an overload of work" this summer, and "Mahler will want to correct such things." Two years later, Athens still fretted over similar petty concerns. A department head, Merle C. Prunty, heard of the division's "undercutting the Athens campus" by offering "twenty hours of work whereas we limit students to fifteen hours." Dean Martin checked with the student and found the rumor to be untrue, but he appreciated Prunty's efforts because "we are ever on the alert for such infractions." [290]

Dean Martin's increasing participation in division affairs and Mahler's appointment as academic dean represented another turning point in Athens/Atlanta relations. Martin's ascendancy signaled a hard line coinciding with the Memorandum of

Understanding's one-year expiration. Yet Dean Mahler's youth as well as Atlanta's suspicions prevented his collegial acceptance. He reported to the UGA president off-campus from his home, and his frequent trips to Athens did not escape division notice. On the other hand, as his written accounts indicate, Mahler was capable, bright, well meaning, and usually fair in his judgments. He served the UGA president well, and under adverse circumstances he made contributions. After a year, Mahler received a special assignment from his president. He would prepare a history of the Atlanta Division using regents records. To avoid suspicion, Mahler claimed to be researching an Atlanta Division history as a New York University doctoral dissertation in education, a task never completed. Later, Mahler *did* submit two detailed reports on the division's internal affairs. At his job, he remained energetic and enthusiastic, and he improved the internal climate at the division. He also worked diligently to prepare for accreditation, and he modified plans for the new building accepted by Sparks but lacking faculty offices.[291]

153

Meanwhile, Chancellor Caldwell, anticipating the 1952 SAC visitation, commissioned his own Atlanta Division study conducted by the UGA's Merle C. Prunty. Concentrating first on business administration, he found the curriculum to be fundamentally strong, "fairly representative of" other urban universities, "and in some areas…more judiciously conceived." But Prunty made a startling discovery. The three-year bachelor of commercial science (B.C.S.) degree, supposedly phased out in 1948 with the implementation of the bachelor of business administration program, survived and during 1950–1951 was awarded to 224 students representing "61% of the business administration graduates." B.C.S. enrollment had continued as registrar J. C. Blair disregarded the catalog and a new general studies Dean, J. C. Horton Burch, along with Sparks, sanctioned the program. Through personal interviews Prunty found students who substituted "back-and-forth between B.B.A. and B.C.S. degree requirements, especially on courses considered 'hard,'" taking pretty much what they wanted to." B.C.S. majors comprised over three-fifths of the business college graduates. Considering the division's American Association of Collegiate Schools of Business (AACSB) approval, continuing the B.C.S. program could well have threatened accreditation. Nevertheless, seven grandfathered B.C.S. candidates completed their degrees as late as June 1956.[292]

Prunty insisted on the B.C.S.'s immediate removal from the catalog to "meet accreditation standards." But as he cut and slashed at liberal arts courses, a significant point seemed to have escaped him. Although unacceptable to him, Athens, the chancellor, and the regents, the Atlanta Division, measured by the number of majors, the "liberal arts" degrees granted, the faculty's composition, and the curriculum, still was basically a general college, as it had been since 1933. His own observations confirmed it. The arts and sciences faculty "handles a majority of enrollments," including "about 7/9ths of the freshman-sophomore [B.B.A.] work," not to mention other programs. "[I]n the long run," Prunty added, the Atlanta Division's "strength or weakness...will be determined in large part by the extent to which the Liberal Arts College becomes a superior instructional unit...[because] it provides the fundamental educational skills and attitudes for every student in the division." Yet only five arts and sciences (A&S) departments had achieved sufficient strength to offer full majors since the extension program ended in 1950 and the division began offering upper-level courses. Prunty thus concluded that the division "*is in no position now to undertake a degree granting [A&S] program.*"[293] It was an arbitrary judgment considering that only twelve months had passed since the Memorandum's signing, an insufficient time to expand faculty and curriculum from junior college to senior-level work.

Prunty also examined the Atlanta Division's "17 'two-year' and four 'oneyear' terminal-vocational programs." Respectable numbers of students had enrolled, but few finished, probably having transferred to the four-year degree where the division's entire curriculum, like a great academic smorgasbord, lay open to them and other lower-level students as well. The lowliest freshmen could sign up for any junior or senior level courses, and they succeeded in passing. "These courses are being reduced to the 'least common denominator...i.e., the freshmen level,'" Prunty justifiably complained, and it amounted to the "subversion of academic standards and abandonment of quality in instruction." Many courses apparently had not been submitted for President Aderhold's approval, a presumptuous act, if true, that should be corrected by resubmitting all the catalog courses. In addition, all nonrequired A&S and education courses should be eliminated.[294]

In sampling student transcripts, Prunty found other serious violations. Course prerequisites went unobserved, because the faculty "permitted students to enter courses without the specified background courses" and the division lacked adequate procedures for enrolling, guiding, and counseling students. Nearly all student advisement fell to the registrar's office, understaffed and il-equipped to "scrutinize the records of every single student, and check all prerequisites." Consequently, students selected whatever courses they wanted "regardless of sound educational practices." Prunty strongly recommended a system of "pre-advisement by selected faculty."[295]

Prunty's faculty assessment echoed many conclusions made previously by the three Southern Association of Colleges visitors. The faculty needed to assume academic responsibility immediately and end the director's sole decision-making. Perhaps faculty responsibility had faltered because of excessive numbers of adjunct or part-time individuals. They handled over seventy-five percent of all enrollees in the business school, compared with A&S's twenty-one percent. Most adjuncts took on more than one five-hour course, and several lacked master's degrees, although "some excellent men [sic] are employed as adjuncts." Higher authorities and even division administrators had "virtually no knowledge of the [adjuncts'] academic qualifications,"

155

who on the average taught over forty-five percent of all division students. Prunty suggested the submission of all part-time faculty appointments to the president for approval.[296]

Prunty's study exhibited considerable insight and objectivity, but he remained a captive of the Athens syndrome of fear and paranoia about the Atlanta Division. Athens should retain control of arts and sciences (A&S) degree programs to avoid the wasteful duplication of "facilities, functions, faculties, and heavy costs," when "the plant in Athens could handle more advanced students at modest cost increments." In fact, he proposed cutting back the division's A&S programs to the sophomore level. So long as the division offered the third year, he warned, agitation will continue for "the fourth year as well." Admittedly, Atlanta area citizens would suffer higher costs "from an additional year's residence in Athens," and perhaps as a solution to the liberal arts problem "an 'urban-life' type major program leading to the A.B. degrees could be developed...[with] specialized types of majors" in the A&S departments.[297]

Given director Sparks's frequent boasts that the division cost the state little money, Prunty explained why its expenses remained lower than any system unit. Large class sizes and high student-teacher ratios, of course, headed his list, along with the excessive number of low-paid, part-time instructors. Even the full-time staff received salaries "lower than in the University as a whole." Because of the limited demand for science programs, the school escaped the high cost of "labs and special apparatus" for music and the arts. The curricula was "fairly simple," while "supporting activities—library, student assistants, secretarial help, supplies, instructional aids...[had been] held to" the minimum. The division also avoided the expense of major programs," and in the absence of "a typical college campus...certain standard costs" did not apply. The physical plant remained "fairly compact and simple...maintenance and janitorial service costs...[were] the lowest in the system," and the division's administration had "relatively few—too few in fact—people."

156

"[E]nrollment, advisement, counseling, registration, guidance and placement activities have been on a strictly minimal (or even nonexistent in some cases) basis."[298]

Finally, Prunty touched on the very sensitive matter of the Atlanta Division's budget surpluses. He thought it unfortunate that after receiving regents funds "budgeted for instructional and operating expenses," the division continued to accumulate surpluses "to the cumulative extent of about $700,000, which is about the size of the present surplus." Money earmarked "to upgrade educational quality" would be used to pay for the new building, about a third of what Atlanta students "were supposed to get but didn't." Sparks over the years built up funds usually for land purchases or buildings. Prunty, like most UGA and system administrators, probably remained ignorant of the true source of these surpluses. As SAC later reported, most "has been derived from tuition payments for veterans."[299] In view of the division's earlier arrangements with the VA, Sparks wisely refrained from answering this criticism.

157

Six months later, five SAC representatives spent four days at the Atlanta Division. Quite remarkably, the school satisfied all twenty-one standards, a tribute to constant SAC pressure that threatened the entire system should the division remain unaccredited. While its state funding still was the lowest in the system, it exceeded the minimum SAC requirements for lower- and upper-division students in the 1951–1952 fiscal year. Surely, support and guidance from the chancellor's office enabled the Atlanta Division to rapidly enlarge and upgrade its full-time faculty. In fact, the visiting team found the number of Ph.D.s "amazing" considering the institution's heavy concentration on junior college level work. Increased state funding also provided updated laboratory equipment and library expansion. Because seventy-five percent of the instruction took place on the junior college level, SAC permitted the state to contribute at a figure below "the [new] perstudent expenditure of $200."[300]

SAC visitors also found other things to praise. They viewed the preliminary work on the foundation of the school's new building on Gilmer Street. They noted "that all admission proce-dures parallel those at Athens." They also saw "evidence of much faculty participation" in preparing the division SAC report, and monthly faculty meetings took place in which "numerous faculty committees" functioned. But graduate work at the division should "be resisted at this time," although the UGA business school had overlooked "the Division's resources" in the Atlanta business community.[301]

The accreditation of the Atlanta Division ended nearly twenty years of doubt and uncertainty ushered in by the 1933 separation of the Evening School from Georgia Tech. Now, perhaps, the fears, doubts, and hostility harbored so long by director Sparks could come to an end. Nevertheless, many division problems, even with accreditation, would remain so long as UGA administrators continued to restrict its development and its growth.

17

SEARCHING FOR AN IDENTITY

To what extent the Southern Association of College's (SAC) accreditation team may have been put off by the Atlanta Division's drab environment can only be a matter of speculation. But as director George Sparks gave them a tour of the Garage, perhaps he communicated his vision of a downtown campus while showing plans for the new general purpose building. Its imprint already had been laid down. After Sparks's death, the edifice would bear his name.

Begun the previous summer with an auspicious ground-breaking ceremony, Korean War shortages and the discovery of underground water halted the construction. Steel pilings and reinforced concrete foundations some thirty feet deep had to be added at great expense. A year passed before the materials could be procured. Originally designed to cover over an acre of land and costing $3,000,000, the three-story structure had an architectural style that copied the adjacent, turn-of-the-century Atlanta Municipal Auditorium with its white marble facing. As the project lagged, regents enthusiasm waned, the director reported, because the excessive cost was judged as "unjust to the other [system] units." Consequently, they halved the state's contribution to $1,500,000. By eliminating "four very necessary items," the total cost, scaled down to $1,835,319, was financed by the school's then $40,000 annual rental receipts. Its 1955

The future Sparks Hall (1955). Courtesy of GSU Archives.

completion left "the entire third floor hulled in as open space" with the loss of fourteen classrooms and the faculty offices.[302]

The Atlanta Division already had enough problems as Athens administrators began attacking its specialized community services. "In our conferences with [division] representatives," University of Georgia (UGA) business Dean James Gates wrote, statewide and regional programs "were to be considered all-University activities." While Gates thought the division should not "be precluded from working directly with organizations" headquartered in Atlanta, "such as the Federal and State Governments," he had evidence of "training and other conferences" involving "personnel outside the Atlanta area," organized without consulting UGA's General Extension Division. In addition, an Atlanta Division representative attended district meetings of the Association of County Commissioners, offering similar contact on a statewide basis. Gates also mentioned the division's Atlanta Marketing Conference for "business-men of the southeastern states," previously collectively sponsored by Athens, Emory, *and* the division. The "duplication of effort" could be a problem, particularly if outsiders got the impression "that the University seems not to know what its left hand is doing."[303]

Gates's communication typified the Athens mindset and fears. The division's central location brought sponsorship of such activities almost as a matter of course, and it refused to stop on the orders of worried Athens administrators. The following February, the division's Third Annual Georgia Credit Clinic attracted region-wide participation, and the Fourth Annual Retailing Clinic, scheduled for October 1952, advertised "to the people of Atlanta and the Southeast." Its advisory committee included major Atlanta commercial groups, such as Davison's and Rich's department stores, the Georgia Chain Store Council, the Chamber of Commerce, and the National Association of Manufacturers.[304]

161

Athens's anxiety may have deepened with knowledge of the widespread praise this activity received from major businesses, including the newly opened Marietta Lockheed aircraft plant and Capital Airlines, whose personnel extolled the conference's management, marketing, and distribution sessions. President Aderhold took particularly strong exception to Clinic advertising that mentioned "Atlanta's downtown University.... It is not a University but a Division of a University." He ordered Dean Thomas Mahler henceforth to approve all division mailing material regarding instruction, even short courses. Besides business contacts, the division inevitably became involved with organizations at the center of state and local power. Its public administration department served the Georgia legislature when in session. Professor Henry C. Pepper daily briefed every new assembly bill, "printed the material, and distributed it to legislators." His staff also prepared abbreviated editions that reduced each bill "to short, candid language."[305]

The UGA president, determined to curb Atlanta's public programs once and for all, prepared "a calendar of proposed courses and conferences." The list showed the division's service programs as having reached nearly 52,000 people during the 1952–1953 academic year, an impressive record of community contact. "All of these activities should be and I hope will eventually be" directed by UGA's "general extension," he wrote the chancellor's office. But to regent Charles Bloch, Aderhold was less circumspect. "[O]ne or two" were "constantly trying to make the general college" into a "four-year program" by reducing UGA's residency requirements. With Dean Mahler's leadership and a cooperative Athens staff, "we must hold the line on the size and scope of the [division's] program." If breached, some "would devote a tremendous amount of effort and energy to build a full-fledged University in Atlanta." Aderhold had faith that Bloch, "the other members of the Education Committee, and the Board as a whole will give me complete backing." Then, as an afterthought, the president wondered if "it would have been as well not to have written these last two paragraphs."[306]

The president harbored similar attitudes toward graduate extension courses, although his campus faculty *was* the extension faculty. Other institutions, such as the University of Michigan, offered evening "graduate residence credit" in a few large cities where as much as seventy-five percent of the masters requirements could be earned. But Athens had no such intention. A proposal for graduate work in Atlanta, submitted after the signing of the Memorandum of Understanding to the graduate faculty's executive committee, aroused little enthusiasm and inspired restrictions that killed the proposal.[307]

But the subject did not go away. Governor Herman Talmadge had been approached "by a number of [area] teachers" with UGA degrees who wanted "a [division] graduate school." His sister-in-law, an Evening School graduate, had to "attend Emory in order to get a Master's Degree" at a cost of $175 per quarter. The "University of Georgia Evening College could do the same for $50.00 per quarter." Talmadge asked the regents to "look into this matter and discuss it at the next meeting." He saw no "reason why a degree could not be conferred from Athens and the work be done here in Atlanta." President Aderhold's quick response gave a lengthy description of the teacher education program in Atlanta. It was "organized and administered through" UGA, and "Atlanta Area" institutions offered the graduate work. Begun "with a few teachers in 1945," the program enrolled 600, with about 400 at UGA. Most were working toward a master's degree "during the regular school year." Although Kappa Phi Kappa, an honorary fraternity, agreed to raise $10,000 annually "to supplement" this activity, Aderhold did not explain how such extremely meager funding, if available, affected individual students.[308]

Aderhold admitted that the program offered "no summer school courses," allegedly because school administrators insisted that "the teachers" go to system campuses. But an Atlanta teacher could earn forty hours at Emory. "[O]ne quarter, or 15 hours work" must be taken in Athens. Overall, the president believed "that the professional needs of [Atlanta area] teachers have been reasonably well met."[309] In effect, despite Aderhold's claims, no convenient system graduate program existed to serve the needs of the Atlanta area's Caucasian teachers.

163

Aderhold's explanation may have satisfied the governor, but Talmadge continued to get complaints, and his intervention may have motivated Athens to consider graduate work in business. Authorized to proceed, resident Dean George Manners completed a graduate proposal in November 1951. In keeping with the spirit of the Memorandum of Understanding, he expected "the Atlanta Division and its staff should be participants." Designed for adults in the evenings, it would be "noncompetitive" with Athens and any other educational institution. It followed closely Chicago's "Executive Training Program (evening)" and "the day programs at MIT and Harvard," which eliminated major or minor fields and the thesis requirement. Manners listed the names of qualified faculty, including Atlantans, nine with doctorates, three

CPAs, and three MBAs, and believed the program could begin by spring 1952.[310]

March found Manners still writing memoranda urging its adoption. July arrived before UGA's graduate executive committee accepted it, pointedly noting "that this is not an Atlanta Division program." Despite the proposal's many clauses asserting Athens's prerogatives, the regents, led by Bloch and Frank D. Foley of Columbus, both Aderhold confidantes, limited it to one academic year, because it "should be started on a trial basis only." "[We] can't have graduate courses all over the state and build up a 'real university,'" Bloch wrote. UGA officials withdrew the application, because it would be impossible for most students to complete the degree.[311]

Manners also had professional problems of his own for outspoken criticism of the Athens administration in his annual report. Aderhold expressed particular consternation about "an administrator" who criticized those above him and "especially challenges" regents policies. We "must have someone in that office who can develop and carry out" the president's and regents' programs, he told Dean Mahler. Manners later attributed his survival to regents secretary L. R. Siebert, who informed Athens that "no papers will be processed" for resident Dean Manners "unless it's a promotion."[312]

While the UGA president tried to curb the resident dean, other Athens administrators imposed tighter restrictions on division course offerings. Twenty-one new arts and sciences (A&S) applications arrived in summer 1952, and Dean S. Walter Martin approved only eight. Although he claimed to have done "an investigation of the actual needs," he seemed to be following a different agenda. "You will notice that none of the [accepted] courses" involved a division expansion, he told Dean Biscoe. "I think their approval falls within" the past policy restricting "new courses." A vetoed course in embryology served all premedical students, and Athens jealously guarded that important field. "You may have had some inquiry about the premedical program

164

from" the Atlanta Division, the UGA president later alerted regent Bloch. "We have had some difficulty keeping one or two" division personnel "straight on this matter." But Dean Mahler "has done an excellent job in keeping the educational program in the Atlanta Division in line" with regents policies. As for the other courses, Dean Martin gave no reason for rejecting them except expansionism. UGA administrators also applied its restrictive policies to new division business courses that involved regents-approved functions.[313]

New courses in radio and television also faced challenge, even though the division's speech faculty had sponsored programs over Atlanta stations for several years. In 1952, they participated in the production of 255 television and 221 radio pieces, varying from fifteen to thirty minutes in length, under the title School of the Air. The program director estimated their airtime value in current market prices to have increased from $10,500 in 1948 to $426,000 by 1952. The programs enjoyed a fair amount of popularity. "[R]equests for copies of the scripts were "far beyond our ability to supply because of our limited facilities." Athens's journalism Dean John E. Drewry professed to "value the work being done in Atlanta" most highly, but approval of the television courses "would be contrary to a Regents' policy" which specified "that the School of Journalism for the University System shall be at Athens."[314]

165

While Athens worked to stop all division expansion, Atlantans wanted more. The chancellor's office received "increasing demands…[for] various vocational training programs" and specialized four-year degrees. The Georgia Hotel Association wanted Tech's poorly patronized hotel management program transferred to the division, a proposal apparently unopposed. The Fulton County health department requested the training of sanitarians, a four-year field entirely different from Tech's sanitary engineering program. Six area hospitals and the Georgia health department pressed for hospital administration that would serve all levels of personnel, with both short courses and degrees. Dean Mahler, who knew of "some twenty [area] people…anxious to get started," succeeded in inaugurating a one-year certificate program, but UGA Dean Biscoe put off deciding whether the programs would be based in Athens or Atlanta.[315]

In the meantime, resident Dean Manners, failing to get a graduate executive degree, began laying a foundation in insurance that would serve the college and the business community for years to come. In the early 1950s, Manners believed, Atlanta had become one of the country's major insurance centers and possibly the largest in the southeast. The several companies with home offices or Southeastern headquarters there, along with many local agencies, had large numbers of employees. A quality insurance program would attract interested people, offer courses for others already in the industry, and provide research and consulting services. The first step involved recruiting a top scholar in a field so relatively new that only a limited number of doctoral specialists existed. Such individuals commanded top salaries beyond the division's resources.[316]

Manners sought help from the insurance industry, first approaching top officials in the Life Insurance Company of Georgia. No shrinking violet as a promoter, he heaped praise on "our School of Business Administration." It was "the largest in the South" and "eleventh in the nation," with ambitions to become the greatest "in the South." The division trained "90 percent of the [metro area's] new C.P.A.'s" and over fifty percent "in the State." The marketing, management, and transportation departments had added doctoral-level faculty, keeping in mind "the selection of men favorable to the ideas supporting our free enterprise system."[317]

Good professors in insurance could command between $8,000 and $10,000 a year, far above the division's budgeted $6,200. Manners asked the company to "consider endowing a chair, supplementing our salary by about $1,500 per year." With his proposal's approval, he recruited Kenneth Black, a University

166

of Pennsylvania doctoral candidate with a Phi Beta Kappa key and foundation support to publish his upcoming dissertation. Three years later, the program's success brought a new three-year agreement making indefinite the industry's financial assistance for salary supplements. Shortly, Manners hoped for a similar relationship with the Atlanta banking community.[318]

As the resident dean promoted important Atlanta business relationships, Dean Mahler completed his 1952–1953 report on the division's activities. He remained upbeat about postaccreditation progress. Enrollment increased six percent to the full-time equivalent of 2,713, although the large number of part-time students raised the total to 5,448. Significant also was the day school's increased size, comprising thirty-three percent of the student body. The average equivalent full-time staff stood at 128.5. In the years ahead, the faculty would increase dramatically if the student-to-teacher ratios declined from 20 to 1 to 16 to 1, as Mahler recommended. Thirty percent of the full-time faculty held doctorates, and twenty-three took graduate work leading to that degree. The dean expressed particular pride in the advisement, guidance, counseling, and hospital administration programs that had his support.[319]

Receiving accreditation had relieved the Atlanta Division of a great burden. At the same time, continued subservience to Athens was becoming an obsession to UGA administrators. Over the next two years, area support for the division began increasing.

167

18

RISING SUPPORT
FOR THE ATLANTA DIVISION

While resident Dean George Manners tied important business groups to the Atlanta Division's future, letters from area residents continued to arrive at the regents office requesting graduate programs and liberal arts degrees. But support also surfaced in unlikely places, such as small-town Georgia. In Swainsboro, the *Forest Blade's* editor praised Emanuel County's seven young people "taking advantage of the wonderful opportunity offered by the Atlanta Division." All pursued "a college education that they could not finance anywhere" else. Unfortunately, those enrolled in liberal arts programs must spend a year in Athens, a financial impossibility. "[T]his growing [Atlanta] University is now fully equipped" to offer arts and sciences (A&S) degrees. Why "deprive Georgia of these future leaders?"[320]

The message had a familiar ring. Letters with similar information continually went out from director George Sparks's office all over the state, and they had an important effect. In November 1954, a Stevens County politician, Ben T. Wiggins, would soon take a job with Sparks's "good friend, Marvin Griffin," the governor-elect. The director wanted statehouse jobs for Georgia's "sons and daughters" who came "to Atlanta." That summer, the Atlanta Division had placed over 400 boys and girls just out of high school. Sparks attached "a list" from Stephens County along with the names of past students. He also mentioned his "long friendship with your [Wiggins's] fine kinswoman, Miss Lucy Marvin Adams," affectionately called "Sweet Lucy."[321]

In south Georgia, a Sparks communication may have inspired an *Alma Times* editorial. That town shortly would have more students at the division than at the University of Georgia (UGA). "Why is the Atlanta Division [the] Board of Regents 'Step Child,'" editor and Evening School alumnus Dean Broome asked. For the year ending in 1952, the school received less than $163 for each of its 6,000 students, "whereas the next lowest," Middle Georgia College, got "more than twice that amount." The UGA's 4,294 students each brought in $448.30, and the 3,323 at Tech, $469.46. The editorial aroused consternation both in Athens and with the regents. Yet the article proved difficult to disparage because the quoted student expenditures were unassailable. President O. C. Aderhold, in testy comments to regent Frank Foley, attributed the editorial to the "false propaganda that goes to the press from…that Division." Difficult to administer, it "had no academic status and could not be accredited until it was put under the University."[322]

At the regents office, treasurer James A. Blissit, an Athens partisan, set out to refute the *Alma Times*. In a polemic to regent Foley, he gave a somewhat muddled account of what had been pitiful state funding and instead attacked the division's surplus, where Sparks was more vulnerable. The director built up funds year after year that "should have been spent" for operation expenses "to upgrade educational quality," including faculty raises. The funds Sparks "saved" went "into the purchase of the" Ivy Street Garage "and toward the new building," Blissit complained. Merle Prunty also had criticized the use of "these surpluses" for construction. Of course, until the 1947 merger, the Evening School under its various names received little state funding, and the so-called "surplus" had accumulated from excessive veterans payments and Sparks's deft management of the auxiliary income.[323]

Both Prunty and Blissit surely knew that without Sparks's managerial talent there probably would have been no building or even a college in downtown Atlanta in 1931, 1937, 1945, or the early 1950s. The regents usually lacked the funds for adequate allocations. Without such physical facilities, Atlanta students, about whom these men expressed such great solicitation, may never have participated in any state-supported education programs. Behind this presumed concern for the students was an agenda heavily influenced by Athens's education politics. Sparks's astounding success in physically building the school seemed to be the true source of their discontent.

Other *Alma Times* charges got a public response from the UGA president, because the paper plunged into another sensitive topic, the state's shortage of teachers. The state education board reported the need for as many as 2,700 teachers and suggested that the Atlanta Division could turn out 200 a year. "[I]nducing people to enter the field of teaching" was the problem, the president scolded, not "adequate facilities for teacher training." He ruled out the Atlanta Division because the regents had designated its mission as business education. Privately, Aderhold thought that "establishing a College of Education" at the Atlanta Division was a "silly and ridiculous" idea. People migrated to the cities for better work opportunities, he told regents chairman Robert Arnold. They never would "go to Atlanta to prepare for the teaching profession when" stenographers and clerks made $3,600 a year, "secretaries up to $4600," and the average teacher, $2,700. Aderhold apparently had little faith in two basic tenets that allegedly inspired people to enter his profession, dedication and professionalism.[324]

171

The Atlanta Division also became an issue in the congressional race of area candidate Iris Blitch, who strongly supported the school. In response, the president blamed "persons who get state jobs around the capitol," but pointedly exempted gubernatorial appointees. He meant mainly personnel in education and health, who then began demanding a university "so that they can get an education while they are on the job." They used "the 'pore' working girl as the basis for their arguments." Aderhold met with this "self-appointed group," and they wanted "A.B. and B.S. degrees" at the division "to take care of their personal needs." Casting the sole blame on civil servants may have been misdirected, however. As Dean Thomas Mahler pointed out in another context, when the division dropped the bachelor of commercial science (B.C.S.) degree, hundreds of students inevitably demanded four-year programs. "We cannot provide" a university-level education "at the back door of every citizen," Aderhold told those complainants. That would favor one group while depriving "such service to the vast majority." Apparently he believed that all qualified Georgians had equal access to the isolated Athens campus.[325]

172

In resisting these pressures, Aderhold rested his hopes on the regents' "strong leadership." They should continue to maintain "a few high quality institutions" rather than "little universities in every community." With "transportation facilities" improving, he saw no need "to bring education of university level to all parts of the state." Chairman Arnold agreed. "We do not have the money to take a Fine Arts course to every farm in Georgia or to make it available for every working woman." While seemingly equating Atlanta's half-million people to scattered Georgia farms and small towns, Arnold also believed that "too many people" sought a "teacher's certificate for a 'safety valve.'" Georgia needed "more career teachers—people who love the profession and are interested in serving humanity as they draw their pay." Ironically, the regents chairman seemed to project an idealism about teaching that eluded the university president. Arnold had another solution for the Atlanta Division. "[W]hat would happen...if we should turn it over to Ga. Tech. Would that make things better or worse?" Aderhold quickly responded with a firm negative to this naive question. It "would necessitate greatly broadening" Tech's "scope, purposes and objectives." From Columbus, regent Frank Foley vowed to "remain alert and consider means of combating and destroying the [Atlanta Division] movement."[326]

As president Aderhold and his confidantes vented their disdain for the Atlanta Division and its supporters, Thomas Mahler, after three years as the division's administrative dean, submitted his findings and observations in two September reports. With refreshing honesty, some of the statements "may not be in line with your thinking," he told Aderhold. Overall, he generally remained impersonal and objective while operating at the division as a total outsider, and his cover letter told of his unhappiness with the assignment. It was his first experience "in a situation where mutual confidence and cooperation are so lacking," with educational situations "largely resolved in terms of personal interest, personal power and prestige, and public effect." That similar pressures existed at Athens apparently did not occur to him. Mahler disliked "very much having to make" his report "outside of channels," yet "I have a new car now and can slip off to see you more frequently, I hope." He had received "veiled hints" of "making too many calls" and "trips to Athens." But his mission seemed worthwhile. The "bulk of the basic progress" had been made since the merger, and it "would be lost quite rapidly" if the division became independent. Mahler gave major credit to Aderhold, although most of the cited improvements preceded that president.[327]

173

Mahler's first report, which dealt with operations, remained factual and objective. While disdaining director Sparks's accumulation of surpluses, he noted rising expenditures for student services and the "rapid increase in the number" of working full-time teachers, from seventeen in 1947 to 116 in 1954. The doctorates increased threefold, from thirteen to thirty-six percent, and part-time people had been restricted to two courses, usually in the "same subjects." Mahler considered faculty improvements as the most outstanding achievement, although resident Dean Manners, not UGA, recruited many of them. The 1949 recession, having ended teacher shortages in many fields, also had affected recruitment. The academic dean praised the improvement in the division's grade distribution, although grade inflation already had been reduced in 1949–1950 prior to

Aderhold's presidency and over two years before Mahler's arrival.[328] Surely, the recruitment of younger full-time faculty with advanced degrees brought higher academic standards.

Mahler tried to stiffen the division's admission and retention policies, which could affect grading practices. The admission of below-average and lower-caliber students made a high attrition rate predictable. But the admissions process continued to be loose and flexible even after Mahler's arrival. With the 1951 establishment of a testing center, entering freshmen registered a "mean I.Q." of only 106, six "points higher than the general population." Mahler concluded that some forty percent of "entering freshmen" ranked below the "top 49 percent of the general population" partly because "we must admit all students with high school diplomas who meet other entrance requirements." But a remedy existed. Student body quality could be controlled by tougher "retention policies and practices," particularly regarding "probation and exclusion," nonexistent before his arrival despite UGA catalog regulations. Mahler's first published exclusion list carried "a large number of students" with even more "placed on probation," sixty percent never again enrolling. Despite opposition from top administrators, the program slowly eliminated poorer students "during the first two years" so that "we have in the upper classes, in general, a much higher caliber student."[329]

His second report, on current problems, was more subjective and personal. The Atlanta Division either should "be a part of the University in the fullest sense" or without such close ties, "be separated." Key division leaders tolerated the relationship "only because of the prestige, status, and general acceptance" that accompanied it. Otherwise, they refused to take problems and "decisions to the president" and handled them by avoiding established channels with the attitude, "Do what you want to until somebody stops you." Some unfairly criticized UGA "almost to the point of enmity," believing that Athens was "trying to smother the Atlanta Division, or prevent its expansion and growth." Actually, "no curtailment of function" had occurred, Mahler believed, while minor expansion came with "the certificate program in Hospital Administration." Of course, in making these judgments, Mahler apparently had no knowledge of the numerous, hostile, in-house, and intra-system communications about the Atlanta Division that circulated among UGA administrators and certain regents.[330]

Mahler thought many problems could be solved if the president had more direct participation in division affairs, "an appropriate office" with a schedule of hours, and personal participation "at all important ceremonial and administrative occasions," including graduation exercises and faculty and administrative council meetings. "All appropriate public announcements" should be "issued under his direction at the Atlanta Division."[331]

175

Not surprisingly, Mahler found division administrators and faculty "supersensitive to all negative" Athens decisions. Often derogatory comments filtered back through students, including a dean's remark that "they were going to 'gut' the Atlanta Division at the first opportunity." An Athens teacher told a class "that the Atlanta Division is nothing but a diploma mill." Athens's rejection of a biology course needed "to complete three years of pre-medicine" seemed like another attempt to curtail and contain division programs. "[I]n some instances," the division had "grounds for believing that [Athens] decisions" lacked objectivity. On the other hand, Mahler claimed that the "top [UGA] administration" had granted the division more leniency than "schools and colleges on the campus."[332]

Mahler criticized the "exaggerated expansionist tendency" in Atlanta that should be curbed. One department claimed "the best faculty in the Southeast in a certain field." Undue emphasis was placed "upon large enrollments as the criterion of success," but admission standards and grading patterns were ignored. As soon as the business school acquired "a minimum staff with the proper academic qualifications," it attempted to develop a separate graduate program. But Mahler understood the effect of Atlanta's growth and development on the college, citing "many pressures from students, their parents, and interested lay-citizens" as well as "much internal staff pressure" for the expansion of programs. The division needed direction "from the top administrative level" to rein in these tendencies. In so doing, Athens administrators and faculty should "'accept' the Atlanta Division" and cease looking on it "as a second-rate institution" and a "dangerous competitor," an approach that "can lead only to conflict and eventual separation."[333]

Finally, Mahler commented on the division's administrative personnel. Some should be eliminated, particularly "one or two key positions" that would be "difficult to handle." He refrained from mentioning director Sparks and resident Dean Manners by name. Much dissatisfaction and bad morale existed among "a number of faculty members" who believed administrators "looked upon [them] as hired hands" without the status due professional men. Many had inadequate office space and little faith that the new building would solve the problem. Mahler, himself, had "little or no effective voice in matters of faculty offices, assignment of space, and parking facilities." The "internal political atmosphere" created discontent, particularly because of "an incipient battle for succession to the directorship" as Sparks approached retirement. Besides the "elimination of certain persons" responsible for the problems, the greatest hope for the future lay "in free and open participation of the faculty in the affairs of the school."[334]

176

Check marks and occasional penciled comments in the margins indicated that the UGA president carefully perused Dean Mahler's two reports. He surely agreed with their insistence that the division remain part of the University of Georgia and that he participate more directly. Subsequent actions, however, revealed how little of the advice actually was heeded as increasing support for the Atlanta Division propelled events beyond the control of him and his regent allies.

19

SEPARATION

By January 1955, the new "modern Division building" was "about ready for occupancy," the *Atlanta Journal* reported in a news item that bore all the marks of director George Sparks's precocious talent for public relations. "In the event that the story...didn't make you see red," UGA department head Merle Prunty wrote to president O. C. Aderhold, "I am forwarding a copy on which you can see some red." Prunty underlined or circled in red ink numerous phrases that offended him, because of "a number of deliberate distortions or misrepresentations." Prunty wanted the *Journal-Constitution* to be "apprised of errors and distortions" in division news stories "and asked to be more careful." There would be "no real end to this kind of publicity until the [division's] public relations work" is channeled through the University of Georgia.[335]

Besides the reference to Sparks as "director of the university," Prunty's crimson pen highlighted several other phrases of public relations puffery: "the only fully air-conditioned college in the South," the purchase of Gilmer Street property "for $150,000 of its own money," "the $600,000 of the school's money...put into the new building," "courses in business administration" not available on the Athens campus, "candidates for the liberal arts degree" being able to earn only "three years credit at the Ivy street school," and finally, "less than half of the money for the operating budget" coming from the state. For some reason

Prunty also took offense at the seemingly innocuous phrase, "working day school students."[336]

Prunty's note provides insight into the Athens mindset as the Atlanta Division continued to grow and capture statewide support. The man who only three years earlier had written for the chancellor an exhaustive and fairly objective study and analysis of the division seemed to be losing perspective. No matter that most of the article's statements, disregarding the hyperbole, were true, the division itself, like the proverbial red flag, seemed to enrage the Athens academic bulls. That the building's dedication in April received a half-hour of live, prime-time television coverage, featuring an address by a former Evening College student, nationally known newscaster Douglas Edwards, surely rankled. But others loved it. "God bless your School in your new building," wrote a Mrs. Harry Epstein, "Mother of Milton." Her letter's salutation, obviously intended for director Sparks, addressed the president of the university.[337]

Long before Prunty's outburst, President Aderhold had been seeking ways to curb the rebellious Atlanta ward. As a member of a Southern Association of Colleges' (SAC's) committee on "standards for accreditation," Aderhold pressed for a revision of Standard Fifteen, which dealt with branches, divisions, or units operating "at a distance from the parent institution and organized primarily for the purpose of offering off-campus instruction." The standards committee and SAC had adopted Aderhold's proposals the previous December. They would "effect certain changes regarding the Atlanta Division over a period of the next few years," Aderhold, undoubtedly with considerable satisfaction, informed the chancellor that February in an exhaustive and detailed Progress Report on the Atlanta Division. Aderhold appended excerpts from SAC's resolution. It required "full faculty control from the home campus both of [branch] curricula and of faculty," with the approval by the dean and department chairman who shall make "regular and systematic visitation." The revised standard centralized "[a]ll admissions"

178

through "the parent institution," including the issuance of "official transcripts," and it dealt in detail with matters from the adequacy of physical plants to extension classes.[338]

Although the Atlanta Division performed functions far more numerous and complex than "off-campus instruction," the UGA president was determined to impose the new standards to the fullest, and his staff began devising plans for "true integration." Since 1947, his Progress Report stated, "Most of the problems and difficulties" in integrating the division "have grown out of personality conflicts," because a few oppose integration and "want only the University's name." Dissatisfied with the regents' functions, "They press for new programs," courses, graduate instruction, "and all the elements that make" a university. Aderhold faulted some of his own faculty for being "arbitrary and antagonistic" toward the division staff. Nevertheless, he claimed "significant progress" in the "instructional program" since the 1947 merger and satisfactory "[a]dministrative relationships" after the Memorandum of Understanding. This "significant achievement" came because the division was "restricted to the Regents-assigned functions while still increasing its courses." Aderhold also took credit for "a large increase in the state appropriation," 569.9 percent for the Atlanta Division and "only 159.42 percent for" UGA. But he used 1947 as the base year when meager division state funding rendered the findings highly misleading.[339]

179

Shortly, the regents treasurer's report to the chancellor revealed a much different financial situation. Total per student spending for the 1953 fiscal year at UGA was $721, and for the division, $339. Since 1948–1949, UGA funding increased by 65.5 percent and only by 39.9 percent in Atlanta, and the "lowest per student expenditure" in any system junior colleges was "$372 or 24.8% more than" the division. Aderhold similarly distorted the state's per capita allocation, which in 1953 stood at only $180 in Atlanta compared with Athens's $717. The president also took credit for increasing library expenditures and circulation, lowering the average class size, improving grade distribution, reforming retention policies, and expanding the full-time faculty. These items had been addressed by Aderhold's UGA predecessors and by Dean Thomas Mahler, leaving such broad claims of accomplishment difficult to sort out. Of course, Merle Prunty's 1951 study for the chancellor called for reforms in all of these areas, and Mahler during his Atlanta sojourn apparently consulted that document extensively. Charitably, the president's Progress Report could be described as being highly selective in content and less than completely forthcoming. Aderhold's "Plans for the Future" clearly envisioned the Atlanta Division's continuance "as an integral part of" UGA, with strict adherence to the regents' functions and integrated "faculty and staff planning." Aderhold also intended to spend "one day a week" in Atlanta and have an office in the new building.[340]

180

The UGA president presented a lengthy and persuasive document with impressive detail. While some statistics and statements were crude and manipulative, others seemed well thought out. It contained claims of progress under Athens's tutelage, some valid and others grossly exaggerated. On its face, it purported to be an earnest statement of goals and objectives. In reality, however, Athens's bold ambitions had been elaborately clothed as serious education policy. The real objective was to retard, halt, and even reverse the development of public higher education in the Atlanta area regardless of the need. Counting on sympathetic regents for support, the UGA president pursued a course previously rejected by several experts, including George Works, George D. Strayer, and two prominent regional education leaders.[341] Whether in taking this aggressive and uncompromising stand Aderhold over-played his hand remained to be seen.

The president's "Plans for the Future" brought no joy to Atlanta. The "proposed [SAC] changes" would "put us right back in that unworkable and unacademic position we were in before," Sparks reported. But Dean Mahler, shortly to leave the Atlanta

Division, believed SAC's committee "did not have in mind a large, complex, well-established branch such as ours," he told Sparks. They had targeted "off campus centers" like Marietta and Columbus. Whether ignorant of his president's SAC activities or simply equivocating, Mahler saw "no need for hasty action of any kind."[342]

Shortly after receiving the Progress Report, the chancellor imparted some unsettling news to Athens. The Atlanta Division's alumni association, representing some 4,000 active graduates, had requested separation. The group's president, Atlanta attorney Thomas R. Luck, Jr., shortly would testify before the Georgia House's University System Committee, and the UGA president should attend. In calling for "complete separation," Luck admitted that the merger had facilitated the division's accreditation, but "in the intervening years" Atlanta students had developed "school pride and spirit." Furthermore, the division's large enrollment included "students from almost every [Georgia] county." Alarmed UGA supporters took this turn of events very seriously. At the regents education committee, Charles Bloch pronounced "The Atlanta situation" as being "very acute." The committee instructed the chancellor to report by April on a plan for the Atlanta division's future.[343]

The UGA president's angry reaction, imparted confidentially to Judge Frank Foley, contained comments demeaning, erroneous, uninformed, and inconsistent. The Atlanta Division operated "from 1913 to 1937 as an evening school" and "was never accredited." Pressure for the 1947 merger came chiefly from the regents office and the Atlanta Division itself, mainly because of complaints from the Veterans Administration. At the merger, "a few retired Atlanta school teachers" constituted "practically the entire" full-time faculty, and "the fees paid for all of this low grade instruction" facilitated the accumulation of all "the state appropriation and part of the student fees" for the purchase of Atlanta real estate. Athens encountered "great resistance" to "improving the quality of the educational program,"

181

and the appointment of Dean Mahler had been primarily responsible for the progressive improvements there. The division, if
separated, would have difficulty in achieving accreditation. On
the other hand, once independent "it will be impossible to prevent it from growing into a full fledged university."[344]

That possibility drove the president's implacable opposition.
The University of Georgia needed only three more years until the
division's "top leadership" changed with director Sparks's
mandatory retirement. In some respects, the separation had nar-
rowed to a struggle between two determined men, both forceful
educational entrepreneurs, with powerful allies among the
regents, legislature, and Atlanta businesses. Of course, Aderhold
personally would "be in favor of separation" if people like Foley
and "our other friends" could serve as regents "for ten years."
With that scenario unlikely, UGA must control "the program
there." By that time "we can make it largely an adult evening
school in Business Administration" and offer "junior college level
work for nonemployed adults." But working adults should "pay
higher tuition rates than" young students attending full-time.[345]

At the state capitol, the legislative committee listened sym-
pathetically to Atlanta Division supporters and directed a
subcommittee of five, under Rep. Ebb Duncan, to study the university system. Their preliminary investigation prompted the
issuance of an interim report labeling the new SAC standards
"highly impractical and prohibitive." The demands involved "a
needless expenditure" of funds and threatened the division's
accreditation. "[B]ecause of a critical and extremely pressing situation," they approved Resolution 121, shortly passed by the full
House, that recommended the Atlanta Division's divorce from
UGA "as a separate unit." Its courses should be expanded to four
years with degrees in business and the arts and sciences "as soon
as feasible." While the legislative action was only advisory, the
division's supporters had won a significant victory. The report's
decisiveness undoubtedly took the UGA president, the regents,
and most system administrators by surprise. Surely the irony in

this outcome did not escape the UGA president, who promoted the new SAC standards to achieve entirely opposite ends. But he kept waging a spirited fight. Meanwhile, regents Foley and Bloch arranged a luncheon conference on higher education with Atlanta newspaper officials. The *Atlanta Constitution* about a month later editorially opposed the separation.[346]

On the Athens campus, twenty-one department heads expressed concern to the president that "A.B. and B.S. degrees will be offered" in Atlanta. They volunteered to meet with the chancellor and regents "if you see fit," or "appear on television." If separation were rejected, they would "willingly try to cooperate with [division] officials" toward a "workable agreement," because Athens's supervision would produce "a better quality of work." Separation would lead to costly duplication and spread "our appropriations too thin." But if it happened, "No name should be given the new unit" in any way resembling the university's. Aderhold had strong support, but so did Sparks. Besides the legislature, alumni, and the student body, the Georgia Association of Credit Management, comprising officers and directors from Atlanta's most influential corporate and government bodies, gave separation a strong endorsement. Support also came from governor Marvin Griffin on the radio program *Georgia News Panorama*.[347]

183

Atlanta newspaper columnists became interested commentators. With the Atlanta Division's headcount the biggest in the system, Margaret Shannon wrote, its "enrollment sagged less in 1949 than the other institutions," and it was "shooting up faster now." The B.A. degree was "the hub of the controversy" and "really sets opponents on their ear. They envision a great emigration from Athens to Atlanta and a consequent weakening of the university." Columnist Jack Spalding labeled it "one of the most serious crises" in the history of a system "nurtured by enormous growth" accompanied by "malnutrition." The system faced shortages of buildings, equipment, and competent faculty amidst the state's remarkable postwar industrial expansion and changing social values. It simply could not keep pace with the rest of Georgia's progress. "Judged by dollars, the University System is pretty small potatoes," with the state apportionment "the smallest in the South. Georgians no longer can say 'Thank God for Mississippi.'"[348]

The submission of the chancellor's findings and recommendations in April intensified the debate. It so alarmed UGA supporters that regent Foley tried unsuccessfully to delay the momentum through a protracted Senate investigation. Caldwell's twenty-four-page, closely reasoned document was amply supported with evidence, and it also relied on previous division studies as well as the chancellor's own knowledge from years as an Athens insider. Caldwell praised the university for the "marked improvement in the division's academic standards" but noted the absence of "a happy and really effective working relationship." He scolded some UGA administrators for ignoring their Atlanta responsibilities and others who treated Atlanta like "a stepchild." He cited a 1950 study that mentioned UGA's failure "to understand the basic problems of adult education...and encourage course offerings aimed at" that group. With the adoption of the 1950 Memorandum of Understanding, however, the division erred by ending "efforts to integrate the institution." Standards deteriorated, more part-time faculty appeared, the student-teacher ratio increased, and library expenditures declined. These reverses also had been accompanied by a drop in the division's state funding, "from $152.00" per student (1951–1952) "to $140.00" (1954–1955). Rejecting large portions of President Aderhold's glowing Progress Report, the chancellor concluded that "most of the progress took place prior to 1952."[349]

Of the five studies undertaken since 1942, four recommended separation. Caldwell's "own thinking" led to the same conclusion in the "best interests of the University System" and Georgia higher education. But he made a clear distinction between "separation" and "function." The division's functions

184

constituted "a separate and independent question." The chancellor advocated separation for several reasons, but he emphasized the new SAC standards, mandatory whether or not the merger continued. In addition, SAC required "full faculty control from the home campus of curricula and of faculty." Caldwell doubted their ability to perform satisfactorily while spending "considerable time in Atlanta." Even worse, they would be returning to the unworkable, pre-1950 "plan of operation" abandoned "on the recommendation of President Aderhold." The chancellor confirmed that UGA must keep all 6,000 student records, involving "needless duplication" and complicating division counseling.[350]

The chancellor also thought Athens had "a negative sort of reason" for keeping "its jurisdiction" over Atlanta. It "desperately" feared the division would "over-shadow the University" and seriously compete for students, a position unacceptable to the chancellor. "[C]ontrol and management of the University System," including the definition of functions, rested with the regents. The division's functions "should be very restricted," but Athens, in making such decisions, had been and would continue to be charged with "allowing self-interest to dictate its policies." Athens's fear that its enrollments and work would be adversely affected should be allayed by the knowledge that eighty-five percent of the division enrollees could not "attend college" without employment, and few would go elsewhere if the business program ended. In addition, the chancellor opposed graduate work because the school still could not yet meet SAC undergraduate standards. It also would need American Association of Collegiate Schools of Business (AACSB) accreditation.[351]

General studies (A&S) took nearly seven pages. The school's "three years of [A&S] work" conformed "to no accepted academic pattern" and should be either two or four years. Recent division surveys counted some 1,300 in general studies seeking A&S degrees and 400 who wanted a B.S. in education. Their numbers "exceeded the [Athens] undergraduate [A&S]

185

enrollment," 1,070 in 1953–1954. The state's "five, four-year [white] colleges" lay beyond commuting distance.[352]

In the final analysis, inadequate state funding was the major impediment to a division A&S function, either at the three- or four-year level. Based on an anticipated enrollment of 4,100, the business school alone needed $492,000 in the upcoming year. Expanding general studies required $328,000 more, a total "minimum State allocation of $820,000." Only $540,000 had been provided, with "[n]o additional funds...in sight." With accreditation unattainable at that level of funding, the division again would jeopardize the whole system. Even the three-year program could not be funded. Advanced courses would be available through the system's extension division.[353]

186

Caldwell, who despite flaws was becoming the system's first truly capable, and, until then, its only outstanding chancellor, had made perhaps one of his most important decisions. In prevailing over the Athens statewide establishment, he demonstrated a mastery of the regents not unlike his earlier handling of the agricultural college's imbroglio. Needless to say, his report infuriated President Aderhold, who faulted Caldwell for failing to give UGA credit for trying "to integrate the program" when "top [division] administrative officials" were the problem. Aderhold particularly resented the "disturbing statement" that "[m]ost of the progress took place prior to 1952."[354]

The UGA president immediately began a campaign to stop separation. A fact sheet boldly contradicted the chancellor's findings. An Athens bookstore operator pitched in. For G. Arthur "Mac" Booth, the UGA president prepared "some notes in line with our discussion in my office." In this document, Aderhold's vision of Georgia higher education focused on the past, when the university system had been established to "reduce the number of units" and coordinate their activities "with the mother institution." Unfortunately, expanding programs "had begun to move [the system] in the opposite direction," with "an indirect de-emphasis of the University." Georgians "unalterably opposed" another large university in Atlanta because the state already had "enough—in fact too many units" to support adequately. If the Atlanta Division survived, he wanted it boxed in forever as a junior college with four years of academic work only in business. Booth rewrote this material to conceal the president's phraseology, and upon Aderhold's approval, he circulated the two-page, single-spaced polemic over his own signature.[355]

Also warming to the task, regent Charles Bloch, a Macon attorney with powerful political connections, believed the chancellor's report was "entirely unrealistic." Some "citizens" deserved a college education more than others. The regents owed a "primary duty and responsibility" to those just out of high school and only a "secondary duty" to others unable to go to college. Those who migrated "to a metropolitan center" seeking a better economic status and had "family responsibilities" deserved praise, but Bloch found it less commendable "if they are merely seeking degrees." Of course, "we recognize that we owe a duty to that group, too."[356]

187

As the education committee's May meeting approached, chairman Foley felt strong pressure for action. He worried about Rep. Ebb Duncan, who, according to an informant, "had pledges from eight regents to take" action that May "without waiting for the [legislative committee] report." But Duncan either cooled off or was bluffing, and the regents still provided no resolution of the issue. When early in June the chancellor's confidential report recommending separation became public, a deeply disappointed UGA president urged the regents to end the merger at their next meeting. With the report's release, he could no longer "administer the program," because division leaders "would not hesitate to go over my head."[357]

In his anger, Aderhold offered proposals even more draconian. His "first preference" would make the whole division a junior college. If the business program survived, it should be limited "to four years" with general studies offered through "a day junior college" and no UGA extension courses. Otherwise, "every junior college in the state would eventually make" a similar request, "a long step towards making each of them a senior college." Aderhold insisted on the immediate elimination of the general studies's third-year level without any "commitment to students" with uncompleted course work. Finally, the name of the school "should carry the junior college idea," but if the regents continued the business program "a part of the name should be 'evening school.'"[358]

By mid-June, regent Foley gave up. "This seems about the best that can be done," he wrote Aderhold. Shortly, he sent for the president's comment a draft of the committee's "Proposed Resolution" on separation. The staff at the chancellor's office was "strongly pro-Atlanta Division," although "the name provoked much discussion." Aderhold suggested the Atlanta State College of Business Administration, because of a "general [regents] policy" that identified system units "either with the town or area of the state." On July 11, the regents formally authorized the separation for September 1, but regent Bloch opposed the name Atlanta. Apparently at his insistence, they chose State College of Business Administration. Avoid competing with UGA, they warned. Pursuant to the chancellor's report on funding, they granted only the bachelor of business administration (B.B.A.) degree and canceled the third year in general studies (A&S), affecting nearly 2,000 students.[359]

While deploring such a grievous loss, the *University Signal* was exuberant over the division's independence.[360] Nevertheless, as Atlanta grew and thrived, the Georgia economy also continued to expand and the university system had to provide better educational services throughout the state. Shortly, the restrictive policies temporarily necessitated by state funding shortages and willed by the Athens establishment proved unacceptable to regional and national accrediting agencies and, ultimately, to the state's leaders and citizens.

188

THE PROBLEMS OF INDEPENDENCE

T he regents resolution granting the Atlanta Division independence brought immediate howls of protest over the new name. Three days later at a called meeting, the faculty peppered Chancellor Harmon Caldwell with complaints. Had the regents considered the effect on recruiting and maintaining the arts and sciences (A&S) faculty? Respected zoologist Dr. Helen Jordan, a research scholar and expert on lizards, vowed never to "read a paper" at a professional meeting "under the name of the State College of Business Administration" (SCBA). The school needed respect like others in the system, she told Caldwell. The registrar worried about the several hundred general studies (SGS) students ready to begin the junior year as offered in the catalog.[361]

Administrators, faculty, students, alumni, and friends "raised a general chorus condemning the name," director George Sparks, soon to assume the title of president, wrote the chancellor. Sparks feared "a wave of" resignations, not to mention the premium in salaries needed "to attract quality staff." Recruitment already had suffered. "We start our independent life under a cloud" burdened also by "inadequate state support." Sparks and the general studies faculty wanted the name Georgia State College. Some 1956 graduates demanded, and, on request, received diplomas labeled "Atlanta Division of the University of

Georgia." By October, the regents added "Georgia" to the name. They also yielded on the abrupt termination of the third year in general studies and allowed a continuance through the 1956 spring quarter for those already enrolled, but at regent Charles Bloch's insistence, the Athens extension service, not the Georgia State faculty, taught the advanced courses.[362]

A chancellor's committee looked into administrative organization and curriculum. The two schools, Business Administration (SBA) and General Studies (SGS), should continue, but they found the college's unitary organizational structure, which radiated around the president, inadequate for such a large unit and suggested decentralization. Not surprisingly, President Sparks resisted. With little enthusiasm for new statutes, bylaws, or general faculty meetings, he implemented the chancellor's changes reluctantly and named Dean Thomas Mahler's replacement only after being directly ordered. He finally chose registrar J. D. Blair over such strong regents objections that the man took the title of acting administrative dean.[363]

While Sparks disdained the administrative changes, regent Bloch, now education committee chair, boldly set out to micromanage the curriculum and curb general studies. Should courses of a cultural nature include philosophy and psychology along with the required science, mathematics, history, and English, he wondered. Offering "a general education" was not Georgia State's mission. Even the SBA's eight fields of concentration seemed excessive, but Bloch backed off when told of the Wharton School's sixteen fields and Northwestern University's twenty. Bloch even questioned the qualifications of the chancellor's committee members. Were these gentlemen "sufficiently trained in matters pertaining" to business schools? The regents education committee "has failed" to implement the chancellor's recommendations, Sparks complained. Building "this institution" would "have to wait until Mr. Bloch's term" expired "next year."[364]

190

Chairman Bloch also waged war on the noncredit courses, especially when gender-oriented. "Self Improvement and Personality Development for Women" drew particular wrath. "[T]hese courses" should be the last, and in the future the college will confine itself "to its functions," Bloch fumed to assistant Chancellor M. Gordon Brown. It had been offered twice before because of great demand, Brown replied. Some 2,000 women had participated in these types of courses, but fewer would be scheduled in the future. Despite Bloch's disapproval, the short courses continued to "Lure Hundreds of Adults" and remained the college's "most popular" offerings, the *Constitution* later reported. Bloch also objected to the student newspaper's dateline, *Georgia State Signal,* and to its innumerable references to "Georgia State" and "Georgia State College." The editors should use the correct name, otherwise the regents would face an expansionist "situation just like" California and Florida. Of course, Georgia State administrators, themselves, belittled this unwelcome moniker despite a 1956 regents resolution requesting that the college "use its full name in all instances."[365] In mock compliance, the institution's official stationery carried an enlarged, high-lighted, centered, and bold "Georgia State College" followed to the right by "of Business Administration" in smaller type.

191

Fear of declining enrollments because general studies was closed to new applicants proved groundless as the business curriculum expanded, including a new center for machine accounting and tabulating studies. The growing enrollment was astounding, attributable partly to nearly 2,400 Korean War veterans. The final count reached nearly 6,300, with a record full-time equivalent of 4,223. Nevertheless, course cutbacks became inevitable when general studies ended that spring.[366]

While the 1955 separation freed Atlanta from UGA supervision, Athens continued a vigilant watch for function infringements even while itself attempting to expand into Atlanta. That August, UGA's journalism school sought to lure away the Atlanta Advertising Club's annual clinic. When club leaders objected to leaving the metropolis, Dean John Drewry offered to conduct the clinic in Atlanta. To an angry Dean George Manners, Georgia State had primacy in regents-assigned fields, and he sent "strong protests to the Chancellor" over this invasion both of "our geographical area and our area of operations." Sister institutions could contribute by invitation, he wrote Drewry, but Georgia State's marketing division, with three full-time doctorates, could handle it, although Athens might participate by agreeing to those premises. Manners also invited Tech and Emory. Dean Drewry eventually retreated while insisting on UGA's prerogative to carry programs to any part of the state.[367]

192

While this episode involved the Atlanta community, Athens's art department questioned Atlanta's coursework. Were six faculty "needed to cover junior division" art work, the chancellor was asked anonymously, although Atlanta officials knew the questioner was UGA's Lamar Dodd. He "willfully distorted the facts" to create trouble, wrote Dean Horton Burch, whose patience over this and other Athens complaints was "wearing thin." The Georgia State art department had only "two men and four part-timers," some teaching in the UGA extension service. Dodd's monitoring continued, though the Atlanta art program was headed by Joseph Perrin, a former student whom Dodd professed to respect. The following summer, Dodd feared that senior level A&S courses had not ended, because Georgia State's summer school prospectus "shows [art] offerings that far exceed our own." Inquiries by the chancellor found the work to be "strictly non-credit." President O. C. Aderhold maintained a similar vigil, leading the assistant chancellor to take "this [A&S] matter up department by department" with Atlanta officials, but no violation was found.[368]

Other, more serious matters also clouded Georgia State's transition to independence. When the grandfathered junior-level program ended in June 1956, declining enrollments followed.

Officials also blamed the college's name for the nearly thirty percent drop, because it left the perception of instruction "limited to offerings [only] in Business Administration." The missing 900 students left an immediate ten percent budget loss projected at $25,000 to $30,000, and $100,000 for the current fiscal year. The decline continued into winter 1957. As "a purely professional school stripped of the mass of undergraduate students," Georgia State was limited to "those phases of education" less profitable, Sparks lamented to the chancellor. At the same time, "we are under the close scrutiny of the Southern Association" in building "up an outstanding professional faculty."[369]

Indeed, during this phase of independence, SAC visits became annual events, which led Sparks to revive his long-standing wariness of that organization. With some trepidation, he invited "a group of well-known educators to inspect us" preliminary to an official visitation the next year. He believed the college to be ready, and this time he got it right. Shortly, SAC officials extended accreditation under the UGA umbrella for three years until Georgia State could qualify on its own. Two visitations later, SAC's October 1956 report may have astounded the doubting president. It surely dismayed UGA officials and their regents' supporters, because SAC strongly rejected as educationally unsound Athens's policies of retarding the Atlanta institution. Indeed, A&S expansion was needed. As "the most important commercial center in the southeast," Atlanta should have a full-service public, downtown college. Regents' fears of encroachment on the University of Georgia were "groundless." At the same time, Georgia State's excellent faculty "cannot be retained under a two-year program," but the college, if expanded, "can render tremendous service" to the entire state.[370]

SAC officials also labeled the business degree, offered without advanced work in other fields, as unique in Southern education and perhaps in the nation. It established "an unrealistic and undesirable pattern," because business majors needed A&S support "beyond the second year" that could not be

193

supplied by a junior college. Consequently, AACSB accreditation also "will be affected" adversely. While this interim report carried tremendous influence prior to a definitive SAC study in 1958, the AACSB situation required immediate attention. Dean Manners shortly discovered that recently revised standards toughened membership requirements. Other degrees besides business *must* be offered before Georgia State could apply. In addition, the AACSB mandated a twenty-to-one student-teacher ratio and a twelve-hour, undergraduate, business faculty teaching load. The university system required fifteen hours.[371]

The regents would do everything possible to deal with the problem, chairman Arnold stated. But their continuing silence undoubtedly spurred Atlanta Rep. M. M. "Muggsy" Smith a month later to call for action. The regents discussed the matter informally several times, the chancellor soothed, but two months more passed without a "positive statement" that we "will or will not have the liberal arts degree," the *Signal* fumed. "[W]e think we have the right to know what our future" holds at "this crucial period." The regents also failed to address the SBA's heavy teaching load.[372]

With approval from two accrediting organizations in limbo, racial uncertainties predictable, and inadequate state funding a fact of life, the business school struggled to hold faculty. Their real income had declined, even as SBA salaries remained less than competitive in academia, and the SBA received no sympathy from general studies where remuneration was even more depressing. The SGS faculty declined to endorse a resolution requesting regents approval of higher SBA salaries. President Sparks did what he could, even "arbitrarily" adding "$200 [for individual raises] hoping the budget would go through anyway." At least in the real estate department, the SBA dean after two years of preparation succeeded in providing salary supplements through private contributions similar to earlier industry funding for the insurance department. In spring 1957, the Atlanta Real Estate Board and fifteen firms contributed $2,500, enabling R. K.

194

George M. Sparks, president 1955–1957, pointing toward the new building that three years later would bear his name. Courtesy of GSU Archives.

Brown to turn down a faculty position at the prestigious Wharton School.[373]

For different reasons, Georgia State also was losing its president in 1957. For several months a search went on for a successor to Sparks, reluctantly facing mandatory retirement. A faculty resolution asked the chancellor and regents for their involvement, because "our feelings" about the candidate's "qualifications and characteristics" should be "taken into consideration." By mid-December, its ad hoc committee informed the chancellor that eighty percent of the faculty's fifty-two members wanted someone with the doctoral degree, administrative experience being essential; college teaching, highly important; research, helpful; and "business experience," desirable but not essential. Most wanted the candidate to have some familiarity with the South. A president also should be skillful in public relations, have knowledge of a city college, show leadership ability, and maintain a good relationship with faculty and students.[374]

While the ad hoc committee proceeded, the chancellor and regents privately pursued Tulane President Rufus Harris, also under consideration at Tech. Although not interested in Georgia State, Harris hoped the two positions could be combined. Shortly, Caldwell informed Harris that Tech's alumni and faculty wanted "an outstanding engineer," and the regents acquiesced while unanimously expressing "the earnest hope that you could be persuaded to assume the presidency of Georgia State." Although the faculty committee had been ignored, they responded to Harris's possible candidacy "enthusiastically and unanimously" in an April resolution. At the same time, a search for other candidates went on. Among the outsiders, eleven made the list, all with terminal degrees. While the large majority of the faculty preferred an outsider, the ad hoc committee mentioned four insiders. But the faculty really wanted Rufus Harris. At a mid-May meeting, they again endorsed him as the person fitting the presidential profile they had adopted. In the event of his withdrawal, the ad hoc committee circulated ballots with the other candidates' names. Of the outsiders, system Vice Chancellor Judson Ward came close to a majority. Among the insiders, Dean Burch, the only degreed in-house candidate, received the strongest faculty endorsement, though far from a majority.[375]

A few days later, Rufus Harris privately revealed his reservations about the Atlanta situation. He found "too much real doubt in the minds of the regents about" Georgia State College. "Its importance is not positively felt or possibly even desired." The state's "educational necessities" and the opportunities in Atlanta were so great that "nothing but grief and anguish will be the lot of anyone who has to cope with them while the policy makers— The Regents—have no real heart for the place." Given Georgia's limited financial thinking about its institutions, Georgia State College "should be organized with Georgia Tech." Harris saw significant savings "in plant and administration." The faculty, though no different in "the total number of teachers," would be significantly improved. "Stronger personnel could be held and obtained."[376]

With Rufus Harris out of the picture, additional names surfaced. But by the end of June, when President Sparks formally stepped down, no replacement had been named. Under the statutes, acting administrative Dean Blair now became acting president. In early July, the appointment of Noah Langdale, Jr., never publicly a candidate and a "veritable dark horse," came as a complete surprise. A Valdosta native of a family well connected politically, the thirty-seven-year-old Langdale held a Phi Beta Kappa key from the University of Alabama where he starred as a football tackle. After four years in the U.S. Navy, he took a Harvard law degree and then an M.B.A. Returning home in 1950, Langdale opened a private law practice, served as an assistant professor of social science at Valdosta State College, and became Valdosta's "man of the year" in 1955.[377]

Explaining the situation to an outside applicant, the chancellor cited the racial climate as the major determinant of the regents action. Negroes had applied for admission and were "quite active," taking depositions for a federal court hearing expected in early fall. Fearful of the outcome, the legislature had ordered the cut off of state funding should racial integration occur. Under the circumstances, the "Regents decided that it would be unfair" to bring "an outside person into a situation that has so many uncertainties." The institution "may be closed in a matter of weeks or months." Consequently, they asked "a man already in the System to assume the presidency...at least for a time."[378] Having begun this assignment under tentative tenure, Langdale stayed over thirty years.

197

21

THE CHALLENGE TO SEGREGATION

When Noah Langdale became the Georgia State College (GSC) president in summer 1957, African Americans had been seeking admissions to the system's segregated white units since 1950 when Horace Ward applied to the University of Georgia (UGA) law school. Legal, admissions, and procedural hurdles fashioned by determined legislators, regents, and UGA administrators, along with Ward's unanticipated military service, brought a six-year delay. Ward lost the case in federal court upon revealing his attendance at the Northwestern University law school. Meanwhile, a 1954 constitutional amendment authorized the governor to close any racially mixed public school system, end state funding, give affected pupils educational grants, and lease school buildings to private groups. The 1956 legislature nullified United States Supreme Court desegregation rulings.[379] This defiance received a mixed reception from Atlanta's two representatives. Hamilton Lokey cast the sole house vote against nullification, and M. M. "Muggsy" Smith later supported local option, permitting complying schools to remain open. Mayor William B. Hartsfield, coining the phrase "a city too busy to hate," had hired in 1948 black police and subsequently integrated public transportation and golf courses. Atlanta University president Rufus Clement joined the Board of Education in 1953. As Georgia's racial stance hardened, the

Atlanta Constitution in March 1956 carried a *New York Times* article portraying Atlanta residents as racially moderate or liberal. Most saw legal segregation's end as inevitable. Yet while the majority of white Atlantans opposed both nullification and the governor's private school plan, they still strongly favored segregation. About a third of Atlantans were black.[380]

In this mixed atmosphere of hostility and ambivalence, six African Americans applied at Georgia State in spring 1956 encouraged by business and community leaders led by Jesse Hill, the Atlanta Life Insurance company president. The applicants held full-time jobs at three highly respected black establishments. They targeted the business school's evening program because its older, mature students seemed less violence prone. Besides legal impediments, they faced formidable regents barriers adopted during the Ward controversy, including the endorsement of two alumni. Applicants in the largest counties also needed a superior court ordinary's, or clerk's, certification. A battery of aptitude and intelligence tests finalized the process. But the regents offered scholarships for graduate or professional work outside the state.[381]

The six applicants, accompanied by an attorney, went first to the Fulton County court house and surprised ordinary Eugene Gunby who expected to deal with batches of applications forwarded by GSC officials following registration. Judge Gunby sent them to the college. On March 23, Thelma Barbee Boone and Edward Jacob Clemons, having submitted college transcripts for transfer credit, visited GSC registrar J. D. Blair. He refused admission without alumni certification, but courteous and conversant, he expressed "his love for the Negro people." His family "worked 95 Negroes" on a South Carolina farm where in boyhood he played with blacks. Sent to President George Sparks, the applicants learned that the two UGA alumni certifying Edward Clemons's good character could not be considered Georgia State graduates just because the UGA and Atlanta Division earlier had been merged. Furthermore, their applications arrived by mail after the spring quarter deadline, and all new applicants must enroll in person. Sparks sent them to the regents office where secretary L. R. Siebert suggested out-of-state aid, which both refused.[382]

On their return to the registrar's office, Thelma Boone attempted to enroll in a noncredit course not requiring alumni certification. As Blair faced the possibility of registering the first black in a system white college, the instructor suddenly canceled his secretarial course allegedly because of low enrollment. Meanwhile, the other four applicants also were rejected. Despite the near closing of the school, President Sparks projected calm and pleasure that Georgia State, unlike Alabama and "miss Lucy [sic]," had avoided riots. It lacked "residential facilities," dining rooms, and "campus life," and had "mature and working" students, he told the *Macon Telegraph*. Registrar Blair also exuded nonchalance. "None of us are panicked here." The faculty "remained broadminded," although the final decision rested with the regents.[383]

201

The faculty's openness described by Blair had little appeal to the president. He had "talked several times" to the chancellor of his fear "of securing teachers from the North and East who might be the least 'tainted' with any anti-segregation ideas." To "screen them the best we can," the college used extensive interviews and employed "Retail Credit reports (the long form)." In view of the "first [integration] effort" last week, Sparks would use "more caution" in building "an outstanding faculty," and Caldwell agreed. But Sparks knew that some faculty and staff were completely trustworthy. Acting Dean of Men William Suttles "helped me work more angles during the 'battle of last week.'" Without "his organizing of courthouse friends we might have had a lone battle to fight in the application of the first two Negro students..." On campus, queried coeds, while anticipating a flood of blacks, expected no violence if they "stayed in their place" and did not "show off." But they would not be accepted socially or as equals. Some males predicted on-site segregation, "two student bodies," and increasing white transfers. One foresaw mob action but not like Alabama. After five years blacks might be accepted amidst continuing resentment.[384]

As spring quarter ended, two of the original black applicants, joined by three others, prepared for challenges that summer. With mimeographed letters to officially designated alumni, the five tried to comply, but they received no replies. Before registration, they hired attorney E. E. Moore, Jr., and soon had a National Association for the Advancement of Colored People (NAACP) pledge of financial support. At the June registration, they encountered repeated rebuffs as face to face they approached alumni, five to nine in number, "floating around the halls with name tags." Ironically, black attempts that summer coincided with the college's severe enrollment decline. Their actions laid the basis for a class action case, *Hunt v. Arnold*, in federal district court that September. It sought a permanent injunction against the regents and Georgia State administrators.[385]

In reporting integration, the *Georgia State Signal* aroused both criticism and support. Editor Al Haskell followed too closely the administration line, six former *Signal* editors and managers charged. Haskell "deliberately played down one of the most vital issues ever to confront the South" and Georgia State. The possible enrollment of several African Americans "is of interest to all," yet Haskell buried the news item "on an inner page." Was this "another example of administrative pressure?" In early October, the *Signal* did give front page coverage to the lawsuit, and Haskell took a strong editorial stand. Segregation was "the only answer to the racial problem," because integration would bring "racial strife." The legislature should privatize Georgia State. Later, Haskell noted proudly that the *Augusta Chronicle* described the *Signal* "as a clear beacon out of a haze of confusion." The *Chronicle's* arch-segregationist editor, regent Roy V. Harris, later reprinted Haskell's editorial and visited the campus seeking additional material.[386]

202

Filing motions, counter-motions, and appeals took over two years after the Hunt case entered federal district court, with plaintiffs seeking to expedite and the defense to delay. In February 1957, the state sought the suit's dismissal because plaintiffs failed to "exhaust their administrative remedies." Lacking the "endorsement of Georgia State alumni" they "improperly took the suit to federal court" before a state court had "passed upon" the regents regulations. Their purposes also were suspect. They sought a test case, not an education. It took Judge William Boyd Sloan until June 10 to dismiss this motion. The regents' expiring terms also brought delay. Plaintiffs' motions that their successors also be listed as defendants required hearings and opened up endless defense arguments. With the announcement that *Hunt v. Arnold* finally would come to trial in December 1958, a legal attack on segregation in the city's public schools also was under way.[387]

203

Successful challenges to segregation carried dire consequences, with GSC's closing inevitable. By early 1958, as the impending litigation's implications began to sink in, the faculty expressed increasing concern. What were the regents' plans should the institution be closed? The chancellor's assurance that current contracts would be honored provided only fleeting solace. Business Dean George Manners embraced their concerns. Perhaps they could "be employed by the Regents office" or by Tech.[388]

At the December trial, Attorney General Eugene Cook's defense team, rejecting plaintiff claims of being deprived of the Fourteenth Amendment's equal protection, took several approaches. Adamantly denying discrimination, they tried to prevent plaintiff's attorneys from extracting from system witnesses acknowledgment that the university system operated racially segregated units. When the regents' 1950s admissions barriers came under scrutiny, individual regents cited "crowded conditions" and enrollment pressure as motives for their action. Law school entrance standards had been tightened in response to Georgia Bar Association concerns over quality, not because Horace Ward had applied.[389]

The defense also devoted considerable time putting the NAACP on trial. Although Barbara Hunt testified to approaching that organization for financial aid only after hiring an attorney, the defense made the most of this relationship. Instead of entering the school "in good faith," Hunt "simply loaned herself to a [NAACP] scheme...to make a test case." The applicant failed to "come in with clean hands." In the meantime, she had been accepted at Lincoln University, and "her case ought to fall on that account." In a meaner mode, the defense took advantage of negative, contemporary attitudes toward divorce and premarital sex, impugning the morals of two female plaintiffs.[390]

(Left to right) Mrs. Myra Elliott Dinsmore, Mrs. Barbara Pace Hunt, and Ms. Iris Mae Welch, plaintiffs in Hunt v. Arnold (Atlanta Daily World, 8 Dec. 1958). Courtesy of GSU Archives.

But testimony of certain defense witnesses proved self-destructive. Late in the trial, the prosecution's outside, NAACP attorney, Donald Hollowell, discovered the initials of registrar J. D. Blair, himself, not a Georgia State graduate, on an alumni certificate. Asked if "it is common custom for the faculty" to act for alumni during registration, Blair "would not say that is true" while admitting that "it is done," but not as a common practice. He denied that faculty had signed student certificates from other counties. When presented with such an application signed by one of his employees, Blair claimed the woman was an alumna. Shown that this service had been rendered by other staff members, Blair weakly explained that they had been approved by the alumni association.[391]

Judge Sloan's seventeen-page decision four weeks later followed by one day another federal court ruling striking down the region's segregated busing. Sloan granted the plaintiffs class

action status and accepted federal jurisdiction. The black applicants, some having completed high school and others with
college work, qualified to make application, but the college still
had "the primary right and responsibility of fixing and passing
upon" admissions. Nevertheless, the court restricted that right by
prohibiting the denial of "admission to qualified Negroes solely
because of their race or color." The out-of-state scholarship program for blacks also violated equal protection. While noting the
alleged immoral character of two plaintiffs, the judge restrained
the defendants from requiring "certificates of character" from
alumni, because "the average Negro" had little opportunity "to
become personally acquainted with the average white person,"
particularly in "a white educational institution." Sloan applied
the decision to the whole system.[392]

205

While Atlanta blacks savored their victory, Georgia's two U.S.
senators were shocked, and Governor-elect Ernest Vandiver
called for the indefinite suspension of all system registration, a
move immediately ordered by chairman Robert Arnold until the
regents met in mid-February. Meanwhile, the "noisy heroics"
anticipated by the *Atlanta Journal* did "prevail" among white
politicians. At the end of his inaugural address, Governor
Vandiver, in a weary and trite simulation of Churchillian rhetoric,
promised to fight "judicial tyranny" in the streets "of every city"
town and hamlet "until sanity is restored in the land." Within
days, legislators enacted several bills implementing the governor's program of complete exclusion. Vandiver could close
individual units and hire defense attorneys. An age law set up
maximum limits for admission, twenty-one for undergraduates
and twenty-five for graduate students.[393]

The Tech and UGA presidents immediately predicted enrollment cuts, particularly in graduate programs. Some students
foresaw damaging effects upon whites as well as blacks. In being
told "what they can and can't do," people were being treated like
Russians, a 1958 alumna wrote. Having entered college at age
fifty-six, she had derived "immeasurable" benefits and self-

confidence and wanted a master's degree. A Dunwoody woman believed the age law perpetrated an "unthinkable wrong," placing limits on both races. No legislature or congress "has the right to tell people when they can attend school."[394]

While the politicians passed laws, the regents began fashioning a system approach to the crisis. In February, they empowered each unit to select or reject students based on "social responsibility, adjustment or personality, sturdiness of character and general fitness for admission to the institution." Segregation "didn't enter the board discussion at all," regents secretary L. R. Siebert assured the press, and the Hunt case was never mentioned. The regents for a long time had been seeking "best prepared students, and we can find those by tests, aptitudes, grades, and interviews."[395]

The new policy initially came from Georgia State president Noah Langdale in mid-November 1958, some three weeks before the Hunt trial began. It grew out of his concern over the quality of students, and he offered it as an addition to existing requirements. "[A]t our graduation ceremonies on June 1," Langdale "worried" that "a rather small fraction of the total number of 'heads' enrolled at this college" were involved, he told the chancellor. With attrition at "around 14%," this high turnover rate was unfair to students and institutions. Recently, a visiting Southern Association of Colleges (SAC) official emphasized the need to review admissions requirements and procedures to get "a more promising ratio of students successfully completing their degree programs."[396]

Langdale's suggested admissions procedures included "character, personality, and moral-worth analyses of each matriculant." Because such perusal took time, applicants must apply by July 1 or thirty-five days prior to each quarter's registration date. Personal interviews would be mandatory. The regents should remove "approved" secondary schools as sources of entering students and accept only those from "accredited" high schools. Langdale stressed proficiency in mathematics and

English. Each college would create an admissions committee to replace its registration committee, which did not review all applicants. In addition, the process placed great "emphasis on psychological testing," and it reserved "the right to view matriculants who" passed all of the tests "but whose promise of successful accomplishment is questionable from the viewpoint of personality and proper psychological reflects." Finally, all "transfer students will be tested as entering freshmen."[397]

In offering this program, Langdale made several stipulations. Every system unit must adopt it "simultaneously," because excluding any would be "grossly unfair." By April, the regents had implemented the program's main features and raised system academic requirements. But in permitting each unit to make admittance decisions, exceptions favorable to white applicants became available. In addition, registration could be suspended when a unit's "capacity" was reached, and unit officials could consider whether an applicant's matriculation would enhance Georgia's "economic welfare."[398]

The governor's age limitations along with new quality standards, the latter introduced abruptly and without careful planning, seriously threatened Georgia State. Under normal circumstances, the simultaneous adoption of such far-reaching changes undoubtedly would have been unthinkable. Yet according to admissions director William Patrick, the new system initially produced excellent results. That March he noted a "most gratifying" response to the toughening of standards. More telephone calls, letters, personal visits, and requests for catalogs came than ever before at that time of year. Students wanted "to attend an institution that has high standards of selectivity and instruction."[399] Within a few months, however, Patrick's optimism vanished.

As the regents freeze on registrations ended, several blacks again sought to enroll that summer at both Georgia State and Tech. Atlanta's increasing attraction to civil rights groups may have influenced this activity. Unlike earlier applicants from the black business community, most in this new group, all female, gave the Friendship Baptist church as their address, and they employed different methods when seeking registration forms, including fictitious names. With the governor's age restrictions in effect, they also were younger. Backers "still insist it's a good law for keeping Negroes out of white colleges," columnist Margaret Shannon wrote, and the governor "has not changed his mind about closing schools. Nevertheless, "while those responsible for closing them may be heroes for a moment, they certainly will be history's villains if lasting damage is done." Events at Georgia State turned somewhat bizarre on May 7 when one James Dennis, representing six of the young women, was expected to meet with admissions officials, Shannon reported. "His arrival was awaited in vain by three Georgia Bureau of Investigation (GBI) agents and one state-employed photographer," who said he came "on instructions from the governor's executive secretary." Vandiver's denial still left the GBI's presence unexplained. Not surprisingly, the man's name turned out to be fictitious.[400]

By registration's end, six had dropped out. The remaining three were ruled ineligible for various reasons, including the lack of high school algebra, too few academic units, no College Entrance Exam Board tests scores and grade transcripts, and late applications. Such glaring lapses seemed to indicate, if not a loss of will, poor preparation, little serious planning, or even possibly a simple desire to make a statement when the odds against success remained so heavily stacked against them. If they had overcome initial hurdles, they still would have faced four hours of testing to determine their ability to do college work, then individual conferences with three faculty. Thirty-five, chosen to conduct these sessions in groups of three, attended preparatory workshops led by the counseling and testing director. Despite appearances of objectivity, one faculty interviewer had no doubt that "they were not going to get in" whatever their qualifications.[401]

Of course, the age requirements also had to be met, although the law exempted teachers, servicemen, veterans, and apparently any others the regents or administrators might so favor. A niece of regents chairman Robert Arnold had no difficulty "being admitted as a student" to the GSC arts program despite her age. By 1962, age limit exceptions became so common that college officials, facing tumbling enrollments, sometimes admitted as much privately. "That they absolutely can not attend" if over the age limit was a "misconception," Patrick wrote a state legislator. The "loss of potential students" amounted to "several thousands" despite "press statements, radio and television news, personal contacts." Patrick believed a great many people still were unaware "that they can be considered for admission in spite of the age limits." No other system unit went to such extremes in screening applicants. In fact, despite Langdale's insistence on strict system inclusiveness, most apparently did nothing. Patrick referred to Georgia State "as a pilot school" selected by the regents to enforce the "stringent new admissions standards."[402]

By spring 1960, the absence of system-wide enforcement caused great alarm at Georgia State over Tech's expansionist activities. Their proposal to begin a night management MBA program would duplicate and harm Georgia State, with registrations already seriously impacted by the age law, Dean Manners warned. President Langdale was more direct. "I have remained quiet about the unique manner in which we have observed the ordinances of our superiors," he wrote the chancellor. "I shall continue to remain quiet." But a Tech evening program "which pays lip service to both" the legislative act and "Regents Regulations will ultimately destroy adult education in the field of management at this College."[403]

The lull in integration efforts at Georgia State during the 1959 fall may have been puzzling, but the *Atlanta Journal* welcomed it. "NO RACE PROBLEMS SEEN NOW AT GSC," the paper headlined. The *Journal* either was unaware of, or ignored,

209

two young Atlanta blacks with impeccable credentials, Charlayne Hunter and Hamilton Holmes, who attempted that fall to enroll at the University of Georgia. They had been turned back because of inadequate dormitory space and late registrations. But attitudes at Athens toward integration already had begun to change. A year earlier, sixty percent of some 200 UGA students, while preferring segregation, chose race mixing over closing. Later, a larger sampling found the UGA faculty favoring integration if the alternative involved shutting down the institution. The 1960 general assembly also witnessed dissent. Would the University of Georgia, itself, be closed? The governor's legislative opponents, although few in number, temporarily removed the cut-off clause in the appropriation bill over the opposition of Augusta representative and regent Roy Harris, who vowed to go to jail in support of segregation.[404]

A few south Georgians also complained about the age law. They had supported it because of administration assurances it would not deter white admissions, but it did. Citing depleted enrollments at junior colleges and at Georgia State, the House University System committee introduced a repeal bill. But the governor, having heard of no serious effects, liked the law, and few dared oppose him on the issue of segregation. That winter, the Georgia State student body declined by 1,062, down twenty-five percent from the previous year and nine times greater than Tech's loss of 129. The overall average student age also dropped, from twenty-seven in 1957 to twenty (day) and twenty-five (night). GSC's losses exceeded all the other system units. In the midst of the winter recruiting season, the president informed his deans that no faculty would be hired for new positions or vacant ones.[405]

By then it was becoming obvious to some that the segregation crisis had changed Georgia State's mode of operation and threatened its survival. A series of *Atlanta Constitution* articles by columnist Charles Moore dissected the school's painful transformation. Once referred to as an educational "cafeteria," Georgia

State had "shut the door to samplers." Moore noted President Langdale's strong defense of the new standards and the complicated registration routine. The president denigrated "cafeteria education." Before the quality reforms, "special" or "irregular" non-degree-seeking students comprised an estimated one-quarter of the enrollment. Lacking the stimulus for better grades, they studied less and were even disruptive. Now, taking courses just to get a better job had ended. While Langdale acknowledged the unmet needs of special students, other things must come first, including library, classroom and multipurpose buildings, an auditorium-gymnasium, and improved faculty salaries.[406]

Moore also examined the age limit requirement, described as "the state's main weapon designed to battle against integration." It really was "two-edged and thus far appears to have hurt the institution as much as it has helped," cutting deeply into Georgia State's enrollment. The school "suffers more than the others." Dr. Sparks's "Philosophy Is Gone with the Wind." Under his leadership, "all a high-school graduate needed to get a degree was the burning desire—an ideal which turned a tiny debt-badgered night school into the multi-million-dollar" Georgia State. A twenty-year-old small-town girl took a job in Atlanta for two years before deciding to attend college. Lacking Georgia State's newly required fourteen hours of academic work, the highest in the state, she had to go back home to pick up extra credits. The age limit also was a tragedy. "By the time young people work and save enough money for college, they are too old to be admitted."[407]

While citizens complained about the exclusion policies and college officials fretted over declining enrollments, "a youthful Negro" apparently in his early twenties "quietly picked up admission forms." This activity coincided with the 1960 arrival of the "direct action" movement in Georgia. As press and college officials prepared to keep tabs on his every move, the integration spotlight began shifting toward Athens. Charlayne Hunter and Hamilton Holmes had renewed their UGA applications each successive quarter. After numerous delays and refusals, their trial opened in Macon federal court on December 13, some two years after *Hunt v. Arnold*. Judge W. A. Bootle in early January ordered their immediate admittance. Faced with growing public opposition and student demonstrations, the governor blinked. The University of Georgia, system flagship and for generations the intellectual cradle and training ground for thousands of Georgia politicians and professionals, remained open. In moving the integration spotlight to Athens, Hunter and Holmes spared Georgia State undoubtedly a less auspicious outcome.[408]

Although Georgia Tech admitted three blacks in fall 1961, President Langdale, with all admissions impediments officially still in place, followed the letter of the law and delayed integration for over a year and a half. Finally, with repeal of the age law in March 1962 and an official chancellor's advisory that system units should cease requiring certificates signed by alumni and ordinaries, Georgia State admitted its first African American student. Annette Lucille Hall, a thirty-seven-year-old Rockdale County public school teacher, attended an Institute on Americanism and Communism sponsored by the regents and the state Education Department that summer. In the fall, Mary Belle Reynolds Warner, a thirty-one year-old mother and housewife with a master's degree in social work from Washington University, transferred from Athens to take courses in music. The college made no announcement and "not the slightest adverse student reaction" occurred. The next year, Georgia State enrolled six blacks (one graduate student) and rejected thirteen others. As more race students subsequently entered, the first African American faculty joined the library staff in spring 1966. Annie L. McPheeters, a 1929 graduate of Atlanta's Clark College with a library science degree from Hampton Institute, had headed a branch of the Atlanta Public Library. Two years later, Harvard-trained Harding Young joined the business school to work directly with minority group businessmen.[409]

Still, blacks immediately did not flock into Georgia State or other system units. By winter 1968, the Atlanta institution's 252 African Americans, only about three percent of the total enrollment, formed the Black Students United (BSU) to promote their campus interests, foster "meaningful and effective" interracial communication, encourage scholarships and recognition of black leadership, and disseminate knowledge and understanding of their culture. The following year, some sort of bonding with the institution seemed to be taking place when the BSU sponsored a homecoming celebration which selected a Ms. and Mrs. Black Georgia State. Meanwhile, a 1968 White House executive order applied affirmative action hiring to all institutions of higher learning with federal contracts. The following year, a high profile black educator, Thomas M. Jenkins, the Albany State College president, accepted a joint appointment working with the chancellor on the creation of a new community college in Atlanta and serving as President Langdale's executive assistant.[410]

213

While resolution of the college integration issue provided no immediate solution to Georgia's or the region's larger racial problems, minorities could now participate more fully in the educational process, one of the most impelling aspects of the American dream. During the state's struggle to prevent integration, both blacks and Caucasians lost educational opportunities. In addition, Georgia State's abrupt abandonment of open admissions and its adoption of the highest entrance requirements in the system brought additional hardship. Besides being a self-inflicted wound, it harmed its own white constituency. It also invited comparison with the state's earlier use of the "quality education' theme to protect the UGA law school from integration. Unfortunately, the GSC's quality program suffered opprobrium at a time when the loose academic system inherited from the Sparks era badly needed improvement. Perhaps this experience foretold that Georgia State's mission of reaching out and providing services to a wide variety of urban constituents could not again be easily abandoned.

Plaza scene (c. 1970). Courtesy of GSU Archives.

By the post-World War II period, Georgia's segregation struggle over public higher education ran counter to all progressive national trends that began with the American Council on Education's call in the late 1940s for the removal of all barriers to educational opportunity. Indeed, the system and Georgia State, while preoccupied with segregation, could never participate to the fullest in the federally subsidized scholarship and fellowship programs made available under the National Defense Education Act of 1958. The demise of racial segregation liberated public higher education to pursue in a national framework a level of quality hitherto more difficult to attain.

22

SURVIVING DURING
THE SEGREGATION CRISIS

Georgia State College President Noah Langdale, Jr., began his tenure at a decidedly difficult time. Although *Hunt v. Arnold* came nearly a year and a half later, the college faced closing at any time if integrated. Under the circumstances, the president, new to academic administration, seemed to emphasize continuity. For years he retained the Sparks staff, including his second in command, J. D. Blair, who lobbied vigorously to retain the job. The president seemed to exert a "hands-on" involvement in college affairs while instructing his deans on the "group approach" to administration in order to "create this 'team' result...badly needed throughout all management efforts." Later, with the 1963 appointment of William M. Suttles as vice president, Langdale "pretty much turned over the academic program to him."[411]

Langdale's style provided a sharp contrast with his aging predecessor. While Sparks relied on public relations and political maneuvering, Langdale's relative youth, dynamism, and oratory afforded a high public profile that seemed to bolster confidence. One participant described him initially as "creative and exciting." A large, gregarious man with an athlete's crew cut and a bombastic nineteenth century oratorical style, he exuded "buoyance [sic] and enthusiasm." Sometimes using nouns and adjectives as

Noah Langdale, Jr., President 1957–1988. Courtesy of the GSU Archives.

verbs, he employed alliterative and nebulous phrases peppered with euphemisms. Georgia State should "professionalize its product, the graduate," he noted, and that "can only come through three steps: discipline, development and dedication."[412]

In initial campus meetings, the president vowed to maintain administrative integrity, keep open channels of communication, and foster teamwork. At the same time, he discovered that the deans and faculty had very decided ideas on the institution's future. He sympathized with the business school's aspirations for graduate programs and promised to make the M.B.A. part of a package deal along with the arts and sciences (A&S). The chancellor thought "[s]ome of the Regents are looking on such a program with greater favor."[413]

Besides new degrees, the faculty had a number of other concerns. The incompetent librarian must be replaced, and in October Langdale authorized the library study that the faculty had been recommending "[f]or four consecutive years." Its critical report brought in William R. Pullen as the new librarian. Perhaps reflecting other pent-up frustrations from the Sparks era, the faculty also wanted improvement in the college's public relations and placement practices, which seldom brought major corporations on campus to recruit seniors and alumni. The faculty also complained about the physical facilities and the usually shared offices lacking privacy.[414]

During the fall, in several reports to the chancellor, the new president pressed for the new programs and developed arguments justifying them. The college faced "LOSS OF ACCREDITATION" without A&S degrees. The absence of graduate programs made faculty recruitment and retention more difficult, caused lagging student enrollment, and adversely affected participation in the ROTC program. The college's name bestowed neither prestige nor a positive identification for alumni and foundation supporters, while "[o]ur sister institutions" greatly benefited from various grants.[415]

The regents that September, in a move the *Atlanta Journal* labeled "a change of heart," authorized arts and sciences (A&S) majors in English, history, political science, and psychology, effective in winter 1958. A month later, the hard sciences, biology, and mathematics received similar authority for fall 1959. In addition, accounting, management, marketing, insurance, and economics could prepare that September to offer the M.B.A. "Mr. Langdale is showing his fellow school presidents...a thing or two about how to get results from the regents," the *Atlanta Journal* commented. The regents' action impressed Southern Association of Colleges (SAC) visitors that October. In their "very favorable" report, Langdale told the chancellor, "every standard had been met." SAC's blessing, along with the expanded A&S curriculum, expedited Georgia State's application for full American Association of Collegiate Schools of Business (AACSB) membership. College officials looked forward to the January 1958 visitation with great anticipation.[416]

217

The AACSB's negative findings stunned administrators and faculty. The school was well organized in preparation for a future urban university, but the evening classes, despite "extreme integration," still remained "the center of gravity." School of Business Administration (SBA) committees, too numerous, youthful, and diverse, reflected the faculty's academic immaturity due to rapid growth. In addition, the faculty's newness, uneven departmental preparedness, low salaries compared to other system units, bad summer teaching, inadequate library for graduate-level work, heavy reliance on objective testing instead of analysis, among other criticisms, all contributed to a certification delay. The visitors also wanted time to evaluate the soon-to-be implemented M.B.A. program. Finally, A&S course offerings would have to be increased.[417]

A disappointed Dean George Manners, whose offer to resign was refused, acknowledged the findings, but it was Georgia State's misfortune to have two of the three AACSB visitors later remove themselves from the decision-making process for personal or professional reasons. Another AACSB visitation in October 1959 brought strong committee approval but a rejection from the executive committee. Manners later claimed to have discovered that Athens business school Dean James Gates, using questionable and even illegal tactics, decisively had influenced the negative decision. After this malfeasance's exposure, AACSB membership came in 1960.[418]

As part of the preparation for four-year and graduate work, the president sought private sector financial support. He did not equivocate when asking various Atlanta businesses, industries, and alumni for over $200,000. The money would help enhance several fields of instruction and supplement faculty salaries. Langdale initially asked Atlanta bankers for $10,000 annually for "educational facilities to 'breed' the super-employee" needed to attract "modern industries and financial institutions" to the area. By January, he doubled the request, with a listing of the new M.B.A. courses. The president also tapped the Atlanta and Fulton County governments for up to "$50,000 per year for 7 years" for a gymnasium that SAC listed as a vital need. He supplemented fundraising and public relations with extensive public speaking throughout the state. In November alone, the *Signal* reported eight speeches to civic, business, and government organizations. Climaxing this activity, the Georgia State College Foundation received a charter early in 1958. Governed by alumni-elected trustees, its goals stressed scholarships, student loans, research, equipment for instruction, publicity, and teacher salary supplements.[419] The involvement of Atlanta community leaders became particularly significant in the years ahead.

The president also launched a major effort to improve faculty pay, then twenty percent below Southern and nonregional institutions. Professors should be paid "within the Tech-Georgia

218

range" because Georgia State competed "for top-grade personnel" with both institutions, not with the state colleges. In fields subsidized by private donations, "industry will give more to aid a high-priced man." In 1961, Langdale inaugurated the first salary supplement program through the Georgia State Foundation. Eight years later, some two-and-a-third million dollars had been raised. Of course, the college still possessed few characteristics of a university or a research institution. The library avoided weekend hours for another six years. Yet a few faculty in both schools received grants and other recognition and engaged in serious scholarship.[420]

Market forces became a complicating factor in determining faculty remuneration. Business school professors, with numerous private sector opportunities in Atlanta, usually commanded considerably more than most A&S faculty. "Our personnel are vulnerable to [local] inducements" from business, government, and sister institutions, Langdale told the chancellor. AACSB salary requirements and reduced teaching loads also had to be acknowledged. But in Atlanta, "even our musicians can be attracted by insurance companies." Athens and Valdosta, on the other hand, did not have firms that could lure "the best teachers from their blackboards." The chancellor apparently ignored Langdale's letter, and the regents tabled his proposals for a year. By spring 1960, even Dean George Manners, while struggling to retain faculty, briefly looked around for a position "where remuneration might be better."[421]

Besides low salaries, the segregation troubles surely influenced faculty attrition. Nevertheless, the new degree programs in 1958 temporarily produced a record fall enrollment of 5,688, up fifty percent in A&S, with eighty M.B.A. students. In November, the regents sanctioned degrees in music and sociology, adding geology-geography and medical technology (para-medicine) in fall 1961. But Athens's sensitivity over journalism and art had been longstanding. The art department cited Georgia State's negative "affect [sic]" on its "further progress and development."

219

Yet Atlanta's rapid business expansion brought a strong demand for art specialists, Dean Horton Burch explained. "[B]ack of every successful advertising campaign or publication effort is a skilled artist." Besides retailers, Atlanta had over "53 advertising agencies, 89 publishers, and 3300 manufacturing concerns," all using art. By fall 1960, "57 students" worked in the GSC art program, but none could "state that they have a major in the subject."[422]

In 1962, Georgia State finally received permission to offer the B.A. degree in art but obtained it at a price. In a deal arranged by a former Athens dean, then-Vice Chancellor S. Walter Martin, Georgia State promised to "end" its requests "for other art degrees - specifically, the B.F.A. [bachelor of fine arts, and] the M.F.A. [master of fine arts]." Chairman Lamar Dodd, in imparting this information to his dean, was "thankful" that "Walter [Martin] is in there." Georgia State later gave bachelor's and master's work in visual arts.[423]

The Athens journalism dean flatly stated that the regents "have an obligation to prevent such competition." Nevertheless, Georgia State had strong arguments to justify the journalism major. "Atlanta is the communications center of the South," Dean Burch later stressed. "Government, labor, science, industry, [and] business become the [students'] laboratory facilities." In offering courses in "advertising, public relations, [and] trade publications," journalism complemented the business school. Nevertheless, the regents education committee deferred to UGA, although the Georgia Association of Broadcasters strongly supported Atlanta. Three years later the regents finally authorized Georgia State's major in journalism provided it did not lead to the creation of a school of journalism.[424]

By winter 1959, as the segregation struggle intensified, the age law and the new admission policies brought Georgia State hard times. Fearing the integration threat would affect state funding, the *Signal* demanded an explanation as well as assurances about Georgia State's future. What had been done to finance a new gymnasium, the old one with a cracked beam having been condemned in 1957? Governor Griffin had promised help from his special fund, but the money "went instead to a sister institution." The plans drawn up for a student center, or multipurpose building, "lie dormant," while some $48,000,000 for capital improvements went mostly to UGA and Tech. If the regents paid scant attention to such complaints, some legislators *did* take notice. A House subcommittee suggested that the multi-purpose building, costing $1,750,000, be given top priority. But the regents had different goals that included $5,100,000 in construction at UGA and $4,650,000 at Tech. That summer, amidst even deeper pessimism about the future, President Langdale gamely sent a "20-year plan" for development to a legislative committee. He still projected future growth and asked for a new library and a student center, but with the 3,800 student body diminished by over a third, the Georgia Building Authority refrained from appointing an architect until fall 1960.[425]

221

Nevertheless, changing attitudes about Georgia State in the Chancellor's office appeared by early 1960. System thinking must "be in terms of an ever-expanding student population," chancellor's assistant Arthur Gignilliat wrote. "Present trends in higher education" favored expansion in areas of high population density rather than trying "to accommodate students away from home."[426] Most Georgia families could not afford the tuition and board involved in going away to college, and Georgia State students faced the most precarious futures. One-third came from high schools outside the Atlanta area "from families with average or lower income." Their only opportunity for college came from institutions such as Georgia State, and their higher education needs could best be accommodated *"in the Atlanta area."* Accordingly, the Georgia State College of Business Administration's name should be "changed at once" to remove the "trade school implications." A&S majors should be offered in several additional departments, and a B.S. degree in medical technology "worked out with the Grady Hospital."[427]

That December, Langdale asked the chancellor for university status, a move shortly seconded by Georgia Senate and House resolutions. Noting other states developing second universities, the president composed seven pages of justification, although the American Association of University Professors (AAUP) chapter as well as the A&S faculty months earlier warned that Georgia State was not yet ready for that status. The president's arguments were vigorously stated. He dismissed the "of Business Administration" moniker with contempt. "[S]uch a suffix ending is commonly referred to when one speaks of high-school-level 'business college' mills.... understood to mean nonaccredited study" and reminiscent of a "cheap private business 'college' operated at night over some drugstore." "[T]he school will benefit bountifully by a title that will open doors and pocketbooks in support of a 'University.'"[428]

Strong opposition in the chancellor's office surprised the president. Giving the name, university, without quality work and additional research activity would not be in the best interest of the educational program, regents secretary L. R. Siebert told a state legislator. Certainly, the regents education committee had "no intention of raising this institution to University Status." Facing a lost cause, the president reluctantly changed the request to Georgia State College. After more study, the regents in December dropped the offensive suffix "of Business Administration." Eventually, they authorized M.A. degrees in English, history, and political science, and a Master of Education (M.E.D.) and Master of Arts in Teaching (M.A.T.), all for fall 1962. The coveted doctor of business administration (D.B.A.) in all fields also passed.[429]

Even as the regents in 1958 began bestowing new degrees, enrollment remained in desperate shape. Between that fall, when 5,668 students attended, and winter 1962 with only 2,393, the school had lost fifty-eight percent (3,275) of its student body. Once again, the president issued what had become familiar instructions: "No new personnel will be recruited or replace-

222

ments added except in physics and mathematics." Nevertheless, Langdale publicly continued to express optimism. Within six years, he predicted 16,000 students, the need for five more buildings, and expansion into a three-block area.[430]

An end to Georgia State's trauma finally seemed in sight. The governor's age law, bane of the school's existence and itself under siege, escaped repeal the previous year only through a veto threat. As the law died in the 1962 legislative session, the chancellor advised that student applicants no longer should be required to submit certificates signed by alumni and ordinaries.[431] Meanwhile, as Atlanta continued to grow and new enrollment pressures strained meager facilities, Georgia State embarked on a period of physical and academic expansion that in the late 1950s had been unimaginable.

223

23

STUDENT AND FACULTY ACTIVITIES AFTER WORLD WAR II

T he GI bill and the postwar education boom opened up new opportunities for the Atlanta Center. The unprecedented growth in the student body, faculty, and plant brought expanded programs. With over 1,000 GIs enrolled, the regular students, mostly working, older, and already familiar with real responsibilities, seemed to mimic the seriousness of the former warriors. But as veterans' numbers declined, the "normal student body" had "a greater interest in a wide variety of student activities," director George Sparks noted. The Southern Association of Colleges (SAC) mandated a "well integrated Student Activity Program." Considering the diversity of the commuting college's student body, SAC rules fashioned for residential institutions may have overlooked the realities of urban higher education. Georgia State in some respects resembled a work-study cooperative without dormitories, and its totally commuting population often resisted efforts by successive student deans as well as academic departments to foster activities more typical of the conventional campus.[432]

The Garage's spaciousness and unique construction quickly had an influence. Its automobile inclines brought the renaming of the *Gateway*, the college annual, to *Rampway*. The ramps inspired humor. "[A]fter half an hour of bull sessions on a

slant," one wit suggested, students could understand how Paul
Bunyan's bovines, "raised on a perfectly smooth, cone-shaped
mountain," developed "legs on one side shorter than the others."
The ramps also could be used to transport semi-round beer kegs,
they wished, and provide roller skating "for students just in or
out of their cups."[433]

Some things remained unchanged. The junior college faculty
still received reminders to test students weekly and write parents
of excessive absences. Mandatory class attendance continued
throughout the 1950s. Rules infractions, disorderly or unbe-
coming conduct, serious illnesses, low academic performance,
and marked deterioration in grades also must be reported, as
well as cutting the weekly and increasingly unpopular student
assembly. In 1953, the *Signal* condemned the callous, vulgar, and
rude conduct at assembly programs. Skipping assembly brought
disciplinary action, and over 300 students received letters that
January. "[A] large number of students" signed slips and "immediately left," Dean Nell Trotter reported, inexplicable because the
band and choir program that day were "very good."[434]

As veteran enrollments declined, student activities accelerated. A freshman orientation dance late in September 1955
preceded sorority and fraternity rushing in October. The annual
homecoming banquet at the fall quarter's end attracted some
500. Off-campus, a Georgia State coed rode a horse down
Peachtree Street in twenty-two degree weather advertising the
film *Lady Godiva*. Besides preparing for final examinations, many
students held Christmas jobs. Greek week in January was followed by an occasional fraternity hayride, and in 1957 an
appreciation dance featuring bandleader Woody Herman supported the Sparks scholarship. The festive March Mardi Gras
brought "pretty girls" riding through the halls and up the ramps
in a gaily decorated jeep. The May Day festival in Hurt Park
attracted some 300 spectators. Coed competition for May Day
queen began in early April, with the runners-up serving in her
court.[435]

Students celebrating Mardi Gras at the gymnasium (c. 1962). Courtesy of GSU Archives.

Not all appreciated such events. Phantom, a two-year transfer student, described the "appropriately misnamed 'Mardi Gras,'" as being "unlike its namesake in every way." "[A] majority of the prizes are 'Teddy Bears.' Childish? It is ridiculous." At "the May Day farce," college students "actually danced around a maypole...a direct insult to the student's mentality." Phantom, apparently a lone dissenter, wisely concealed his identity. At Georgia Tech, a student critical of the dormitory food was threatened with legal action. Students sharing Phantom's pessimism may have been few, but one freshman class dance attracted only twenty-five participants. Nevertheless, they "had a good time," and Dean Nell Trotter believed "their next class event will show improvement." Of course, student programs depended upon the activity fee, and the two dollars authorized in 1952 proved inadequate. The student body "voted affirmatively" for an increase three times, Sparks wrote the chancellor in 1955, and he wanted a variety of new programs for the "boys and

Pan Hellenic Coffee. Courtesy of GSU Archives.

girls." A new four-dollar fee, approved that year, lasted until 1962 when it reached six dollars.[436]

Some student activity could be public spirited and inexpensive. After the new building's completion in 1955, student leaders organized a "Keep the Building Beautiful Campaign" featuring posters, slogans, and announcements in the *Signal*. That December they scrubbed walls, floors, and classrooms and continued the campaign during the upcoming year. Elsewhere, twenty-five fraternity members cut grass and cleaned around buildings at the Hillside Cottages, a children's home. While refraining from attacking such worthy activities, Phantom had faint praise for Georgia State's administration. The "inter-fraternity council" and "intra-mural sports" could not function because the school gymnasium had become "a money-making interest." Student activities often faced cancellation.[437]

Opening college facilities for public purposes also antago-
nized the local American Association of University Professors
(AAUP) chapter. At the request of Atlanta officials, Sparks
planned to close the library for the temporary and free use of
Junior Chamber of Commerce (JCC) conventioneers in hopes
that the city might install lighting and infrastructure improvements around the new building. A possible gift of $25,000 also
was mentioned. Citing public relations motives, Sparks sarcasti-
cally "dismissed the idea that" the AAUP would "go off
half-cocked" if they knew what was involved. Although in the
end the library remained open, the JCC still used part of it along
with the gymnasium. While Phantom concluded, undoubtedly
unfairly, that the administration operated "like a dictatorship in
a kindergarten" rather than "a true university," complaints about
heavy oversight occasionally came from other students. Night
school president Bill Capes told the *Signal* that the administration handled many powers delegated by other colleges to
students and alumni.[438]

After the University of Georgia merger ended, one student-
wide task involved the selection of new school colors to replace
the red and black. Voting separately in January 1956, a majority
of both night and day students chose black and white, symbolic
of the night and day schools, with the runner-up, black and gold.
Later, the day students in assembly again endorsed black and
white with Panthers as the college nickname. A night school poll
in May again turned up a plurality for black and white, and student leaders demanded action. They voted twice, the *Signal*
complained, yet the dean refused to turn "it over to the student
activities committee" of five faculty and the two student body
presidents for a recommendation. Instead, another student vote
would be taken. In truth, the committee and the administration
regarded colors like black and white as "unsatisfactory in deco-
rating the Lounge for student dances and affairs." After faculty
artist Joseph Perrin prepared samples for display in the dean's
office and publication in the *Signal*, the committee picked two

229

combinations, blue and gray and yellow and gray and called for another vote. Two-thirds of the voting students chose blue and gray, which became the school colors.[439]

In this controversy and in many other matters the *Signal* had become an important messenger that held the student body together. Although Phantom thought the paper "consists of 90% tripe" of little interest "to the majority," only twice did rival publications appear. In fall 1948, the underground *Lantern* railed briefly against student council ticket raffles as illegal "lottery rackets." Later, in the 1960s, student radicals circulated the "Altus," a typed, photocopied sheet commenting on military and social issues.[440]

230

The late 1940s recession challenged all student publications. Both the *Signal* and the *Rampway* ended 1949 with large deficits. After failing to break even over seven issues, the *Signal* had to seek college support. Over time, though, the *Signal* did achieve recognition. In 1958, it received a national first-class rating along with twelve other college papers. Thirty-eight, all over 1,000 in circulation, entered the competition. Seven years later, the *Signal* for two consecutive years won the Georgia Press Association's top award as the best newspaper in the state's senior college division. Unlike the Sparks years, no complaints of administrative pressure appeared during this period, but President Langdale in 1962 made his policies perfectly clear to the *Signal's* staff advisers. "I must hold the three of you responsible for the content." "[T]here will be no matters of a vulgar, obscene, sexual, fanatical, or radical nature in any of our publications." This brief admonition signaled the appearance of an administrative style increasingly used during the 1960s in which the president began delegating almost all of his responsibilities, holding the recipients "strictly accountable" for completing them.[441]

Student jobs, financial problems, and family diversions, among other distractions, surely explained the absence of campus cohesion. But so did the loss of the gymnasium for over a decade and the absence of a separate student center until the mid-1960s. The new Camp Center (named after Professor J. C. Camp) functioned mainly as a service area with food and a bookstore, informal meeting and game rooms, and a small theater. It also had space for the dean of students's offices, college-sponsored groups, and sororities and fraternities, which paid "very low rentals" for small chapter rooms. One department head challenged in vain the practice "of giving economically privileged student groups [subsidized] State owned space" not available "to all other students."[442]

The lack of dormitories also affected student activities. Administration officials clearly understood that the regents and UGA frowned on dorms for the Atlanta unit despite generous federal loan policies during the postwar period. In their absence, some students endured long commutes of fifty miles or more. Dean England advised one male student to try rooming in the YMCA. After arriving in Atlanta, another was instructed to find an inexpensive hotel or motel and come to the office to check the files on available housing.[443]

231

While only inconvenient for males, housing could be much more complicated for single, day school women who must reside in supervised living arrangements unless staying with family "related by blood." Besides the YWCA, the dean approved substitute dorms, such as the Churches Homes for Business Girls, operating eight Atlanta facilities that often mixed working girls and with coeds, sometimes in walk-through sleeping rooms. The dean admitted receiving many complaints of noise and poor food. Yet "I do not see how we can let girls choose their own housing," Trotter wrote in 1963, although the University of Wisconsin changed five years earlier "and makes no effort to provide [female] dormitory housing."[444]

Night school women had *no* residential restrictions, a fact that undoubtedly accelerated coed transfers out of day school. Trotter repeatedly tried to get some kind of college-run living arrangements, but failing, she resolved to enforce conventional residential regulations and even sought unsuccessfully to apply them to single night school women. The result was an endless obsession with suspected student deceit, administration sleuthing, requests for coed "personal sheets" from the registrar's office, and the checking of the Churches Homes files, among other monitoring activities. "Once a girl has been admitted, it is almost impossible to exercise supervision," Trotter fretted, and a coed's age made no difference. On the other hand, the vast majority of Georgia State women who attended without housing restrictions enjoyed liberties denied UGA coeds.[445]

In compliance with administration instructions to report rules infractions, a constant watch for violations and especially for moral turpitude went on. A sophomore working in the library "announced her secret marriage" several months earlier to another student. They expected a baby at the end of the summer. "I am of the opinion that both…are subject to the disciplinary rule," Trotter told Dean William Suttles. The "increasing number of married pregnant women in our Day Student body" also alarmed the women's dean. "I believe…it would be well for these pregnant students not to attend college after they have been enceinte for six months." Of course, coeds "wearing a mini, mini, mini skirt" also brought disapproval, as did women art students entering the cafeteria in slacks and shorts, attire forbidden except in the studio. Many colleges enforced female dress codes into the 1960s. UGA women while on campus concealed their gymnasium uniforms with opaque raincoats, and majorettes at football games covered their abbreviated costumes when not performing. More surprising was Trotter's ire at a Georgia State coed who protested with fifty others at the inauguration of Lester Maddox as governor. An inked-in arrow pointed to the girl in an *Atlanta Constitution* group photo, and parts of the story were underlined. While Trotter's prescribed activities often cast her more as a benevolent warden than a respected educator, this recipient of Atlanta's 1962 Woman of the Year (WOTY) award in education believed that Betty Friedan's controversial *The Feminine Mystique* "will be very helpful, both to women

232

colleagues, and women students." She requested a copy for the library.[446]

The arrival of "student activism" at Georgia State "brought many changes in dress, housing patterns, and student mores," Dean Trotter wrote in her memoir. The student protest movement—contemporary with civil rights sit-ins, the Students for a Democratic Society's (SDS) 1962 Port Huron statement, and the Berkeley "free speech" activity—was further fueled by the Vietnam War. Activism arrived relatively late at Georgia State when in 1967 the Committee on Social Issues (COSI) applied for recognition as one of seventy-eight student organizations. Claiming support from fifteen faculty and three department heads, the application expressed the need for "interesting and challenging ideas" through the presentation of lectures and debates. Its issues agenda closely mimicked the SDS, and two years later COSI officially became one of that "New Left" protest organization's hundreds of chapters.[447]

That year COSI flyers and speakers targeted the war and the draft. An August march ending at Hurt Park attracted some 500 protesters. A few days later at UGA about 300 students occupied the academic building for two days. At Georgia State, despite the president's deepest fears, protesting students never took over even a classroom. By November, a disappointed COSI chairman felt that "his organization's growth has been stunted by the nature of an urban commuter college." During 1968, COSI's drive against the ROTC dovetailed an April faculty petition with seventy-five names opposed to compulsory ROTC. According to COSI's flyer, the "Altus," 750 students also joined the effort. The issue received added notoriety after the ROTC organized an ill-conceived downtown faculty rifle shoot only days after Martin Luther King, Jr.'s, assassination followed by urban riots. The faculty turned the matter over to the college standards committee. Having discovered that the U.S. Army did not require students to join ROTC, the committee advised each school to abandon that feature. Three years earlier compulsory ROTC had ended at

233

Georgia Tech partially for administrative reasons, a move unrelated to the armed services or the war effort.[448]

Other COSI efforts seemed equally unproductive. "We do not expect to close" Georgia State, COSI announced as it politely requested faculty cooperation during an international student strike, but the activity scarcely produced a ripple. In May, COSI presented two showings of the fifty-minute documentary *Revolt at Columbia University* in the student center without either obvious administration opposition or strong student support. Switching its social agenda, COSI began denouncing the low wages paid at the physical plant and cafeteria, but so did 750 students and faculty at Tech in an action apparently taken independently of the protest movement. COSI also urged a boycott of Levi's Jeans over the issue of union recognition at the Blue Ridge, Georgia, plant.[449]

The muted reactions both of Chancellor George Simpson and Dean of Men Kenneth England to the student protest movement helped calm a situation of increasing administration apprehension. In November, the chancellor created a system committee on student affairs with a student advisory council. He urged preventive efforts in dealing with UGA-type sit-ins but also stated that "we should learn how to live with aberrations." At the same time, the chancellor oversaw the adoption of a regents resolution affirming freedom of expression but deploring "irresponsible disruption and obstructive action by students and faculty." Such activity, including "physical occupation of a building" or the use of "verbal or written obscenities," could bring serious disciplinary action.[450]

Dean England outwardly treated the Committee on Social Issues the same as any other campus organization. Assembly rooms became available for COSI lectures, and negotiated student center demonstrations against campus armed services recruiters took place. After a COSI complaint to the *Atlanta Constitution* that "you can sell cookies...here [at Georgia State] but not ideas," the hawking of leftist literature at cost went on in

234

certain corridors. COSI's anti-war "Altus," with its militant language, also circulated. Later that year the dean officially invited "the president and every top administrator" to attend a campus, COSI-sponsored coffee for black Georgia anti-war activist Julian Bond.[451]

Dean England's outward calm contrasted with the administration's alarm fed by reports of revolutionary student activity elsewhere. "You will need to record" the American Council on Education's estimate of the SDS workshop on explosives, the president told a subordinate. After an August trip to Columbia and New York Universities, the president found "the situation is worse than I imagined." Lists identifying radical publications accumulated in administration files, including Georgia State's "Altus" and Emory's *Great Speckled Bird*, the latter unsuccessfully prosecuted by Fulton County for obscenity.[452]

235

Meanwhile, serious charges against the SDS appeared in national publications, such as *Readers Digest*, featuring phrases like "campus totalitarians" and charging Communist infiltration. While such reports provided little insight into COSI except its attempts to manipulate issues, Langdale seemingly became obsessed with student demonstrations. He communicated with college presidents throughout the country and spent a good deal of time ascertaining his legal options if confronted with a problem. At one point, the administration seriously considered setting up a secure room in the basement of Sparks Hall. If equipped with telephones and stocked with supplies and food, it could serve as a command post in case violence erupted. On the other hand, to an alarmed local banker and a state politician, who wanted to "get this group out of Georgia State" and "prevent" radicals "from using the University as a forum," Langdale gave a short lecture on the First Amendment and recent judicial opinion. [453]

But COSI rejected the radicals' emphasis on anti-war activity and focused primarily on "small issues." It gradually became, in most respects, just another campus organization but decidedly dissident, with a social and student agenda that to the watchful administration still spelled mischief. Even without COSI's prodding, student opinion already had begun to change. Students should serve on faculty search committees selecting deans, the *Signal* declared in August 1967. While Vice President William Suttles disagreed, he offered them an advisory role. By summer 1969, statutory changes were under way authorizing student appointments to all college and faculty committees.[454]

A *Signal* demand for teacher evaluations by students also was implemented in fall 1969 after faculty and student hearings. Meanwhile, *Signal* editor John Allgood helped convince Governor Lester Maddox to appoint a Georgia State graduate as a regent. In accepting that seven-year assignment, W. Lee Burge, president of Equifax, became Georgia State's first alumnus on that body. Calls for university status soon followed along with the suggestion that it was time to establish a college honors program. This unprecedented burst of student participation continued during 1969, now with direct participation by the Committee on Social Issues and Students for a Democratic Society (COSI-SDS) through their representative on the students' general council. A January COSI-SDS motion for SGA control of the student activity fee, estimated at over $200,000 annually, lost overwhelmingly, but it may have moved Langdale with the *Signal's* blessing to appoint the SGA treasurer as the only student on the seven-member activity fee committee. In addition, a newly created student review committee considered requests for funds from various campus organizations.[455]

The increasing student involvement in the 1960s saw parallel developments in faculty affairs. Bolstered locally by the expanding influence of their national professional associations, faculties sought more power in governance, resource allocation, and budget allotments, especially salary decisions. At the same time, they experienced additional pressure to complete their doctorates, engage in scholarly research and publish, adopt interdisciplinary approaches, develop new fields and courses, and

236

also help solve society's problems. In these pursuits, they increasingly became oriented toward disciplines and departments while administrators focused their efforts internally.[456]

These changes had sweeping effects on institutions such as Georgia State. Pressure for higher doctoral ratios from accrediting groups, such as the Southern Association of Colleges and the American Association of Collegiate Schools of Business intensified as the college added arts and sciences (A&S) degrees and graduate programs. By 1964, sixty-two percent of the teaching faculty had earned doctorates. A few business faculty unsuccessfully demanded scholarly output—articles, research reports, books—as standard obligations. Nevertheless, until university status came and the 1960s teacher shortage abated in the early 1970s, faculty members with doctorates in most departments still had little fear that the absence of scholarly productivity would adversely affect their promotions or graduate teaching assignments.[457]

237

Until the end of the 1960s, before the adoption of recruiting procedures and affirmative action, the "old boy network" usually guided faculty hiring. Candidates with or without doctoral degrees who knew influential people sometimes sought positions through the back door. The assistant chancellor knew an "outstanding" retired Army colonel interested in "science teaching" and thanked President Sparks "in advance" for examining "such opportunities." Georgia's lieutenant governor recommended a friend to be director of speech and grammar and contacted both Langdale and the chancellor for their "endorsement and recommendation." A newly hooded Tulane Ph.D., unhappily teaching at a small state college, rather than applying directly through departmental channels, unsuccessfully approached administration and system contacts about a Georgia State teaching position, as did a candidate's prominent father, who was headmaster of a prestigious Atlanta private high school.[458]

Among the faculty, several achieved recognition beyond their promotions. Kenneth Black (insurance) became Georgia State's first regents professor in 1959, an honor also achieved in the late 1960s by historian Joseph O. Baylen. James Lemly did extensive contract work for the Georgia Department of Transportation and also gave advice on transportation problems in Ghana, Nigeria, and Pakistan. Two other business faculty, economist Jack Blicksilver and management's James Chapman, received grants and summer appointments at the Harvard Business School. Artist Joseph Perrin won local and regional recognition for his paintings and community service. Accountant and attorney Catherine Miles, the only female department chair, became the 1968 Atlanta Woman of the Year in education. Management's Michael Mescon, supported by local business interests, founded and held the chair of private enterprise, which sponsored educational programs on Americanism and Communism. Meanwhile, then-Dean Suttles, an ordained Southern Baptist, became the 1959 rural Minister of the Year and President Langdale, the 1962 Georgian of the Year.[459]

238

Of course, the possession of doctorates and recognition of achievement could not erase financial disparities between the business and A&S faculties. Besides the market's positive effect on business professors' incomes, the SBA also benefited from mandated AACSB standards. The A&S faculty began complaining in 1960. Five years later they formally resolved that the teaching load of fifteen class contact hours for everyone "is detrimental to effective instruction, scholarly development and research, and recruitment." Georgia State, despite advanced graduate work, kept the regents classification of college. The University of Georgia and Georgia Tech, with class-one ratings, generally escaped the fifteen-hour teaching requirement. Athens department heads by 1965 ordinarily carried only five-hour classroom loads, half those at Georgia State.[460]

AACSB standards became a model that ultimately benefited A&S faculty but in a manner totally unexpected in the business school. Early in 1967, Dean Manners discovered that some A&S department heads taught only five hours. In addition, combining graduate and undergraduate courses yielded ten hours of teaching credit for some A&S professors, as did the teaching of large freshman classes and graduate seminars. "We know that there are some advantages we enjoy by virtue of the AACSB in the Business School," he wrote the vice president, but this situation involved the purveyance of "distortions and untruths." Faced by "a consistent barrage of frank criticism from my colleagues in Business...that I don't know what's going on," Manners demanded the equal reduction of SBA teaching loads. Such costly changes required thirteen new faculty positions "to support our developing doctoral program." At the same time, Manners heatedly insisted that the SBA's larger average class size, twenty-nine in business compared to seventeen in A&S, be considered as well as the teaching load.[461]

239

Although the business dean in the past strongly supported A&S programs, inter-school rivalry for influence and resources had been building up for over six years. "[I]nstitution objectivity" was needed in the place of "bluff and guff, concealed information, distortions, prevarications, dissembling, and the continued piling up of rumors, near-rumors, and untruths," Manners fumed. These alleged aberrations were attributed primarily to the A&S dean, who "made decisions and concealed the facts." He brought about significant changes while having no "budget, no organization, no procedure, no accounting." Manners already had suggested to the state treasurer the need "for the restitution of State moneys improperly expended" on that school. The controversy illustrated unforeseen and changing circumstances.[462] A&S, always numerically larger and now with its own graduate programs and faculty development goals, had become a major player.

Faculty involvement in nonacademic matters also increased. In 1963, Georgia State's AAUP chapter began pressuring the administration for a faculty senate. Despite the chancellor's reservations and the in-house statutes and bylaws committee's doubts, an advisory senate, presided over by the vice president, began meeting in 1965. This unwieldy body, consisting of all tenured faculty above the rank of assistant professor, barely functioned. Lacking appeal procedures to the regents and usually poorly attended, its meetings could be ended by simple quorum calls. In 1967, the SAC institutional self-study recommended its replacement by a representative body with delegated faculty powers, a change arriving after the receipt of university status.[463]

Under the leadership of two faculty members, Arthur Waterman and Gerald Davis, the AAUP and its executive committee became deeply involved in faculty affairs. As a result, a professor facing disciplinary action or dismissal received a faculty committee hearing attended by counsel, with a full stenographic report of findings and recommendations, a copy to be forwarded to the regents. The AAUP also called the administration's attention to several other matters: salaries and salary payment procedures, promotions, teaching loads, committee assignments, fringe benefits, the insurance and retirement plan, the handling of parking, faculty discounts at the bookstore, the allocation of the student activity funds, the rights and freedom of students, and tenure for assistant professors.[464]

Two other problems—the interviewing of faculty candidates and the comprehensive credit check—had become particularly sensitive. President Sparks probably recruited and interviewed every faculty applicant, and during the segregation crisis his fears led to the use of a comprehensive credit check to investigate personal matters, including a candidate's finances and character. It continued during the succeeding troubled decade of student protests. At AAUP insistence, the practice ended in 1969 except when a dean considered it desirable.[465]

The lengthy and cumbersome interviewing process touched faculty candidates at all ranks. The visitor generally met separately with the departmental search committee, chair, and faculty. Further interviews followed with the dean and the vice president. Finally, President Langdale insisted on seeing all candidates, a complicating factor because of his heavy schedule of public speaking and his generally unconventional and often intimidating interviewing practices. According to one department head, this process consumed "approximately $20,000 worth of time...that could have easily been saved by more streamlined procedures."[466]

The AAUP challenged the interviewing system in 1967 seeking simplification and a reduction in administration participation. While the South's and Georgia's earlier political and social environment still caused some candidates to be concerned about academic freedom, Atlanta's progressive reputation greatly aided in recruitment. Yet Georgia State's interviewing process worried the AAUP about "our image in the academic community." It recommended the use of caution to avoid "embarrassing or personal questions involving psychological, political, religious and social attitudes." Some social science faculty saw the process as guaranteeing the recruitment of a "safe, non-boatrocking" faculty.[467]

241

The Southern Association of Colleges' 1967 visiting committee found that interviewing involved "a great deal of 'red tape' and time-consuming effort on the part of too many busy people." The SBA faculty took action after Dean Manners discussed the problem with the chancellor and unanimously restricted interviewing to candidates "at the associate and full rank," a process later applied by the administrative council to the whole college. This issue along with many others, once incorporated into SAC's institutional self-study, got the administration's attention.[468]

While this ambitious AAUP agenda often brought change in the conduct of faculty affairs, a serious problem during 1966–1967 in the political science department defied attempts at either mediation or resolution. The issue involved the retention of a bright, popular, but sometimes contentious and immature new faculty member. To new chairman Karl O'Lessker and most of the department's ten members, the only applicable standards of judgment were professional competence, classroom performance, and scholarly achievement, all fulfilled. Opposing the reappointment, Dean Horton Burch cited several lapses primarily involving uncooperative behavior with the administration. Unmentioned were charges that the young man at a public meeting had sharply challenged the chancellor on his policies for Georgia State's development. While the dean accepted "classroom performance as a number one criteria," some faculty "are so difficult to work with that their retention is inadvisable."[469]

During the controversy, the issue inspired press releases, flyers, letters, and student protests in support of the department. The refusal to renew the contract led to the resignations of five other faculty, including the dynamic and scholarly chairman.[470] While the administration's goal of compatibility predominated, the gutted department faced difficult times in the face of increasing enrollments, a seller-friendly job market, and new degree programs seeking regents approval. But the administration's aversion to "trouble makers" in an age of continuing change and protest had been openly challenged. Ironically, at that time Georgia State avidly sought university status, a title suggesting the existence of a robust scholarly environment in which such nonacademic, faculty eruptions ordinarily would receive scant administration attention.

24

ATLANTA AND GEORGIA STATE: PROSPERITY, GROWTH, AND UNIVERSITY STATUS

A s Georgia State students and faculty went about their activities during the 1960s, they witnessed constant change in
their urban college and community. The traditional nineteenth
century central city, surrounded by densely populated residential
areas, gave way to a polycentric metro area with mini-cities on
Atlanta's periphery. Only some 497,000 (thirty-five percent) of
the area's 1,387,000 people in 1970 lived in the central city, while
676,000 resided in the urban fringe.[471] Students, who in an earlier era walked to classes from their downtown jobs, now often
commuted from the suburbs.

Various forces propelled growth away from the central city.
While Atlanta's pre-eminence as the major southeastern distribution center went unchallenged, hundreds of new firms,
particularly service industries requiring cheaper land for storage
and fabrication with easy access to truckers, located in the industrial suburbs. In addition, a modest manufacturing sector
evolved around transportation, including assembly plants for
automobiles, mobile homes, and aircraft. Both ground and air
transportation drove much of this growth. By 1970, trucking
became the second largest Georgia employer, with eighty

terminals and over 180 motor carriers. They moved the south-east's agricultural, manufactured, and petroleum products over a highway system touching perhaps forty million people in overnight deliveries of some 500 miles. Trade, both wholesale and retail, and services explained well over forty percent of the city's employment by the 1970s. In the midst of this motorized activity, the city approved a public transportation system under the Metro Atlanta Rapid Transit Authority (MARTA). Additional thousands of air passengers touched Atlanta, by 1970 ranking the city second in emplaned passengers and third in aircraft movement.[472]

The city's vertical expansion continued in the postwar period. Eleven tall buildings went up, many near Georgia State College. Some exclusively served the needs of commerce, such as the 1960 Merchandise Mart, which was joined during the next decade by an apparel mart, the Omni International Hotel, and the World Congress Center, among others, increasing Atlanta's room inventory from 4,000 to 14,000 by 1974. These, along with a new civic center, highlighted the rising importance of conventions and tourism. In addition, Georgia State's own construction program included new buildings and a plaza. Atlanta also attracted major league football, basketball, and baseball. By the end of the decade, Atlanta could seriously challenge both Chicago and New York in the number of convention delegates. In this expansion, Atlanta promoters in government and the private sector continued to provide strong leadership. The Chamber of Commerce and Mayor Ivan Allen, Jr., endorsed urban renewal and public housing, consulted with race leaders, and eased the Jim Crow stigma by supporting public school integration. In 1974, Atlantans even persuaded the Organization of American States to meet for the first time outside of the D.C. area. Promoters quickly, if somewhat prematurely, began labeling Atlanta an "international city."[473]

For Georgia State College, the 1960s in many ways became its golden decade. Physical expansion accelerated as lot-by-lot it

244

acquired costly downtown real estate. Housing and Urban Development (HUD) grants after 1959 facilitated the acquisition of the south side of Decatur Street and additional land a decade later, with a million dollars in urban renewal funds. Shortly, prices climbed as high as $500,000 an acre. The Garage, named Kell Hall in 1964 for the founder, and the Gilmer Street building, christened Sparks Hall in 1960, ultimately were joined by a student center; the 900,000-volume Pullen Library; business administration and general classroom buildings; a gymnasium/sports arena; a fine arts center; an urban plaza; and an urban life center, all by the early 1970s. As the student population reached nearly 13,000, the new buildings relieved only yesterday's congestion. Additional space continually had to be rented in nearby office buildings.[474] Faculty and students still coped with crowded hallways and cramped office space. They taught and learned from early morning to late evening in small, usually packed classrooms, and queued up to check out books in the cramped Sparks Hall library. And until the mid-1960s, they ate in the small Sparks basement cafeteria or found fast food in the dated Kell Hall refectory. Change for them undoubtedly came at a snail's pace.

245

Recovery from the segregation crisis was slow and sometimes painful. In 1959, as the age law and the president's quality standards ended adult service programs, unhappy legislators called for the resumption of noncredit courses, especially remedial work in mathematics, the sciences, and English. Two years later, President Noah Langdale proposed a school of general studies offering cultural, remedial, vocational, and professional courses. He predicted an enrollment of 400 students in the initial ten classes. General studies, receiving regents approval three years later as "separate and distinct from other schools" in curriculum and administration, was combined with them academically. Its students could receive associate level "certificates," and their courses were transferable for academic credit. Described by one administrator as "a sub-standard, but acceptable necessity," general studies aroused considerable faculty opposition. An AAUP resolution feared it would diminish the college's reputation and harm the "recruitment of first rate faculty." Certainly, only the best students should transfer to the core institution. Nevertheless, it reaffirmed Sparks's philosophy of community service and also fit into the emerging concept of an urban university.[475]

While the faculty fretted over general studies, new academic programs seemed a certainty. The push for additional departments, undergraduate majors, and graduate programs by ambitious deans and department heads also came from the bottom up as younger faculty joined the ranks. The Atlanta community contributed. In a network of contacts, many business groups, teacher organizations, and government and public health officials made the college aware of their educational needs. A 1963 Georgia Hospital Association resolution noted that the area demand for master's-level employees justified graduate programs at Georgia State. The regents a few months later responded with an advanced degree in hospital administration but provided no immediate funding.[476]

Developments in the business school between 1958 and 1962 had brought an array of master's degrees, including actuarial sciences, the only such program in the Southeast. The doctorate of business administration (DBA) also received authorization. Shortly, Georgia State's first doctor of philosophy (Ph.D.) degrees became available in business education and economics. Meanwhile, the SBA's computing and data processing center officially opened in 1959, providing the fundamentals of programming to students and new research capabilities to the faculty. By 1968, 1,000 students worked in the program. The next year a system decision not to place a centralized computer at Athens left Georgia State and other units free to continue their activities.[477]

While the SBA fleshed out degree programs, A&S tried to catch up. With masters in English, history, and political science approved for 1962, new requests focused on the sciences, music, and the visual arts. Although the regents' sluggish response disappointed, encouragement came from another quarter. A governor's commission on improvement of education, while warning against overlapping system programs, mentioned Georgia State in the same category as UGA and Tech. Thus, when the chancellor's office initiated a 1963, unit-by unit analysis of system-wide expansion known as the Role and Scope Study, Georgia State administrators called for a "quality-oriented Urban University." Shortly, the regents reclassified Georgia State to a higher position, between categories one and two, and increased its budget. Later, in his Role and Scope report to the chancellor, Vice President William Suttles projected breath-taking expansion, with twelve schools in addition to A&S and SBA. Nevertheless, the continuing lack in A&S advancement was alarming and suggested little regents enthusiasm. "[O]ur people" have been "living on promises," and the "psychological environment" at Georgia State has deteriorated, Langdale warned the new chancellor, George L. Simpson, late in 1965.[478]

247

While the deans and faculty concentrated on academic proposals, the administration dealt with physical expansion. By early 1963, the college's needs still had a low regents priority. Considering "the millions...spent during the past five years for" system construction, Langdale was "appalled" at the "scarcity of support for" Georgia State. On a ratio basis, "we usually end up getting an amount for buildings and improvements equal to the lowest fraction of funds." Library space had become so cramped that the president pressed "for some kind of a building at least partially completed." The library was "filled to capacity in only three short

William M. Suttles, Vice President, 1963–1988 (c. mid-1970s). Courtesy of GSU Archives.

years" after Sparks Hall's completion with additional material stored in the Garage basement. *"Every time a single new book is put on the shelf,"* librarian William Pullen reported, *"another book must be removed and placed in storage."* Yet by fall, the president could report only slow progress on the student activity building and merely preliminary work on the library. The six-story library, with ground-level parking underneath, eventually went up in two stages. The delayed, three top floors were added upon receipt of a matching federal grant of $867,316 under the Higher Education Act of 1965. The regents approved a fine arts center in 1964 but left the building out of the bond issue. Four more years passed without funding. The completion of the library's sixth floor in summer 1970 brought some relief to the congested campus.[479]

248

As Georgia State's needs mounted, Langdale sent the chancellor a surprisingly pointed assessment of the college's plight. The institution lost good teachers and hired "the ones we rather not have" because of money shortages. At the same time, "Tech and Georgia have been spending large sums of money for outstanding people." In expanding its campus, Georgia State also had lost out. While Tech purchased land with state money, Georgia State had to finance its expansion "by curtailing operations," including the percentage for raises. The regents refused money for a gymnasium "unless we used the term 'Multi-purpose building'" and crowded more facilities "into one structure." When its cost was estimated at $4,000,000, "We were told we could have $2,000,000," so only one-half of the building for student services could be built. Yet without "a facility for meetings, sports, Physical Education, etc." Georgia State's accreditation could be questioned at the upcoming 1965–1966 SAC self-study. Of course, "you and I know that schools like Valdosta State College receive money to build adequate and sometimes costly gymnasiums." In March, the regents did authorize the physical education building, but they deferred further action. Similar to the library's federal funding, a $1,000,000 grant came to the rescue in 1967, providing one-third of the cost. Meanwhile,

Pullen Library and Plaza. Courtesy GSU Archives.

student organizations began moving into the new student center in fall 1964, freeing up Sparks Hall for twenty-two offices.[480]

As Georgia State planned its space needs, a faculty committee's suggestion for a plaza between Sparks Hall and the new library site shortly was incorporated into the master campus plan. The plaza concept stressed beautification and the easy movement of students on three walkways over the auto and truck traffic on busy Decatur Street. The plaza, built in the early 1970s, preserved existing parking areas and added overhead "platforms" connected both by short steps and wide ramps. With a large fountain, trees, landscaping, benches, and pedestrian bridges, the plaza "doubled the available space," unified the campus, and afforded "opportunities for aesthetics."[481]

While the plaza provided a campus atmosphere, the space underneath for autos brought some relief, if not a solution, to serious parking shortages. "[P]arking for us is the limiting factor of the entire college's growth," Langdale believed. As plans for

Atlanta's rapid transit system unfolded during the mid-1960s, the president successfully pressed for Georgia State's "own station." With the plaza and the new buildings under construction, the parking shortages worsened. "It is imperative that we secure, as quickly as possible, parking structures for this campus," Langdale wrote a regents official. Without a solution, "we shall suffer a decrease in enrollment." In summer 1969, the college turned to nearby Atlanta Stadium where 1,000 spaces were available.[482]

By fall 1965, new business administration classrooms had been approved in addition to fine arts and physical education facilities. But with exploding enrollments, 6,000 in 1964, 8,000 the next fall, and a projected 10,000 for 1966, more structures were justified, Langdale told the regents. The master plan, eighty percent completed by summer 1966, called for two other $4,000,000 buildings. One, a ten-story general classroom approved in October 1967, ultimately attracted over $800,000 in federal funds. The other was a new science facility, but the regents, who shortly began pouring money into the University of Georgia's science departments, put off approval of Georgia State's new science building for over two decades, severely limiting federal grants weighted heavily toward scientific research.[483]

In the academic realm, as the approval of A&S degrees continued to lag, Chancellor Simpson signaled an unwelcome change toward Georgia State. The University of Georgia and Georgia Tech, with the only top quality departments, would get most of the money, he told Atlanta area legislators in fall 1966. Furthermore, the chancellor planned to turn Georgia State into a "great complex of teacher training." The chancellor's statement was alarming and involved programs at both the masters and doctoral levels. Only the psychology master's degree for fall 1967 passed, but regents approval of two new schools, education and allied health sciences (AHS), seemed to confirm the chancellor's priorities. At the same time, Simpson became intrigued with an

"Urban Life" program proposed by Georgia State officials that September. Whether Urban Life (UL) was seen as a way around Athens's generally successful blocking of the arts and sciences at Georgia State could not be ascertained. Urban Life would create an institute to give SBA and A&S undergraduate and graduate degrees, but the focus would be distinctly different from the existing programs. In a handwritten postscript, Simpson added, "we must design curriculum for the job, not for the professional fads of a few people." Within weeks, the regents authorized the school of general studies to give BS and associate in science degrees in urban life, effective for fall 1967. In May, a program in police science was added.[484]

The Urban Life concept originated shortly after World War II when the American Council on Education urged academia to begin dealing with changing public needs and to provide equal educational opportunity. In the 1960s, urban universities in the northeast got involved with municipalities and antipoverty work. In Milwaukee, an interdisciplinary department of urban affairs in 1963 began training specialists who could respond to the city's professed need for research and knowledge in solving problems. HUD experts believed that the study of urban politics lagged behind the natural sciences and agriculture, with their field stations, data centers, and observatories, and urged the use of similar approaches to urban research. The National League of Cities endorsed the concept in 1965. As city halls stated their needs to the universities, useful research assistance could be provided. That same year, the Higher Education Act offered financial assistance for urban universities to develop educational programs aimed at their communities.[485] Georgia State's urban life program represented a belated response to those developments.

But immediate regents action seemed to focus on Georgia State's growth rather than urban life programs. In fall 1965, the regents ordered a study of the college's enlargement. Considering the "continuing growth of Atlanta," pressure on Georgia State "to offer programs at the graduate level would be inevitable."

251

Even as the regents met, Georgia State's graduate enrollment, at 775, included ninety in doctoral programs. In response, Simpson created the Committee on Academic Growth (CAG) with members from Georgia State and the regents office, plus Tech, Emory, UGA, and Albany State. Since Georgia State's mission lacked clear definition, CAG would examine the terminal degrees to be instituted and investigate possible public service functions. Meanwhile, the previous summer, the regents had approved masters work in chemistry, computer science, and insurance, and the Ph.D. in business administration.[486]

The regents expected CAG to study both the "high road" (graduate programs with emphasis on the Ph.D.) and the "low road" (general studies). Disappointed with Georgia State's slow progress in offering services, regents approval of graduate programs would depend upon some movement in public service. The chancellor directed CAG to focus on three main areas: new Ph.D. programs with a timetable, professional programs, such as health, and service to the Atlanta community, including non-credit courses.[487]

Urban problems increasingly preoccupied the nation during the waning days of President Lyndon Johnson's Great Society. As the various Committee on Academic Growth groups deliberated, the American Political Science Association's president told Emory and Georgia State audiences that colleges focusing on housing, job restrictions, and equal educational opportunity could relieve the urban crisis in ten years. While various groups in CAG discussed the role of the urban university, others listened to oral presentations supporting Georgia State's requested programs, many already having been submitted to the regents. In this exercise, the regents and chancellor seemed to be using CAG as an urban filter, so to speak, screening the college's requests for quality, content, and, especially, relevance to the urban university concept. Nevertheless, most SBA and A&S departments, while loyal to their disciplines but wary of change, cooperated. The visual, performing, and communicative arts justified their proposals by citing Atlanta's "[t]remendous developments" that demanded personnel and professional training. Other departments also pointed to Atlanta's growth as a rationale for their curriculum proposals. The history department had many fields to offer but decided to specialize in urban and labor history. The English department stressed urban literature.[488]

While proposals for the "high road" came easily, Georgia State's service role required lengthier study. This task went primarily to CAG's seven "internal [GSC] members." "[A]fter careful planning and deliberation," they recommended the establishment of an "urban life center" for groups of scholars assembled from different disciplines, renaming general studies as "urban studies." In fact, the president in February already had hired a dean, Alex B. Lacey, Jr., for the Urban Life program. The urban life center would coordinate the college into an effective force in helping to master urban problems. The chancellor accepted the urban life concept as a way of "educating the disadvantaged and less able students." Go both roads, his vice chancellors added: Consider service as a major area while pursuing academic excellence. Above all, Georgia State should be a downtown community college answering to the central city's needs in the way that "some of the new junior colleges" performed similar services "in other areas."[489]

With CAG's work nearly completed, the regents in June approved doctoral degrees in English and history. For 1969, CAG recommended Ph.D.s for political science, sociology, and biology "with great urgency," and the Ed.D. (doctor of education) in several fields. Terminal degrees in the hard and natural sciences, the health sciences, education, urban studies, and social work should come later. In addition, CAG recommended several new schools in art, music, and computer science for 1969. Thereafter, new schools should "provide many educational services expected of an urban university." Besides journalism, social work, theater arts, and public health, other sweeping additions would include law, library science, communications, medicine, and dentistry.[490]

253

CAG's urban filter proved sufficiently porous to produce degrees and programs beyond even the wildest dreams of many Georgia State supporters. Of course, all required regents action.

As CAG finished reporting in summer 1968, HUD funds established six urban observatories at "key universities" to "explore every aspect of urban life and collect the data" for "dissemination to public officials." HUD contracted with the National League of Cities to select the six locations. With the upcoming 1968 election and a possible change in administrations, time became a factor. Consequently, only fifty-one entries were considered, including some from leading universities. Thus, from the beginning, political uncertainty cast a shadow over the program. During that summer, Dean Lacy waged a major campaign to capture an observatory for Georgia State, with full mayoral and city support, Washington lobbying, and the astute use of inside information. When Georgia State was selected in December, HUD officials indicated it would stress "hard research" in governmental structure, land use, housing, urban renewal, education, and police-community relations. Estimated federal funding at "about $100,000 a year" would be supplemented with some $30,000" from local sources."[491]

Having won the observatory, Georgia State required a major effort to produce results, including "physical resources," such as a new urban life center, and "[i]mmediate [state] funding." In the meantime, the Observatory and sister projects leased space in a nearby private building. During 1969–1970, various U.S. agencies directly or indirectly provided $566,876 in support, which attracted other largesse: $200,000 from the Ford Foundation for graduate training programs and $63,827 from the city and private groups, for a total of $830,703. As the highly proclaimed "partnership" between the city and "our colleges and universities" got underway, the Observatory organized a databank and library, and solicited project proposals from city department heads and area college faculty. But of twenty-two suggested projects the first year, only two could be funded at some $66,000.

Both, involving surveys of citizen participation, aroused little enthusiasm in city government. The Observatory, eventually starved of federal funding, by one account suffered from mismanagement and ultimately disappeared.[492]

The college's Urban Life programs, on the other hand, enjoyed immediate popularity, with 530 registrants, a master's degree, and numbers of enthusiastic students on internships with city agencies. At the same time, SBA and A&S faculty frequently served on UL committees and taught courses attended by numerous UL students. Despite Urban Life's appeal, however, the traditional faculty's loyalty, for the most part remained staunchly rooted in their fields and academic disciplines.

The UL center, unlike the other colleges, also stressed public service. Initially it focused attention on Vine City, "Atlanta's largest metro area in need." After months of academic surveys and personal contacts with "great numbers of people," a "massive clean-up effort" in July 1969 attracted some 200 students and a $3,000 cash award from a major bank. The event activated two fraternities, independents, the ROTC, an anthropology class, faculty, and administrators. With the college under attack by student radicals, this activity projected an institutional social consciousness and demonstrated to the regents Georgia State's commitment to service.[493]

The Urban Life center was only the latest example that demonstrated the symbiotic relationship between Georgia State and Atlanta. It began when the downtown Evening School started offering courses to businesses and their young employees. During the Depression, hundreds of young Atlantans and rural Georgians came for the educational opportunities. For most, Evening College was the only chance they would ever have. As Atlanta grew and prospered in both postwar periods, so did the Evening College. Particularly after World War II, thousands of veterans, government workers, teachers, and young business employees attended the school. Later, as the Atlanta Division of the University of Georgia, its independence from

255

Athens could happen only with widespread Atlanta support. The explosion of academic programs in the 1960s surely followed rapid urban growth. As its president pointed out, the college's economic impact was significant. The Georgia State community spent "more than $46 million" in 1969. Its students, "an overwhelming majority" working "either full or part-time," earned nearly the same amount, paid over $5 million in federal taxes, and spent more than $2,500,000 on tuition, not including books and supplies. The after-tax payroll of faculty and staff amounted to nearly $6,500,000.[494]

By 1969, the city had a full-fledged urban university in all but name. As Chancellor Simpson that summer invited the president to apply for university status, the institution could assume a title commensurate with its rank as Georgia's third major system institution. Its five schools, two of them larger than most state colleges, themselves became colleges in the new university. Its completed six-story library shortly added a research function for graduate students with the establishment of the Southern Labor Archives. That and a noncredit labor studies program received strong support from local and regional labor groups, an entirely new constituency for an institution founded to teach only commerce.[495]

Georgia State by that time had become a major graduate center devoting thirty to forty percent of its resources to that pursuit. About 1,000 graduate students were expected in the field of education alone, with "an aggregate total of nearly 2,800." Having "passed through the years under the names of" both Tech and UGA, President Langdale noted, Georgia State historically had "been in a university-connected entity." It recruited faculty "for university teaching," and its graduate students would benefit "in their succeeding life patterns" with the word "university" on their transcripts. So would the institution, since "Federal grants and other sources of gifts or matching funds" were more "readily available where the title of 'University' is applicable."[496] Georgia State University's future could be even more dynamic than its recent past.

BIBLIOGRAPHICAL ESSAY

Most of the unpublished material for the early years before 1932 is located in the Georgia Tech Archives (GTA). It includes faculty minutes, presidents' reports, annual announcements, executive committee minutes, and bulletins, among others, as well as the published campus newspaper, *Technique*, and yearbook, *Blue Print*. Other documents for the early period appear in the extensive George M. Sparks Papers (1925–1957) at the Georgia State University Archives, Special Collections (SCGSU).

From 1932 until Sparks's presidency ended in 1957, his papers are indispensable in documenting and understanding Georgia State University's predecessor institutions—Evening School, System (or Atlanta) Center, Atlanta Division of the University of Georgia, the Georgia State College of Business Administration, and Georgia State College. Sparks's accumulation of letters, besides his own contacts, involved the correspondence of many other officials and their offices, including the regents, Georgia Tech, and the University of Georgia. Fortunately for the historian, some of the revelations in Sparks's personal correspondence reveal his tactics and motives in a useful and surprising way. Besides letters, Sparks seemed to have filed every official report, resolution, and proposal as well as faculty minutes. Apparently the piles of letters and documents that reportedly accumulated on Sparks's desk did not suddenly disappear into the trash as one eye-witness surmised. Of course, the records of the board of regents at the Georgia Department of Archives and History (GDAH) are also a basic source after 1931. More than any other, they provide a continuous documentary account for the entire study. The more abbreviated George E. Manners Papers (SCGSU) are important because of his key role during the merger in dealing with the various Athens adminis-trators. Registrar J. D. Blair's Papers provide a useful but more limited perspective. The William M. Suttles papers are particu-larly important during the 1960s when he became vice president.

Knowledge of the Atlanta Division-Athens merger (1947–1955) is substantially enhanced by the documents of the three University of Georgia presidents from this era, which are available in the archives department of the UGA Russell Library. The Harmon Caldwell Papers detail the first failed attempt to integrate the Atlanta Division with UGA. This experience may have influenced Caldwell when, as chancellor in 1949, he dealt with the Atlanta Division fairly and with hardheaded sympathy. The Jonathan C. Rogers Papers reveal both turmoil and more failure during that president's short year-and-a-half tenure. Finally, the O. C. Aderhold Papers provide a key to understanding why this ill-conceived union could never succeed. Aderhold's highly confidential correspondence with influential regents, dis-dainful of the Atlanta Division and determined to block its expansion, contain some indiscretions as surprising as some of those made by Sparks. In-house memoranda and other commu-nications also display the hostility of top Athens administrators. Besides the president's papers, UGA Records Management pro-vided useful information on other key Athens administrators.

Although the Noah Langdale Papers (1957–1988) extend far beyond the scope of this study, their initial twelve years are indis-pensable. Also useful were several collections from various administrative offices, including the dean of men, dean of women, school of business administration, vice president for financial affairs, college of business administration, college of arts and sciences, library, the GSU print collection involving the

University Senate Committee on Planning and Development and the campus *Signal*. The principal material for the segregation conflict is available in the National Archives Southeast Region (NASR), *Hunt v. Arnold*, Case No. 5781. The War Manpower Commission Labor Market Survey is available in RG 211, NASR.

Despite the wealth of documents, oral interviews usually add color and perspective as well as content to any historical account. The late George E. Manners, Evening School student in the early 1930s and later dean of the business school until the 1970s, gave at least two long interviews to the Georgia State University archival staff and devoted two other lengthy sessions to Gary M. Fink and the author. Unfortunately, he was the only then top surviving administrator who agreed to do so. The author is grateful to other administrators and faculty for their generous oral contributions, including Joe B. Ezell, Melvin Ecke (late), V. V. Lavroff (late), and Gerald H. Davis. Finally, authors are always mindful of the contributions of the publishers, in this case the work of Director Marc Jolley and the editorial staff of Mercer University Press.

NOTES

INTRODUCTION

1 Statistical analysis courtesy of GSU Office of Institutional Research; *Carnegie Classification of Institutions of Higher Education* (2000) www.carnegiefoundation.org.

2 *Undergraduate Catalog, 2000–2001*, Georgia State University (Atlanta GA: Office of the Registrar, May 2000) 196.

3 *The Student Handbook, 1998-1999*, Georgia State University, revised May 1998.

CHAPTER 1

4 Fac. min., 16 September 1913–1914, 7, 20 September 1913–1914, 12, Tech *Bulletin*, no. 11, n.d. [c. 1914]: 160, Georgia Tech Archives, hereinafter cited GTA; Marion L. Brittain, *The Story of Georgia Tech* (Chapel Hill NC: UNC Press, 1948) 52; Robert C. McMath, Jr., Ronald M. Bayor, James E. Brittain, Lawrence Foster, August W. Giebelhaus, and Germaine M. Reed, *Engineering the New South: Georgia Tech, 1885–1985* (Athens GA: UGA Press, 1985) 123–24; George A. Works et al., *Report to the Board of Regents of the University System of Georgia* (1933): 54, Department of Archives, Special Collections, GSU, hereinafter cited SCGSU.

5 L. C. Marshall, "The School of Commerce," *Higher Education in America* (Boston: Ginn, 1930) 78; Willis S. Rudy, *The College of the City of New York* (New York: City College Press, 1949) 3–5, 41, 313–16, 326; Walter S. Matherly, *Business Education in the Changing South*, (Chapel Hill, NC: UNC Press, 1939); John Brubacher and J. Willis Rudy, *Higher Education in Transition*, (New York: Harper & Row, 1976) 168–70; David O. Levine, *The American College and the Culture of Aspiration, 1915–1940* (Ithaca, NY: Cornell University Press, 1986) 36–37; Richard Freeland, *Academia's Golden Age* (New York: Oxford, 1992) 36–37; Martin Klotsche, *The University of Wisconsin-Milwaukee, an Urban University*, 1972) 4, 26.

6 Truman A. Hartshorn, S. Davis, G. E. Dever, P. R. Allen, and S. Bederman, *Metropolis in Georgia: Atlanta's Rise as a Major Transaction Center* (Cambridge MA: Ballinger, 1976) 2; Timothy J. Crimmins, "The Atlanta Palimpsest: Stripping Away the Layers of the Past," *Atlanta Historical Journal* 26 (Summer–Fall 1982): 17; Karen Luehrs and Timothy J. Crimmins, "In the Mind's Eye: The Downtown as Visual Metaphor for the Metropolis," *Atlanta Historical Journal* 26 (Summer–Fall 1982): 178, 186–87; Don Doyle, *New Men, New Cities, New South: Atlanta, Nashville, Charleston, Mobile, 1860–1910* (Chapel Hill NC: UNC Press, 1990) xvi, 15, 143–45, 152, 222; Thomas M. Deaton, "Atlanta During the Progressive Era" (Ph.D. diss., Emory University, 1969) 264–65; Deaton, "The Chamber of Commerce in the Economic and Political Development of Atlanta from 1900 to 1916," *Atlanta Historical Bulletin* 19 (1975): 24.

7 *The Emory University Catalog* (1918–1920), Special Collections, Woodruff Library, Emory University, 221–22; fac. min., 14 January 1916, 57, GTA; Clarence A. Bacote, *The Story of Atlanta University, A Center of* Service, *1865 –1965* (Atlanta: Princeton University Press, 1969) 275; Levine, *American College*, 79; Deaton, "Chamber of Commerce," 22; Matherly, *Business Education*, 77.

8 Matherly, *Business Education*, 172; Philip N. Racine, "Atlanta's Schools: A History of the Public School System, 1869–1955" (Ph.D. diss., Emory University, 1969) 97; Deaton, "Atlanta During the Progressive Era," 293, 296; Timothy J. Crimmons, "Bungalo Suburbs: East and West," *Atlanta Historical Journal* 26 (Summer–Fall 1982) 86; Melvin W. Ecke, *From Ivy Street to Kennedy Center: Centennial History of the Atlanta Public School System* (Atlanta GA: 1972) 142–44.

9 Stuart Galishoff, "Germs Know No Color Line: Black Health and Public Policy in Atlanta, 1900–1918," *Journal of the History of Medicine* 40 (January 1985): 23–24; Clifford Kuhn, Harlon E. Joye, and E. Bernard West, *Living Atlanta: An Oral History of the City, 1914–1948* (Athens: UGA Press, 1990) 111, 130–31, 232–33; Florence Fleming Corley, "Atlanta's Techwood and University Homes Projects: The Nation's Laboratory for Public Housing," *Atlanta History* 31 (Winter 1987–1988): 19.

10 Dana F. White, "The Black Sides of Atlanta: A Geography of Expansion and Containment, 1870–1970," *Atlanta Historical Journal* 26 (Summer–Fall 1982): 215; Kuhn et al., *Living Atlanta*, 12, 19–28; see also, Gary M. Fink, *The Fulton Bag and Cotton Mill Strike of 1914–1915, Espionage, Labor Conflict, and New South Industrial Relations* (Ithaca NY: ILR Press, 1993); Deaton, "Atlanta During the Progressive Era," 277; Doyle, *New Men*, 262.

11 Fac. min., 7 March 1912, 9 May 1912, *Annual Announcement* (1912–1913) 8, 80–81; *Annual Announcement* (1913–1914) 158, 159, 161, 204; *Annual Announcement* (1915–1916) 7, 9, GTA; Mrs. W. S. Kell, interview by Edward E. Baker, n.d., in "Baker: A General History of the Georgia Evening College" (B.C.S. thesis, University System of Georgia Evening College, 1939) 8; *Technique*, 23 October 1917; *Blue Print* (1915): 9.

12 *Annual Announcement* (1913–1914) 161, GTA; Clio C. Norris, "The Beginnings of Education for Business at the University of Georgia" (Ph.D. dissertation, UGA, 1968) 112, 122–25, 143–44; McMath, Jr., et al., *Georgia Tech*, 123.

13 *Annual Announcement* (1913–1914) 163, fac. min., 20 September 1913, 12; 30 September 1913, 20; 7 November 1913, 50; 23 February 1914, 193; *Technique*, 23 October 1914, GTA; Marshall, "School of Commerce," 82–85; McMath, Jr., et al., *Georgia Tech*, 124.

14 *13th Census* (1910) vol. ix, *Manufactures*, 284; *Atlanta City Directory* (1918) 1248; *Annual Announcement* (1913–1914) GTA: 161–62; In the absence of the Evening School's records, enrollment figures have been taken from three often incomplete and conflicting sources: the official reports of the Tech presidents to the trustees, the GST *Bulletins*, and the secondary account of Marion L. Brittain, Tech president during the 1920s and 1930s. Georgia Tech recorded no on-campus commerce enrollments until 1923, when the *Bulletin* began reporting the number of students in each school or department. Report of the Trustees (June 1914): 61–62, (June 1915):11, (June 1916): 28, in *President's Report, 1899–1931*, GTA; Brittain, *Story of Georgia Tech*, 52.

15 Schedule of Evening Classes for the Fall Term...The Walton Building and the Campus, printed, n.d. [c. 1915) Second Term Schedule, 1915–1916, Georgia Tech's School of Commerce stationery, n.d. [c. 1932–1933) box 9, folder 126, Sparks Papers, SCGSU; Report of the GST (1915–1916): 33, (1916–1917): 13, 26, 48, in *President's Report, 1899–1931*; *Blue Print* (1916); George E. Manners, in discussion with author, 6 April 1996; *Technique*, 23 October 1917, GTA.

16 Fac. min., 4 January 1917, 175, GTA, Report of the GST (1917–1918): 56, in *President's Report, 1899–1931*, min., Board of Trustees, 10 June 1918, GTA; D. I. "Red" Barron, interview in Kuhn et al., *Living Atlanta*, 164–65, n.d. [c. 1988]; *Technique*, 13 November 1917, 3; *Technique*, 27 November 1917, 6; *Blue Print* (1917), GTA; *Atlanta Constitution*, 11 November 1917; Richard Teach, "History of IMMS," unpublished MS, n.d., 5.

17 Min., ex. Comm., 1 June 1920, GTA; *Technique*, 14 May 1918, 7; *Atlanta City Directory* (1918): 1070, (1919): 1155, (1920): 429; Brittain, *Story of Georgia Tech*, 52; Franklin M. Garrett, *Atlanta and Environs: A Chronicle of Its People and Events II* (Athens GA: UGA Press, 1954), 706.

18 Levine, *American College*, 23–24, 48; McMath, Jr., et al., *Georgia Tech*, 125; Thomas G. Dyer, *The University of Georgia: A Bicentennial History, 1785–1985* (Athens GA: UGA Press, 1985) 159, 172.

19 Report of GST (1917–1918): 32–34, (1918–1919): 69, (1919–1920): 9, 54, in *President's Report, 1899–1931*; GST Bulletin (1917–1918): 18, (1918–1919): 4, (1919–1920): 22–23; *Technique*, 23 October 1917; *Technique*, 14 May 1918; *Technique*, 27 April 1979, 7; Norris, "Business at the University of Georgia," 152, 158; Rudy, *College of the City of New York*, 439, GTA.

CHAPTER 2

20 Truman A. Hartshorn, S. Davis, G. E. Dever, P. R. Allen, and S. Bederman, *Metropolis in Georgia: Atlanta's Rise as a Major Transaction Center* (Cambridge MA: Ballinger, 1976) 2–3; Douglas L. Fleming, "Atlanta, the Depression, and the New Deal," (Ph.D. diss., Emory University, 1984) 6–7, 38; Clarence N. Stone, *Regime Politics: Governing Atlanta, 1946–1988*, (Lawrence KS: University of Kansas Press, 1989) 25–26.

21 *Technique*, 19 October 1923, 8, GTA; Fleming, "Atlanta," 6–7, 20, 38; Hartshorn et al., *Metropolis in Georgia*, 2–3; Karen Luehrs and Timothy J. Crimmins, "In the Mind's Eye: The Downtown as Visual Metaphor for the Metropolis," *Atlanta Historical Journal* 26 (Summer–Fall 1982): 188–89; Elizabeth A. Lyon, "Business Buildings in Atlanta: A

Study in Urban Growth and Form," (Ph.D. diss., Emory University, 1971) 460–61; Stone, *Regime Politics*, 25–26.

22 Dana F. White and Timothy J. Crimmins, "How Atlanta Grew: Cool Heads, Hot Air, and Hard Work," *Atlanta Economic Review* 7 (January/February 1978): 33; Howard L. Preston, *Automobile Age Atlanta: The Making of a Southern Metropolis, 1900–1935* (Athens GA: UGA Press, 1979) 119; Phillip Hoffman, "Creating Underground Atlanta, 1898–1932," *Atlanta Historical Bulletin* 12 (September 1968): 55–66; Fleming, "Atlanta," 7–9; Hartshorn et al., *Metropolis in Georgia*, 9.

23 Fleming, "Atlanta," 7–9; Clifford Kuhn, Harlon E. Joye, and E. Bernard West, *Living Atlanta: An Oral History of the City, 1914–1948* (Athens GA: UGA Press, 1990) 87, 93–95; Timothy J. Crimmins, "Bungalow Suburbs: East and West," *Atlanta Historical Journal* 26 (Summer–Fall 1982): 84, 88; Andrew Marshall Hamer, "Urban Perspective for the 1980s," *Urban Atlanta: Redefining the Role of the City,* ed. Andrew Marshall Hamer (Atlanta: GSU College of Business Administration, 1980) 9; White and Crimmins, "How Atlanta Grew," 23; David O. Levine, *The American College and the Culture of Aspiration, 1915–1940* (Ithaca, NY: Cornell University Press, 1986) 45, 53, 59, 69–71, 113, 115.

24 Teach, "IMMS," 7; L. C. Marshall, "The School of Commerce," in *Higher Education in America* (Boston: Ginn, 1930) 94; Philip N. Racine, "Atlanta's Schools: A History of the Public School System, 1869–1955" (Ph.D. diss., Emory University, 1969) 195–96; Fleming, "Atlanta," 43–44; Levine, *American College*, 78; Robert C. McMath, Jr., Ronald M. Bayor, James E. Brittain, Lawrence Foster, August W. Giebelhaus, and Germaine M. Reed, *Engineering the New South: Georgia Tech, 1885–1985* (Athens GA: UGA Press, 1985) 165; Thomas G. Dyer, *The University of Georgia: A Bicentennial History, 1785–1985* (Athens GA: UGA Press, 1985) 194–95, 211.

25 *Emory University Catalog* (1919–1920): 49; *Blue Print* (1920–1932); Henry M. Bulloch, *A History of Emory University, 1836–1936* (Atlanta GA: Cherokee, 1972) 372; Levine, *American College*, 124. In a 1938 address, the Evening School registrar reported the 1932 enrollment at 418 men and 106 women. Baker, "General History," 52; Walter J. Matherly, *Business Education in the Changing South* (Chapel Hill NC: UNC Press, 1939) 81.

26 Enrollment statistics varied depending on the source. This account has used the reports of the president, supplemented when needed by the Tech *Bulletin*. Report of GST (1920–1921): 3, (1921–1922): n.p., (1922–1923): 27, (1923–1924): 452, (1924–1925): 6, (1926–1927): 11, in *President's Report, 1899–1931*, GTA; *Bulletin* (1932): 264; George Sparks to President Marion Brittain, 15 May 1929, Sparks to Brittain, carbon, n.d. [c. December 1929) box 20, folder 256, Sparks Papers, SCGSU; *Blue Print* (1920–1932) GTA; Julia Kirk Blackwelder, "Mop and Typewriter: Women's Work in Early Twentieth Century Atlanta," *Atlanta Historical Quarterly* 27 (Fall 1983): 21.

27 *Blue Print* (1920–1932) GTA.

28 Marshall, "School of Commerce," 86, 100–101, 106; Matherly, *Business Education*, 181.

29 Fac. min. (26 March 1921): 116, (29 March 1921): 121, (3 March 1922): 299, (21 April 1921): 131, 158, (23 March 1922): 315, (27 April 1922): 335, GTA; George Sparks to City Epworth League, 20 September 1929, Sparks to B. S. Embry, 18

November 1930, George A. Bland to Sparks, 30 November 1931, box 39, folder 463, Sparks Papers, SCGSU; Levine, *American College*, 120.

30 *Technique*, 9 November 1923, 5; *Technique*, 25 April 1924, 3; *Technique*, 9 Jan 1925, 4; *Technique*, 15 May 1925, 8, GTA.

31 John M. Watters to prospective students, box 30, folder 376, Sparks Papers, SCGSU; Report of GST (1924–1925): 14, 24, in *President's Report, 1899–1931*; *Technique*, 21 November 1924, 3, GTA; George Manners to Merl Reed, 5 March 1999, in possession of the author.

32 *Pandora* (1921); *Evening Signal*, Russell Library, UGA, 7 November 1934, 1; Report of GST (1922–1923): 18, 19, (1924–1925): 13, in *President's Report, 1899–1931*; fac. min., 25 September 1924, 12, GTA, *Blue Print* (1924–1926); *Atlanta Journal*, 14 May 1925, 13.

33 Fred B. Wenn to Mr. Superintendent, 26 August 1925, box 30, folder 376, George Sparks to Philip Weltner, 16 January 1933, box 31, folder 397, Sparks to Marion Brittain, carbon, n.d. [c. December 1929], box 20, folder 256, R. R. Johnson to Charles M. Snelling, 29 September 1936, box 32, folder 405, Sparks Papers, SCGSU. The new address, 92 ? Forsyth, became 106 ? Forsyth after downtown street numbers changed in 1928. *Atlanta City Directory* (1927): 486, (1928): 1449; Report of GST (1926–1927): 11, in *President's Report, 1899–1931*.

34 *Technique*, 25 March 1927, 2; for a contemporary photo of Sparks, see also *Blue Print* (1930): 118, GTA; George Manners, interview by Les Hough and Joe Constance, 7 March 1986, 28, George M. Sparks, biographical sketch, box 11, folder 160, Sparks Papers, SCGSU; academic information, typescript, n.d. [c. December 1934) box 16, gen. files, 1934–1939, folder, RG33–1–51, GDAH.

35 *Blue Print* (1927) GTA; George M. Sparks to Marion Brittain, carbon, n.d. [c. December 1929) box 20, folder 256, Sparks Papers, SCGSU; fac. min., 3 March 1922, 300; *Technique*, 29 February 1924, 1; *Technique*, 24 October 1924, 5, 7, GTA.

36 *Technique*, 19 October 1923, 8; *Technique*, 7 November 1924, 6; *Technique*, 13 January 1928, 7; *Blue Print* (1921): 108, GTA; McMath, Jr., et al., *Georgia Tech*, 132–33; Kuhn, et al, *Living Atlanta*, 260, 263, 286, 296, 304–305, 313–14; Kenneth T. Jackson, *The Ku Klux Klan in the City, 1915–1930* (New York: Oxford Press, 1967) 37.

37 T. M. McClellan to Teachers, n.d. [c. 1928–1929], box 30, folder 376, George Sparks to Marion Brittain, 15 May 1929, Sparks to Brittain, carbon, n.d. [c. December 1929], box 20, folder 256, Sparks Papers, SCGSU; academic information, typescript, n.d. [c. December 1934) box 16, gen. files, 1934–1939, folder, RG33–1–51.

38 Academic Information, typescript, n.d. [c. December 1934], gen. adm. records of the chancellor, box 16, gen. files 1934–1939 folder, RG33–1–51; George Manners, interview by Les Hough and Joe Constance, 7 March 1986, 29; George Manners, in discussion with the author and Gary M. Fink, 2 February 1989, 27–28, SCGSU.

39 George M. Sparks to Marion Brittain, carbon, n.d. [c. December 1929) box 20, folder 256, Sparks Papers, SCGSU; George Manners, interview by Les Hough and Joe Constance, 7 March 1986, 16, SCGSU; Manners to Merl Reed, 5 March 1999, in possession of the author.

40 L. W. Robert, Jr., trustees' ex. comm., to R. R. Johnson, 14 August 1930, box 1, day-to-day operations folder, Evening School of Commerce of the Georgia School of Technology [Plan of Operation or Bylaws], n.d. [c. early 1931) typescript, box 20, folder 256, Sparks Papers, SCGSU; George Manners to Merl Reed, 5 March 1999, in possession of the author.

CHAPTER 3

41 George Sparks to E. H. Folk, 31 January 1930, box 20, folder 256, George Manners, interview by Les Hough and Joe Constance, 7 March 1986, 14, R. R. Johnson to Charles M. Snelling, 29 September 1936, box 32, folder 405, Sparks Papers, SCGSU; Scrapbook loaned to Laura Cantrell by B. M. Busink, a former teacher, originally possessed by Mrs. Fred J. Paxon, quoted in Cantrell, Atlanta Division, 27; Audit, year ending June 1930, Records of the Office of the President, 6–7, GTA.

42 R. R. Johnson to Charles M. Snelling, 29 September 1936, Johnson to Marion Brittain, 23 March 1931, box 32, folder 405, Johnson to Brittain, 23 March 1931, letter to Ben F. Noble, 4 May 1931, Robin Adair to Johnson, 5 May 1930, John W. Zuber to Johnson, 21 January 1931, box 1, day-to-day operations folder, Sparks Papers, SCGSU; George Manners, interview by Les Hough and Joe Constance, 7 March 1986, 32, SCGSU.

43 R. R. Johnson to M. L. Brittain, 5 May 1930, Brittain to Johnson, 7 May 1930, box 1, day-to-day operations folder, Sparks Papers, SCGSU.

44 Misc. notes seeking contributions, 16–22 July 1930, R. R. Johnson to Marion Brittain, 23 March 1931, anonymous (on GTES stationery) to Johnson, 30 June 1930, Johnson to Ladd Lime & Stone Company, 22 June [July] 1930, Atlantic Ice and Coal Company to Johnson, 16 July 1930, box 1, day-to-day operations folder, Sparks to Lacy E. Bradford, Sparks to Robert S. Calhoun, Sparks to Robert H. Peavy, and Sparks to Frank J. Shipp, all dated 1 July 1931, box 39, folder 463, Sparks Papers, SCGSU; George Manners, in discussion with the author and Gary M. Fink, 2 February 1989, 35–36, SCGSU; Douglas L. Fleming, "Atlanta, the Depression, and the New Deal," (Ph.D. diss., Emory University, 1984) 98–99.

45 R. R. Johnson to C. J. Bowen, 5 November 1931, Johnson to George W. Nix, 25 February 1931, Johnson to J. O. Conoly, 21 March 1931, Johnson to Clifford R. Smith, 23 April 1931, box 1, day-to-day operations folder, George M. Sparks to Johnson, 17 January 1931, box 20, folder 256, Johnson to Sparks, 7 December 1931, list of firms and individuals subscribing… to the building fund, 1 May 1931, box 19 folder 253, Sparks Papers, SCGSU; Marion L. Brittain, *The Story of Georgia Tech* (Chapel Hill NC: UNC Press, 1948), 52.

46 R. R. Johnson to Charles M. Snelling, 29 September 1936, box 32, folder 405, list of firms and individuals subscribing…, box 19, folder 253, George Sparks to Marion Smith, 29 November 1945, box 32, folder 405, dedication (Building) 1931, box 10, folders 3, 128, Sparks Papers, SCGSU; *Atlanta Constitution*, 7 May 1931, 8–9.

47 Fleming, "Atlanta," 72–73, 88, 111, 117–88, 136–37, 208; Leslie L. Hanawalt, *A Place of Light: the History of Wayne State University*, (Detroit MI: Wayne State University Press, 1968) 27.

48 Julia Kirk Blackwelder, "Quiet Suffering: Atlanta Women in the 1930s," *Georgia Historical Quarterly* 61 (Summer 1977): 83, 114–15; Clifford Kuhn, Harlon E. Joye, and E. Bernard West, *Living Atlanta: An Oral History of the City, 1914–1948* (Athens GA: UGA Press, 1990) 202–204; John Hammond Moore, "Communists and Fascists in a Southern City: Atlanta, 1930," in *Hitting Home: The Great Depression in Town and Country*, ed. Bernard Sternsher (Chicago: Quadrangle Books, 1970) 85–104; Fleming, "Atlanta," 71, 80, 89; Florence Fleming Corley, "Atlanta's Techwood and University Homes Projects: The Nation's Laboratory for Public Housing," *Atlanta History* 31 (Winter 1987–1988): 17; Peter E. Arnold, "Public Housing in Atlanta," *Atlanta Historical Bulletin* 13 (September 1968): 9–18.

49 George Sparks to Marion Brittain, 16 December 1930, Sparks to Brittain, draft, n.d. [c. winter, 1931) box 20, folder 256, Sparks Papers, SCGSU.

50 Evening School of Commerce of the Georgia School of Technology [Plan of Operation or Bylaws], n.d. [c. early 1931) typescript, box 20, folder 256, Sparks Papers, SCGSU; *Technique*, 20 November 1931, 1.

51 George Sparks to Marion Brittain, 16 December 1930, Sparks to Brittain, draft, n.d. [c. winter 1931) Evening School of Commerce [Plan of Operation or Bylaws], typescript, n.d. [c. early 1931) box 20, folder 256, Brittain to Sparks, 9 June 1931, box 17, folder 225, Sparks Papers, SCGSU; *Bulletin*, 18 (April 1931): 263; *Bulletin*, 29 (April 1932): 264, GTA; *Technique*, 20 March 1931, 1, *Technique*, 11 December 1931, 1; Walter J. Matherly, *Business Education in the Changing South* (Chapel Hill NC: UNC Press, 1939) 15–16, 111, 115.

267

52 George M. Sparks to Marion L. Brittain, n.d. [c. December 1931], Brittain to heads of departments, 19 April 1932, Annual Report, 29 April 1932, box 20, folder 256, Sparks Papers, SCGSU.

53 J. R. McCain to Carnegie Corporation, 22 October 1932, box 19, folder 237, Sparks Papers, SCGSU.

54 J. G. Stipe to T. M. McClellan, 15 August 1933, box 18, folder 233, Sparks Papers, SCGSU.

CHAPTER 4

55 Office of the director to the faculty, n.d. [c. spring 1933) box 12, folder 162, Sparks Papers, SCGSU; *Annual Report of the Regents of the University System of Georgia* (1932): 1, 3, 5, 13, hereinafter cited Regents, *Annual Report*; Thomas G. Dyer, *The University of Georgia: A Bicentennial History, 1785–1985* (Athens GA: UGA Press, 1985) 195, 204–205; Robert C. McMath, Jr., Ronald M. Bayor, James E. Brittain, Lawrence Foster, August W. Giebelhaus, and Germaine M. Reed, *Engineering the New South: Georgia Tech, 1885–1985* (Athens GA: UGA Press, 1985) 100–101, 176; Robert Preston Brooks, *The University of Georgia Under Sixteen Administrations, 1785–1955* (Athens GA: UGA Press, 1956) 178–79; Cameron Fincher, *Historical Development of the University System of Georgia* (Athens GA: Institute of Higher Education, UGA, 1991) 5, 9–10, 15; Merle Curti and Roderick Nash, *Philanthropy in the Shaping of American Higher Education* (New Brunswick NJ: Rutgers U. Press, 1965) 117; Barbara Ann Scott, *Crisis Management in American Higher Education* (New York: Praeger, 1983) 34; see also Raymond Blaine

Fosdick, *Adventure in Giving: The Story of the General Education Board, a Foundation Established by John D. Rockefeller* (New York: Harper, 1962).

56 Besides George Works, the survey team included Chicago Dean Charles H. Judd; Presidents Edward C. Elliott (Purdue), George F. Zook (Akron), and L. D. Coffman (Minnesota); and a large staff of specialists. L. D. Coffman, Edward C. Elliot, Charles H. Judd and George F. Zook, *Report to the Board of Regents of the University System of Georgia* (1932) 9, Record Group (RG) 33–1–32, box 1, Georgia Department of Archives and History (GDAH) hereinafter cited Works *Report*; Scott, *Crisis Management*, 34–35, 74; Curti and Nash, *Philanthropy*, 213–214; Louis Round Wilson, *The University of North Carolina under Consolidation, 1931–1963, History and Appraisal* (Chapel Hill NC: UNC Press, 1964) 18, 22.

57 Works *Report* (1932): 7–8, 12–14; Regents, *Annual Report* (1932): 3, 13; Dyer, *University of Georgia*, 214–15.

58 In 1930, Atlanta's population was 270,366, but over 434,000 resided in the four-county metropolitan area (Fulton, DeKalb, Cobb, and Clayton), comprising about fifteen percent of the state's population. Other major cities and their counties included Savannah, 85,0255 (Chatham, 105,531); Macon, 58,829 (Bibb, 77,042); Augusta, 60,342 (Richmond, 72,990); Columbus, 43,191 (Muscogee, 57,558); Albany, 14,507 (Dougherty, 22,306); and Athens, 18,192 (Clark, 25,613). *Fifteenth Census of the United States: 1930* (U.S. Government Printing Office, 1932) 464, 466, 467, 469, 472, 474; Works *Report* (1932): 7–8; Fred J. Kelly and John H. McNeely, *The State and Higher Education* (New York: Carnegie Foundation, 1933) 182.

59 Works *Report*, (1932): 15–16; Dyer, *University of Georgia*, 214; Kelly and McNeely, *The State and Higher Education*, 182.

60 Works *Report* (1932): 26–27, 32, 48, 54, 57, 69; McMath, Jr., et al., *Georgia Tech*, 175–76; Dyer, *University of Georgia*, 202–204.

61 Works *Report* (1932): 64–69.

62 Ibid.

63 Business enrollments, at 1,316 during 1919–1920, increased to 7,943 in 1935–1936. Walter J. Matherly, *Business Education in the Changing South* (Chapel Hill NC: UNC Press, 1939) 131–32, 141, 158–60.

64 George Sparks to Hughes Spalding, 26 July 1934, box 31, folder 398, Sparks to Philip Weltner, 26 October 1933, folder 397, Sparks Papers, SCGSU; "Proposed Outline of Policy To Govern the Work in The Evening School," typescript, n.d. [c. early 1934) box 16, gen. files 1934–1939 folder, RG33–1–51, GDAH.

65 Regents, *Annual Report* (1932): 8, 16; Regents, *Annual Report* (1935): 21–22, SCGSU; Sandy Beaver to Philip Weltner, 29 August 1933, Marion Smith to Weltner, 23 August 1935, box 1, RG33–1–35; Dyer, *University of Georgia*, 216; Phinizy Spalding, *The History of the Medical College of Georgia* (Athens GA: UGA Press, 1987) 160; William Ivy Hair, James C. Bonner, and Edward B. Dawson, *A History of Georgia College* (Milledgeville GA: Georgia College, 1976) 153.

66 *Bulletin* 29 (April 1932): 264; George Sparks to Marion Brittain, n.d. [c. late 1932) "Resolution of the Student Council," 14 July 1933, box 20, folder 256, Manget Davis to Board of Regents, 20 April 1933, box 31, folder 397, Sparks Papers, SCGSU; McMath, Jr., et al., *Georgia Tech*, 176–79; Dyer, *University of Georgia*, 217–18.

67 "Ten Reasons Why the Board of Regents Should Not Abolish the School of Commerce at Georgia Tech," n.d. [c. April 1933) box 17, folder 225, Sparks Papers, SCGSU.

CHAPTER 5

68 George Sparks to M. L. Brittain, n.d. [c. December 1931) box 10, folder 256, Sparks to Philip Weltner, 26 October 1933, box 31, folder 397, Sparks Papers, SCGSU. In his letter to Chancellor Weltner, written over a year later, Sparks gave a sketchy and chronologically confusing summary of his activity. It is the only source known to the author.

69 George Sparks to Philip Weltner, 26 October 1933, box 31, folder 397, 22 May 1934, box 31, folder 398, Sparks Papers, SCGSU.

70 Ibid.; Thomas G. Dyer, *The University of Georgia: A Bicentennial History, 1785–1985* (Athens GA: UGA Press, 1985) 204; Marion L. Brittain, *The Story of Georgia Tech* (Chapel Hill NC: UNC Press, 1948) 207.

71 Hughes Spalding to the chancellor et al., 18 March 1933, box 31, folder 397, office of the director to the faculty, n.d. [c. March 1933) box 12, folder 162, Sparks Papers; George Manners, interview by Les Hough and Joe Constance, 7 March 1986, 21, SCGSU.

72 George Sparks to Philip Weltner, 26 October 1933, box 31, folder 397, 22 May 1934, folder 398, Sparks Papers, SCGSU; *Evening Signal*, 2 October 1933, 2; 6 November 1933, 1.

73 R. P. Stephens to Philip Weltner, 5 June 1935, box 15, Degree Advisory Council 1934–1937 folder, RG33–1–51, GDAH; George Sparks to W. F. Caldwell, 15 December 1933, box 31, folder 397, Sparks Papers, SCGSU; *Evening Signal*, 2 October 1933, 2; *Atlanta Constitution*, 1 October 1933, 14.

74 G. H. Bogg to Philip Weltner, 13 October 1933, box 37, folder 446, Sparks Papers, SCGSU.

75 M. L. Huntley to board of regents, 22 December 1933, box 15, gen. file, 1934–1939, folder, RG33–1–51, GDAH; John McCain to Marion Smith, 15 May 1934, box 36, folder 424, Sparks Papers, SCGSU; William A. Cook, "A Comparative Study of Standardizing Agencies," *North Central Association Quarterly* 4 (December 1929): 378.

76 Philip Weltner to M. L. Huntley, 6, 17 January 1934, box 15, gen. files, 1934–1939, folder, RG33–1–51.

77 Report of "Findings, Conclusions and Recommendations of the Committee on Student Activities," typescript, n.d. [c. spring 1934], box 38, folder 447, Sparks Papers, SCGSU; R. P. Stephens to Philip Weltner, 5 June 1935, box 15, Degree Advisory Council folder, RG33–1–51; Dyer, *University of Georgia*, 207.

78 George Sparks to Philip Weltner, 29 March 1934, with attached typescript from *The University of Oregon State System of Higher Education Bulletin*, n.d., 264, box 15, degree advisory council folder, RG33–1–51.

79 USG School of Commerce, 6 April 1934, typescript by R. P. Brooks, box 15, Degrees Advisory Council, 1934–1937 folder, RG33–1–51; Recommendations, n.d. [c. April 1934) attached to Brooks to George Sparks, 12 April 1934, box 38, folder 447, Sparks to Philip Weltner, 15 May 1934, box 31, folder 398, Sparks Papers, SCGSU; *Evening Signal*, 23 May 1934, 2.

80 Marion Brittain to Philip Weltner, 2 June 1934, S. V. Sanford to Weltner, 4 June 1934, box 15, Degrees Advisory Council, 1934–1937 folder, RG33–1–51.

81 Min., Advisory Council, 28 June 1934, R. P. Brooks to George Sparks, 4 July 1934, box 13, folder 172, Sparks Papers, SCGSU; Philip Weltner to Sandy Beaver, 23 April 1934, box 15, Degree Advisory Council, 1934–1937, folder, RG33–1–51.

82 George M. Sparks to Charles M. Snelling, 8 July 1934, 1 August 1934, Sparks to Hughes Spalding, 26 July 1934, box 31, folder 398, Sparks to Snelling, 1 July 1934, box 17, folder 225, "Academic and Economic Reasons Why the University System Evening School Should be Located in Downtown Atlanta," unsigned, typescript, n.d. [summer 1934) box 18, folder 328, Sparks Papers, SCGSU.

83 "Academic and Economic Reasons Why the University System Should be Located in Downtown Atlanta," unsigned, typescript, n.d. [summer 1934], box 18, folder 328, Sparks Papers, SCGSU.

84 Ibid.; Evening School of Commerce, distribution of Evening School Funds, 12 May 1926, box 39, folder 468, Sparks Papers, SCGSU.

85 George Sparks to Charles Snelling, 1 August 1934, Sparks to Hughes Spalding, 26 July 1934, box 31, folder 398, Sparks Papers, SCGSU.

86 Ibid.; Brooks, *University of Georgia*, 187; Robert C. McMath, Jr., Ronald M. Bayor, James E. Brittain, Lawrence Foster, August W. Giebelhaus, and Germaine M. Reed, *Engineering the New South: Georgia Tech, 1885–1985* (Athens GA: UGA Press, 1985) 163–64; Marion L. Brittain, *The Story of Georgia Tech* (Chapel Hill NC: UNC Press, 1948) 106.

87 George Sparks to Hughes Spalding, 26 July 1934, box 31, folder 398, Spalding to Philip Weltner, 31 July 1934, box 31, folder 398, Sparks Papers, SCGSU.

88 George Sparks to Charles Snelling, 8 July, 1 August 1934, box 31, folder 398, Sparks Papers, SCGSU.

89 Ibid.; Hughes Spalding to Philip Weltner, 31 July 1934, Spalding to Charles Snelling, 8 August 1934, box 31, folder 398, Sparks Papers, SCGSU.

90 M. C. Huntley to S. V. Sanford, 18 December 1934, box 16, gen. files, 1934–1939, folder, RG33–1–51.

CHAPTER 6

91 Douglas L. Fleming, "Atlanta, the Depression, and the New Deal," (Ph.D. diss., Emory University, 1984) 134, 139–42, 144, 156; Fleming, "The New Deal in Atlanta: A Review of the Major Programs," *Atlanta Historical Journal* 30 (Spring 1986): 23–45.

92 Fleming, "Atlanta," 203, 236, 242.

93 Ibid., 184, 185–87; Truman A. Hartshorn, S. Davis, G. E. Dever, P. R. Allen, and S. Bederman, *Metropolis in Georgia: Atlanta's Rise as a Major Transaction Center* (Cambridge MA: Ballinger, 1976) 2–3.

94 Fleming, "Atlanta," 173, 176, 183, 313, 322.

95 Regents, *Annual Report*, 1933, 13; Hughes Spalding to Philip Weltner, 31 July 1934, box 31, folder 398, George Sparks to Weltner, 16 January 1933, folder 397, Sparks to C. F. Palmer, 20 October 1933, box 20, folder 256, Sparks Papers, SCGSU; Thomas G. Dyer, *The University of Georgia: A Bicentennial History, 1785–1985* (Athens GA: UGA Press, 1985) 175; Robert C. McMath, Jr., Ronald M. Bayor, James E. Brittain, Lawrence Foster, August W. Giebelhaus, and Germaine M. Reed, *Engineering the New South: Georgia Tech, 1885–1985* (Athens GA: UGA Press, 1985) 182–83.

96 Fac. min., 5 December 1936, box 13, folder 172, J. Houstoun Johnston to Hughes Spalding, 15 December 1933, box 31, folder 397, Hallman Realty to Spalding, 9, 24, January 1934, George M. Sparks to Philip Weltner, 16 January 1934, folder 398, Sparks to L. R. Siebert, 12 July 1935, box 34, folder 446, "Schedule of Annual Payment Necessary to Meet the Government's Requirement for Repayment of Loan," 22 November 1933, box 36, folder 422, Sparks Papers, Regents, *Annual Report* (1933): 18, SCGSU; *Atlanta Journal*, 9 November 1933; 15 November 1933; *Atlanta Constitution*, 9 November 1933; 10 November 1933; 13 December 1933; 15 December 1933; 17 December 1933; *Evening Signal*, 11 December 1933; 16 February 1934; 23 May 1934; 10 December 1934.

97 *Atlanta Constitution*, 15 January 1935, 1, 4; Regents, *Annual Report* (1934): 18, SCGSU; Fleming, "Atlanta," 25, 142; McMath, Jr., et al., *Georgia Tech*, 193–94.

98 *Atlanta Constitution*, 15 January 1935, 1; 19 January 1935, 1, 4; 20 January 1935, 2; McMath, Jr., et al., *Georgia Tech*, 193–94.

99 *Atlanta Constitution*, 4 February 1935, 1; 6 February 1935, 2.

100 Regents, *Annual Report* (1935): 12, 29, *Annual Report* (1936): 61, "Resolution of the Regents," 28 January 1935, box 32, folder 399, Sparks Papers, SCGSU.

101 Regents, *Annual Report* (1935): 29, *Annual Report* (1936): 45, George Sparks to L. R. Siebert, 12 July 1935, box 34, folder 446, Sparks to Hughes Spalding, 11 December 1935, box 32, folder 399, Sparks Papers, SCGSU; George Manners, in discussion with the author and Gary M. Fink, 2 February 1989, 17, SCGSU; *Atlanta Constitution*, 20 January 1935, 1; Dyer, *University of Georgia*, 218; Brooks, *University of Georgia*, 180–81; McMath, Jr., et al., *Georgia Tech*, 182–83.

CHAPTER 7

102 *Evening Signal*, 23 May 1934, 2; "Report of Findings, Conclusions and Recommendations of the Comm. on Student Activities," typescript, n.d. [c. 1934), box 38, folder 447, "Enrollment," typescript, box 9, folder 256, George M. Sparks to Philip Weltner, 2 May 1934, box 31, folder 398, Sparks Papers, SCGSU; John Brubacher and J. Willis Rudy, *Higher Education in Transition*, (New York: Harper & Row, 1976) 359–60.

103 George M. Sparks to Philip Weltner, 2 May 1934, box 31, folder 398, Sparks Papers, SCGSU.

104 John McCain to Marion Smith, 15 May 1934, box 36, folder 424, Sparks Papers, SCGSU.

105 George M. Sparks to M. C. Huntley, 2 November 1934, Huntley to S. V. Sanford, 18 December 1934, box 36, folder 424, Sparks Papers, SCGSU.

106 Philip Weltner to S. V. Sanford, 26, 29 December 1934, George Sparks to Weltner, 29 December 1934, gen. adm. records of the chancellor, box 16, gen. file, 1934–1937, folder, RG33–1–51, GDAH.

107 George Sparks to Philip Weltner, 29 December 1934, Weltner to S. V. Sanford, 26, 29 December 1934, gen. adm. records of the chancellor, box 16, gen. file, 1934–1937, folder, RG33–1–51.

108 Philip Weltner to S. V. Sanford, 29 April 1935, Sanford to Weltner, 1 May 1935, Weltner to Sanford, 7 May 1935, box 16, gen. file, 1934–1939, folder, RG33–1–51.

109 "Proposed Outline of Policy to Govern the Work in the Evening School," n.d. [spring 1935], box 16, gen. adm. records of the chancellor, gen. files, 1934–1939, folder, RG33–1–51; Regents, *Annual Report* (1937): 91; George Manners, interview by Les Hough and Joe Constance, 7 March 1986, 30–31.

110 Recommendation of the committee on education, typescript, n.d. [August 1935], box 17, folder 225, Sparks Papers, SCGSU; Sparks to Sanford, 8 July 1935, Sanford to Sparks, 26 July 1935, box 15, Degree Advisory Council, 1934–1937, folder, RG33–1–51.

111 S. V. Sanford to George M. Sparks, 26 July 1935, telegram, board of regents to dean Alfred Powers, 3 August 1935, "Powers to Board of Regents," 6 August 1935, box 15, Degree Advisory Council, 1935–1937, folder RG–33–1–51; Sparks to Sanford, 2 August 1935, box 37, folder 443, Sparks Papers, SCGSU.

112 Snelling did not have a similar regard or affection for Sanford. See unsigned letter, [George Sparks to] Dear Sam [Leonard Siebert], n.d. [c. fall 1935], box 32, folder 400, and Sparks to Hughes Spalding, 11 December 1935, folder 399, S. V. Sanford to Sandy Beaver, 9 August 1935, box 17, folder 225, Sanford to Beaver, 21 August 1935,box 17, folder 225, Sparks Papers, SCGSU.

113 S. V. Sanford to Sandy Beaver, 21 August 1935, meeting of the board of regents, n.d. [23 August 1935], typescript, box 17, folder 225, Sparks Papers, SCGSU; Regents, *Annual Report* (1935): 70; David O. Levine, *The American College and the Culture of Aspiration, 1915–1940* (Ithaca, NY: Cornell University Press, 1986) 99, 162–63.

114 George Sparks to Charles Snelling, n.d. [September 1935], Sparks to Snelling, 16 October 1935, box 32, folder 399, Sparks to S. V. Sanford, 2 August 1935, box 37, folder 443, J. R. McCain to Marion Smith, n.d. [c. winter 1936] box 32, folder 400, Sparks Papers, SCGSU; McCain to Snelling, 21 December 1935, Smith to Sandy Beaver, 13 February 1936, Beaver to Sanford, 13 February 1936, regents min., 10 March 1936, box 15, Degree Advisory Council, 1934–1937, folder, RG33–1–51.

115 Occupations of Graduates of Class of 1936 [as of] June 30, 1937, box 37, folder 443, Sparks Papers, SCGSU.

116 George Manners, interview by Les Hough and Joe Constance, 7 March 1986, 34.

CHAPTER 8

117 George Sparks to Sandy Beaver, 15 October 1936, box 36, folder 431, annual report, December 1940, box 3, folder 31, John E. Drewry to Harmon Caldwell, 17 March 1938, Caldwell to S. V. Sanford, 18 March 1938, R. P. Stephens to Caldwell, 23 April 1938, box 16, gen. file, 1934–1939, folder, Edwin D. Pusey to Sanford, 23 September 1943, box 28, Education, 1943–1952, folder, RG33-1-51; Regents, *Annual Report* (1939): 113, Sparks to Caldwell 17 May 1938, box 17, folder 225, Sparks Papers, George Manners, in discussion with the author and Gary M. Fink, 29 September 1989, SCGSU.

118 *Evening Signal*, 6 September 1935, 1; George Manners, in discussion with the author and Gary M. Fink, 2 February 1989, 5, SCGSU.

119 Doris DeLay to George Sparks, 29 January 1940, box 18, folder 226, University System of Georgia, summer school schedule, 1942, box 9, folder 126, Sparks Papers, SCGSU; George Manners, in discussion with the author and Gary M. Fink, 2 February 1989, 27, SCGSU.

120 Charles T. Taylor to George Sparks, 20 July 1942, Myron F. Lewis to Sparks, 5 August 1943, Glenn N. Sisk to Sparks, 15 August 1945, William E. Hinrichs to Sparks, 15 November 1945, Rev. Jack P. Speer to Sparks, 3 December 1946, box 12, folder 165, Sparks Papers, SCGSU; George Manners, in discussion with the author and Gary M. Fink, 2 February 1989, 5, 27, SCGSU.

121 George Sparks to Charles Snelling, 31 October 1935, box 32, folder 399, Sparks to Sandy Beaver, 15 October 1936, box 36, folder 431, Sparks to S. V. Sanford, 29 October 1937, box 3, folder 31, Sparks Papers, SCGSU; Regents, *Annual Report* (1936): 85.

122 Fac. min., 5 December 1936, box 13, folder 172, George Sparks to Hugh Spalding, 11 December 1935, Sparks to Miller Bell, 16 September 1937, Leonard Siebert to Charles Snelling, 18 July 1936, box 32, folder 400, Sparks Papers, SCGSU, George Manners, interview by Les Hough and Joe Constance, 7 March 1986, 30.

123 James W. Merritt to Cason Callaway, 25 August 1936, regents min., 18 September 1936, box 32, folder 400, fac. min., 10 September, 30 October 1936, box 13, folder 172, Joe E. Shaw to George M. Sparks, 29 May 1945, box 6 folder 65, Sparks Papers, SCGSU; Regents, *Annual Report* (1937): 11; *Evening Signal*, 5 October 1936; 18 January 1937.

124 George Sparks to Miller Bell, 16 September 1937, box 32, folder 401, T. M. McClellan to W. W. Noyes, 27 September 1938, folder 402, Sparks to Charles M. Snelling, 30 November 1938, box 17, folder 225, Sparks Papers, SCGSU; Regents, *Annual Report* (1939): 13, 95; *Evening Signal*, 18 January 1938; 24 January 1938; 10 September 1938.

125 "Georgia League of Nursing Education to Prospective Students in the Pre-Nursing Course," 8 July 1935, box 28, folder 358, Sparks Papers, SCGSU; Evelyn Brown [pseudonym] to S. V. Sanford, 27 October 1937, box 16, gen. files, 1934–1939, folder, RG33-1-51.

126 D. D. Joiner to S. V. Sanford, 5 May 1936, box 17, folder 225, Sanford to Joiner, 7 July 1936, box 17, folder 225, resolution, Fulton County Teachers' Association, 12 June 1939, L. R. Siebert to Committee on Education, 11 August 1939, box 32, folder 403, Sparks Papers, SCGSU; Sanford to W. H. Baskin, 8 July 1936, box 15, Degree

Advisory Council, 1934–1937, folder, Siebert to Miss Vivian McLendon, 18 September 1939, box 16, gen. file. 1934–1939, folder, RG33–1–51.

127 Regents, *Annual Report* (1939): 114; George Sparks to S. V. Sanford, 3 January 1940, box 3, folder 31, Sparks Papers, SCGSU; resolutions adopted by [UGA] administrative council, 5 January 1945, 7, gen. adm. records of the chancellor, box 17, Proposal... 1944, folder, RG33–1–51.

128 George Sparks to Mrs. Nettie Evans, 24 January 1940, box 18, folder 225, Sparks Papers, *Junior Collegiate*, SCGSU (Atlanta Center) 30 April 1942; George Manners, interview by Les Hough and Joe Constance, 7 March 1986, 38–39.

129 Besides Fulton, DeKalb, and Cobb, five additional counties now comprised the official metropolitan area by 1943, including Clayton, Douglas, Cherokee, Bartow, and Paulding. *Sixteenth Census of the United States, 1940, Population*, 2nd ed., 185, 364, 383; Andrew Marshall Hamer, "Urban Perspective for the 1980s," *Urban Atlanta: Redefining the Role of the City,* ed. Andrew Marshall Hamer (Atlanta: GSU College of Business Administration, 1980) 7–8.

130 Labor market survey of Atlanta, 28 December 1942, labor market development report, 15 April 1943, report, 10 September 1943, Bureau of Program Requirements, War Manpower Commission, Atlanta folder, industries having war contracts expiring in March 1943 or later, min. and decisions of regional and essential commissions, 4 February 1943, gen. contract folder, Record Group 211, National Archives, Southeast Region, East Point, GA, hereinafter cited RG211, NASR; Merl E. Reed, *Seedtime for the Modern Civil Rights Movement: The President's Committee on Fair Employment Practice, 1941–1946,* (Baton Rouge LA: LSU Press, 1991) 190, 193, 223–25; see also, Merl E. Reed, "Bell Bomber Comes South: The Struggle by Atlanta Blacks for Jobs During World War II," *Labor in the Modern South,* ed. Glenn Eskew (Athens GA: UGA Press, 2001) 102–34.

131 *Evening Signal,* 14 October 1940; 26 February 1941; USG Center, annual report, 1941, box 3, folder 31, fac. min., 18 September 1942, box 13, folder 172, Sparks Papers, SCGSU.

132 Fac. min., 8 December 1941, box 13, folder 172, Sparks Papers, SCGSU.

133 Regents, *Annual Report* (1942–1943): 69; fac. min., 18 September 1942, box 13, folder 172, Sparks Papers, SCGSU, 1942; *Evening Signal,* 23 January 1942; see also David N. Portman, *The Universities and the Public, A History of Higher Adult Education in the United States* (Chicago: Nelson-Hall, 1978) 135, 137; John Brubacher and J. Willis Rudy, *Higher Education in Transition,* (New York: Harper & Row, 1976) 225; *Evening Signal,* 23 January 1942, 1; *Junior Collegiate,* 22 January 1942, 1.

134 Regents, *Annual Report* (1942): 69; USG Center, annual report, 1942–1943, box 3, folder 31, Sparks Papers, SCGSU.

135 Labor market development report, 15 April 1943, Atlanta folder, Reports, Analysis, Compilations, Georgia, Region 7, RG 211; annual reports, 1942, 1943–1944, box 3, folder 31, Sparks Papers, SCGSU; *Junior Collegiate,* 18 February 1943, 1.

136 S. V. Sanford to George Sparks, 5 January 1944, box 40, folder 477, Sparks Papers, SCGSU; annual report, 1942–1943, box 3, folder 31, Sparks Papers, SCGSU; Regents, *Annual Report* (1943–1944): 67, 157.

137*Evening Signal,* 6 December 1944, 1; Regents, *Annual Report* (1943–1944): 158–60; Carter V. Good, comp., *A Guide to Colleges, Universities, and Professional Schools in the United States,* (Washington, D.C.: American Council on Education, 1946) 314.

138 Regents, *Annual Report* (1944–1945): 37–38.

CHAPTER 9

139 Student Council et al. to Hughes Spalding, 10 May 1933, box 17, folder 225, Sparks Papers, SCGSU.

140 Ibid.; George Manners, in discussion with the author and Gary M. Fink, 2 February 1989, 14–15, SCGSU.

141 George Manners, interview by Les Hough and Joe Constance, 7 March 1986, 20, 23, B. F. Wells, Jr. to Hughes Spalding, 10 May 1933, Student Council et al. to Spalding, 10 May 1933, Fred B. Wenn to W. V. Skiles, 28 August 1931, Skiles to George Sparks, 21 September 1931, box 17, folder 225, Sparks Papers, SCGSU; *Evening Signal,* 19 March 1934, 1; 2 November 1936, 1.

142 Committee on Student Activities report, 19 October 1933, box 11, folder 151, George Manners, interview by Les Hough and Joe Constance, 7 March 1986, 17–18, Sparks Papers, SCGSU; *Evening Signal,* 2 October 1933, 3.

143 Walter R. Benson to local businesses, n.d. [spring 1936], Atlanta Gas Light Company, reply, 29 May 1936, Retail Credit Company, reply, 6 May 1936, Committee on Student Activities report, 19 October 1933, box 11, folder 151, Sparks Papers, SCGSU; George Manners, interview by Les Hough and Joe Constance, 7 March 1986, 17–18, SCGSU.

144 (Georgia Tech) *Technite,* December 1926, October 1930–October 1932, GTA; *Evening Signal,* 2 October; 6 November 1933, 3; *Evening Signal,* 9 December 1935, 2; George Manners, interview by Les Hough and Joe Constance, 7 March 1986, 24; John Brubacher and J. Willis Rudy, *Higher Education in Transition,* (New York: Harper & Row, 1976) 136–37.

145 Committee on Student Activities report, 19 October 1933, box 11, folder 151, H. Reid Hunter to George Sparks, 20 May 1935, box 17, folder 225, Sparks Papers, SCGSU; *Evening Signal,* 23 March 1936; 2 May 1938, 1.

146 *Evening Signal,* 2 May 1938; 2 December 1938; 29 January 1941; Francis M. Osteen to Charles Snelling, 23 May 1935, box 38, folder 447, Sparks Papers, SCGSU.

147 *Evening Signal,* 6 November; 11 December 1933.

148 *Atlanta Journal,* 19 September 1937, 6A; *Atlanta Constitution,* 11 December 1933, 7; 23 May 1934, 12; George Manners, interview by Les Hough and Joe Constance, 7 March 1986, 24, SCGSU.

149 George Manners, interview by Les Hough and Joe Constance, 7 March 1986, 26, SCGSU; *University Signal,* 22 February 1946, 1.

150 *Junior Collegiate,* 2 December 1935; 24 January 1936, 1; *Atlanta Journal,* 17 November 1941, 11; fac. min., 30 October 1936, box 10, folder 172, register of student activities, girls of the Junior College of Atlanta, 1936–1937, George Sparks to Joe Alexander, 6 November 1937, Atlanta Junior College fac. meeting, 28 January 1938, box 6, folder 75, Sparks Papers, SCGSU; Tommie Dora Barker to Merle Walker, 15 March 1937, box 2, corres., 1938–1948, folder, RG73–4, SCGSU.

151 Craighead and Dwyer, 1931–1938, typescript, n.d. [1938], box 9, folder 122, Sparks Papers, George Manners, interview by Les Hough and Joe Constance, 7 March 1986, 20, SCGSU; *Evening Signal*, 2 June 1937; 1 September 1937; David O. Levine, *The American College and the Culture of Aspiration, 1915–1940* (Ithaca, NY: Cornell University Press) 75; Baker, "General History," 53.

152 Fac. min., 7 December 1935, box 13, folder 172, Sparks Papers, Regents, *Annual Report* (1939): 95, Regents, *Annual Report* (1941): 43, SCGSU; *Evening Signal*, 2 November 1936; William Ivy Hair, James C. Bonner, and Edward B. Dawson, *A History of Georgia College* (Milledgeville GA: Georgia College, 1976) 183–84.

153 Fac. min., 19 March 1935, 7 December 1935, box 13, folder 172, Sparks Papers, SCGSU; Levine, *The American College*, 201; Michael S. Holmes, *The New Deal in Georgia*, (Westport CT: Greenwood Press, 1975) 45.

154 *Evening Signal*, 5 June 1939, 1; W. O Cheney to George Sparks, 9 June 1942, box 39, folder 463, Sparks Papers, SCGSU.

155 Annual report, George Sparks to S. V. Sanford, 29 October 1937, box 3, folder 31, W. C. Parker to George Sparks, 8 April 1940, box 18, folder 226, Sparks Papers, SCGSU; Regents, *Annual Report* (1939): 113; Levine, *American College*, 62–63.

156 G. B. Strickler to T. M. McClellan, 17 June 1938, box 32, folder 402, Retail Credit Scholarship, box 39, folder 463, Sparks Papers, SCGSU.

157 Nell Trotter to John Dreyer, 24 November 1937, box 2, corres., 1938–1948, folder, G73–4, SCGSU; *Junior Collegiate*, 1 November 1939, 2; *Evening Signal*, 29 January 1936, 1; 30 March 1936, 1; 22 January 1937; *Junior Collegiate*, 9 March 1937, 1.

158 George Sparks to J. E. Rogers, 20 April 1938, box 6, folder 75, Sparks Papers, Annual Report, 1942, box 3, folder 31, SCGSU; *Evening Signal*, 25 March 1938, 1; 25 May 1942, 1.

159 *Evening Signal*, 1 June 1936, 1.

160 Fac. min., USGES, 4 February 1935, box 13, folder 172, Sparks Papers, SCGSU. Graduates Carl Herbig, Ewell Jackson, Howard Johnson, and Clyde Kitchens met with McClellan to organize the association, and Johnson became the first president. *Evening Signal*, 7 March 1938, 1; 25 March 1938, 1; 14 November 1938, 1.

161 *Junior Collegiate*, 16 November 1935, 1; 30 October 1935.

162 *Evening Signal*, 20 September 1937, 1; 14 October 1940, 1; *Georgia State Signal*, 16 October 1956; *Junior Collegiate*, 9 March 1937, 16 November 1938; George H. Boyd to Harmon W. Caldwell, 12 July 1948, box 1, grad. school, deans subject file, 1947–1954, adm. corres. to 1950 folder, UGA Records Management; George Sparks to Caldwell, 9 September 1949, box 34, folder 412, Sparks Papers, SCGSU; Gerald H. Davis, in discussion with the author, 30 November 1999, 6–7.

163 Fac. min., 29 November, 28 December 1933, 4 February 1935, box 13, folder 172, Sparks Papers, SCGSU.

164 Fac. min., 30 October 1936, box 13, folder 172, Annual Report, George Sparks to Charles M. Snelling, 30 June 1938, box 17, folder 225, Sparks Papers, SCGSU.

165 Fac. min., 30 October 1936, box 13, folder 172, Sparks Papers, SCGSU.

166 *Evening Signal*, 23 April 1943, 3; annual report, 1943–1944, box 3, folder 31, T. M. Forbes to George Sparks, 31 August 1942, R. O. Young to Sparks, 27 October 1942, box 18, folder 226, Sparks Papers, SCGSU.

167 Fac. min., 7 March, 10 September 1936, box 13, folder 172, Sparks Papers, SCGSU.

168 Atlanta Junior College, fac. meeting, 10 May 1938, box 6, folder 75, Sparks Papers, SCGSU.

169 Fac. min., 15 January 1940, box 6, folder 76, Sparks Papers, SCGSU.

170 Ibid.

171 Fac. min., 15 February 1940, box 13, folder 172, Sparks Papers, SCGSU.

CHAPTER 10

172 Annual report, 1942–1943, box 3, folder 43, annual report, 1940, fac. min., 8 December 1941, box 13, folder 172, Sparks Papers, SCGSU. For an excellent account of Talmadge's attacks on University System faculty and administrators, see Thomas G. Dyer, *The University of Georgia: A Bicentennial History, 1785–1985* (Athens GA: UGA Press, 1985) chapter 10; James F. Cook, "The Georgia Gubernatorial Election of 1942," *Atlanta Historical Bulletin* 18 (Spring–Summer 1973): 7–19.

173 Fac. min., 8 December 1941, box 13, folder 172, Sparks Papers, George Manners, interview by Les Hough and Joe Constance, 7 March 1986, 30, SCGSU; George Sparks to S. V. Sanford, 29 January 1943, box 51, study of potential for accreditation, 1943, folder, RG33-1-51, GDAH; Cook, "Election of 1942," 8.

174 George Sparks to S. V. Sanford, 29 January 1943, box 51, study of potential for accreditation, 1943, folder, RG33-1-51, GDAH.

175 Ibid.

176 George A. Works and Norman Burns, "The University System of Georgia Center" (December 1943) 2, Sparks Papers, SCGSU; English, *Emory University*, 44–45; Thomas H. English, *Emory University, 1915–1965* (Atlanta: Emory University, 1966).

177 Works and Burns, "University System of Georgia Center," 2–3, 5, box 30, folder 382, Sparks Papers, SCGSU.

178 Ibid., 2–3, 5–7; Regents, *Annual Report* (1943–1944): 157–58.

179 Works and Burns, "University System of Georgia Center," 10.

180 "Occupations of Graduates of Class of 1936," 30 June 1937, typescript, box 37, folder 443, Sparks Papers, SCGSU; George Manners to John W. Hall, March 1961, draft, box 15, folder 11, Manners Papers, George Manners, in discussion with the author and Gary M. Fink, 2 February 1989, 5, SCGSU.

181 Works and Burns, "University System of Georgia Center," 10; "Summary of Thinking Regarding the Operations of the Atlanta Division," n.d. [c. September 1954], typescript, box 3, Atlanta Division, confidential folder, Aderhold Papers, University Library, University of Georgia Libraries, hereinafter cited, UGL; Allan

Cartter, "Qualitative Aspects of Southern University Education," *Southern Economic Journal* 32 (July 1965): 40.

182 This organization should not be confused with the later amalgamation of the black Atlanta University and several other west-side institutions under the name Atlanta University Center. "Some Reactions to the Proposal that the Atlanta Evening College and Junior College be Made a Part of the University of Georgia," typescript, single spaced, n.d. [spring 1944], gen. adm. records of the chancellor, box 17, proposal, 1944 folder, RG33–1–51; Merl E. Reed, "The Struggle for State-Supported Higher Education in a Southern Regional Center: Atlanta and the 'Mother Institution,' 1944–1955," *Georgia Historical Quarterly* 80 (Fall 1996): 566; English, *Emory University*, 43–45.

183 "Some Reactions," [spring 1944], box 17, proposal, 1944, folder, RG33–1–51.

184 Excerpt, regents min., 31 August–1 September 1944, typescript, box 18, folder 227, Sparks Papers, SCGSU; resolution adopted by [UGA] adm. council, 5 January 1945, gen. adm. records of the chancellor, box 17, Proposal, 1944 folder, RG33–1–51; J. Martin Klotsche, *The Urban University and the Future of Our Cities*, (New York: Harper & Row, 1966) 95–96; see also Frederick M. Rosenstreter, *The Boundaries of the Campus: A History of the University of Wisconsin Extension Division, 1885–1945*, (Madison WI: University of Wisconsin Press, 1957) 161, and George M. Woytanowitz, *University Extension*, National Univserity Extension Association and the American College Testing Program, 1974, 121, 123, 154.

185 Excerpt, regents min., 31 August–1 September 1944, typescript, box 18, folder 227, Sparks Papers, SCGSU.

186 Resolutions adopted by the [UGA] adm. council, 5 January 1945, Harmon Caldwell to S. V. Sanford, 17 October 1944, box 17, adm. council folder, RG33–1–51; excerpt, regents min., 8 November 1944, box 18, folder 227, Sparks Papers, SCGSU.

187 S. V. Sanford to the regents, 8 December 1944, box 17, Proposal, 1944 folder, RG33–1–51; Rosenstreter, *University of Wisconsin Extension Division*, 94, 95, 124, 160–61; G. Stuart Demarest, *Faculty Organization at Rutgers*, Chicago Center for the Study of Liberal Education for Adults (1955) 1–24.

188 Resolutions adopted by the [UGA] adm. council, 5 January 1945, 3, 5, RG33–1–51 B417, GDAH.

189 George Sparks to Marion Smith, 12, 18 February 1945, box 32, folder 405, Sparks Papers, SCGSU.

CHAPTER 11

190 David Henry, *Challenges Past, Challenges Present: An Analysis of American Higher Education Since 1930*, (San Francisco: Jossey-Bass, 1975) 56–63.

191 USG Center, annual report, 1941, George Sparks to Marion Smith, 12 February 1945, box 32, folder 405, "A Resolution by the Board of Regents of the University System of Georgia," n.d. [8 August 1945], 3, box 6, folder 65, Sparks Papers, SCGSU; Thomas Evans Coulton, *A City College in Action* (NY: Harper & Brothers, 1955) 47; Leslie L. Hanawalt, *A Place of Light: the History of Wayne State University*, (Detroit MI: Wayne State University Press, 1968) 225.

192 Report on the Georgia Evening College to Governor Arnall, 5 April 1945, box 15, RG33–1–51; excerpts from the *Atlanta Constitution*, 7 April 1945, and the *Atlanta Journal*, 8, 10 April 1945, in George M. Sparks to F. A. Sams, 31 May, 6 June 1945, box 6, folder 65, Sparks Papers, George Manners, interview Les Hough and Joe Constance, 7 March 1986, 36, SCGSU; *University Signal*, 31 May 1945, 1; Numan V. Bartley, *The Creation of Modern Georgia* (Athens GA: UGA Press, 1990) 216.

193 Joseph S. Shaw to George Sparks, 29 May 1945, Sparks to Marion Smith, 3 November 1945, box 6, folder 65, Sparks to William Freeman, 20 June 1945, Ivy Street Garage University Center to George Levy, 15 February 1946, box 36, folder 433, excerpts from regents min., 11 July 1945, box 32, folder 405, Sparks Papers, George Manners, 24 March 1986, 49–51, SCGSU; John Brubacher and J. Willis Rudy, *Higher Education in Transition*, (New York: Harper & Row, 1976) 231–32.

194 After the regents learned that the building could be purchased for $296,000, they authorized that amount in August 1945. The Atlanta Center's Annual Report for 1946 stated the cost of the Ivy Street Garage's "self-liquidating program" at $301,000. Regents resolution, n.d. [8 August 1945], box 6 folder 65, annual report, July 1946, typescript, box 3 folder 32, Joseph Shaw to George Sparks, 29 May 1945, box 6, folder 65, Sparks Papers, SCGSU; George Manners, interview by Les Hough and Joe Constance, 24 March 1986; Flanders, *New Frontier* (Atlanta: Division, UGA) 40.

195 George Sparks to F. A. Sams, 6 June 1945, Sparks to C. J. Smith, 13 June 1945, Sparks to Marion Smith, 5 July 1945, box 6, folder 65, Sparks to William Freeman, 20 June 1945, box 36, folder 432, George Manners, interview by Les Hough and Joe Constance, 24 March 1986, 50, Sparks Papers, SCGSU.

196 George Sparks to A. L. Etheridge, 14 July 1945, regents resolution, n.d. [8 August 1945], George to C. J. Smith, 14 July 1945, regents resolution, n.d. [8 August 1945], 1–2, box 6, folder 65, Sparks Papers, George Manners, 24 March 1986, 50, SCGSU; notes on conversation with George Manners, 5 March 1999, in possession of author.

197 Several other smaller establishments completed the roster of tenants. Manager, Bolling Jones Building, Inc., to George Sparks, 30 June 1945, Sparks to C. J. Smith, 13 June 1945, Sparks to Marion Smith, 5 July 1945, Sparks to George A. Levy, 4 December 1945, box 6, folder 65, Robert B. Troutman to Marion Smith, 14 December 1945, box 32, folder 405, Sparks to Marion Smith, 1 July 1946, annual report, 1946, SCGSU; Sparks to Marion Smith, 11 March 1946, excerpt from regents min., 12 June 1946, box 33, folder 406, excerpt from regents min., 14 August, 1946, L. R. Siebert to Sparks, 13 September 1946, box 33, folder 407, Hal Hulsey to William K. Meadow, 21 July 1948, Jean McDonald et al. to Sparks, 28 June 1946, Siebert to Sparks, 16 January 1947, box 36, folder 433, Sparks Papers, SCGSU; Richard G. Axt, *The Federal Government and Financing Higher Education*, (New York: Columbia University Press, 1952) 132.

198 The catalog with the original tuition error could not be located. Bulletin, Atlanta Division, UGA, 1947–1948, 22; University and Administrative Catalogs/Bulletins, box 64, statement of estimated income ending 30 June 1947, 1948, 1949, 1950, vice president for financial affairs, box 18, folder 6, report of examination, University System Center, 30 June 1947, vice president for financial affairs, audit, box 9, folder 3, G75–20; George Sparks to Ed Green, 31 October 1945, "Report Upon University of Georgia System Center," 1 July 1946, box 6, folder 65; Leonard Siebert to Sparks, 7

July 1947, quoting regents min., 11 June 1957, box 33, folder 409, Sparks Papers, SCGSU; oral interview by Les Hough and Joe Constance with George Manners, 24 March 1986, 51, George Manners, in discussion with the author and Gary M. Fink, 2 February 1989, 2–4, SCGSU.

199 George Sparks to Faber A. Bollinger, August 13, 1945, Sparks to Marion Smith, 14 August 1945, Sparks to Tucker and Howell, 3 October 1945, box 6, folder 65, Sparks Papers, SCGSU.

200 George Sparks to Marion Smith, 16 August 1945, Sparks to Faber A. Bollinger, 13 August 1945, Sparks to Ed Green, 31 October 1945, box 6, folder 65, W. B. Hartsfield to George Sparks, 14 August 1945, box 36, folder 432, Sparks Papers; George Manners, interview by Les Hough and Joe Constance, 7 March 1986, 30–31, SCGSU.

201 Leonard Siebert to the Heads, 31 October 1945, 18 March 1956, box 32, folder 405, Sparks Papers, SCGSU.

202 George Sparks to Marion Smith, 21 September, 13 October, 3 November, 11 December 1945, box 6, folder 65, 5 April 1946, box 33, folder 406, University System Center, Surplus Property, n.d. [fall 1945 and spring 1946], typescripts, box 31, folder 213, University of Minnesota, Center for Continuation Study, 12 November 1947, 2, box 38, folder 448, Sparks Papers, SCGSU; *(GSC) University Signal,* 10 November 1945, 1.

203 George Sparks to Marion Smith, 5 April 1946, Sparks to Miller Bell, 8 July 1946, box 33, folder 406, "Report Upon the University System of Georgia Center," 1 July 1946, 4, box 6, folder 65, Sparks Papers, SCGSU.

204 "Report Upon University System of Georgia Center," 1 July 1946, George Sparks to C. J. Smith, 6 December 1946, box 6, folder 65, "Report on Air Conditioning Equipment for Georgia Evening College," 28 August 1946, box 13, folder 213, Sparks to Marion Smith, 29 May 1947, box 33, folder 408, L. R. Siebert to Presidents, 17 August 1946, box 17, folder 213, Sparks Papers, SCGSU; *University Signal,* 24 September, 29, 3; 23 October 1946, 1; Axt, *Federal Government and Financing Higher Education,* 136–37.

205 "Report Upon University System of Georgia Center," 1 July 1946, Sparks to C. J. Smith, 6 December 1946, box 6, folder 65, "Report on Air Conditioning Equipment for Georgia Evening College," 28 August 1946, box 13, folder 213, Sparks Papers, SCGSU; *University Signal,* 24 September 1946, 1; Axt, *Federal Government and Financing Higher Education,* 137.

206 For a listing of the lots that the director in 1948 hoped to acquire, see George Sparks to L. R. Siebert, 12 January 1948, Sparks to L. E. Siebert, 13 October 1945, box 6 folder 65, regents resolution, 14 December 1945, box 32, folder 405, Sparks to Marion Smith, 5 April 1946, box 33, folder 406, Sparks Papers, SCGSU.

207 Sparks to Marion Smith, 29 May 1947, box 33, folder 408, Alvin Biscoe to James Gates, 13 July 1948, box 20, folder 260, Sparks Papers, SCGSU.

208 J. C. Wardlaw to L. R. Siebert, 24 October 1946, gen. extension, 1946–1951 folder, box 29, RG33–1–51.

209 "Report Upon University System of Georgia Center," 1 July 1946, 4, 5, George Sparks to Marion Smith, 8 November 1945, box 6 folder 65, Sparks Papers, SCGSU.

CHAPTER 12

210 Andrew Marshall Hamer, "Urban Perspective for the 1980s," *Urban Atlanta: Redefining the Role of the City,* ed. Andrew Marshall Hamer (Atlanta: GSU College of Business Administration, 1980) 6–7; Truman A. Hartshorn, S. Davis, G. E. Dever, P. R. Allen, and S. Bederman, *Metropolis in Georgia: Atlanta's Rise as a Major Transaction Center* (Cambridge MA: Ballinger, 1976) 4–5; Bradley R. Rice, "If Dixie Were Atlanta," in *Sunbelt Cities: Politics and Growth Since World War II,* eds. Richard M Bernard and Bradley R. Rice (Austin TX: University of Texas Press, 1983) 33–34.

211 United States 17th Census, *Census of Population, 1950* (Washington D.C.: 1952); Rice, "If Dixie Were Atlanta," 34, 36; Richard S. Combes, "Aircraft Manufacturing in Georgia: A Case Study of Federal Industrial Investment," 10, unpublished paper presented on 6 June 1998 at a conference on Southern industrialization held at the Georgia Institute of Technology, in possession of the author; Hartshorn et al., *Metropolis,* 15–16.

212 The University System Center was officially named the Atlanta Division of the UGA by the regents on 7 April 1948. Excerpt from regents min., 4 April 1948, box 6, folder 68. The faculty committees were curriculum, admissions, standing, honors, and student activities; and the departments: biology, business administration, chemistry, economics, history, languages, mathematics, physics, psychology, and sociology. Min., ex. council, 25 January 1946, min., dept. chairs, 29 May 1946, box 13, folder 172, Sparks Papers, SCGSU.

213 L. R. Siebert to George M. Sparks, 19 February, 2 April 1946, Sparks to Siebert, 6 May 1946, box 33, folder 406, Sparks Papers, SCGSU.

214 George Sparks to L. R. Siebert, 8 April 1946, box 33, folder 406, Sparks Papers, SCGSU.

215 Ibid.; M. C. Huntley to George Sparks, 5 April 1946, box 40, folder 477, Sparks Papers, SCGSU.

216 George Sparks to W. Wilson Noyes, 2 May 1946, vice president for financial affairs, box 18, folder 7, G75–20, Sparks to L. R. Siebert, 6 May, 12 July 1946, box 33, folder 406, Sparks Papers, SCGSU.

217 Sparks to L. R. Siebert, 12 July 1946, box 33, folder 406, Sparks Papers, SCGSU.

218 George Manners, interview by Les Hough and Joe Constance, 24 March 1986, 52, Manners, "Reminiscences," 381–82, SCGSU.

219 "Recommendations of the Atlanta Division," n.d. [spring 1947], box 6, folder 73, Sparks Papers, SCGSU.

220 Ibid.

221 Regents min., 7 March 1946, box 33, folder 406, Sparks Papers, SCGSU.

CHAPTER 13

222 George Manners, interview by Les Hough and Joe Constance, 24 March 1947, 56, SCGSU.

223 Thomas G. Dyer, *The University of Georgia: A Bicentennial History, 1785–1985* (Athens GA: UGA Press, 1985) 291–93; see also Merl E. Reed, "The Struggle for State-

281

Supported Higher Education in a Southern Regional Center: Atlanta and the 'Mother Institution,' 1944–1955," *Georgia Historical Quarterly* 80 (Fall 1996).

224 Dyer, *University of Georgia*, 261–62; Phinizy Spalding, *The History of the Medical College of Georgia* (Athens GA: UGA Press, 1987) 80–81, 123.

225 Alvin B. Biscoe to George Sparks, 24 July 1947, box 6, folder 68, Sparks Papers, George Manners, interview by Les Hough and Joe Constance, 24 March 1986, 52–53, SCGSU; "Survey of the Atlanta Division of the University of Georgia," n.d. [January 1955], typescript, 1–3, Exhibit "A," box 3, Atlanta Division, 1954–1955, folder, Aderhold Papers, UGAL.

226 "Survey of the Atlanta Division of the University of Georgia," n.d. [January 1955], typescript, Exhibit "A," box 3, Atlanta Division, 1954–1955, folder, Aderhold Papers, UGAL; bylaws of the UGA Atlanta Division, n.d. [summer 1947], typescript, box 6, folder 70, Sparks Papers, SCGSU, min., gen. fac. meeting, 17 October 1947, box 30, gen. file, 1948 folder, RG33–1–51, GDAH; Alvin B. Biscoe to Leon P. Smith, 22 December 1957, Smith to heads of departments, 4 May 1948, box 13, Atlanta Division, 1947–1957, folder, Suttles Papers; *University Signal*, 22 September 1947, 1; 15 October 1947.

227 Alvin Biscoe to George Sparks, 2 August 1947, box 6, folder 68, Sparks Papers, SCGSU, Biscoe to Leon P. Smith, 22 December 1947, box 13, Atlanta Division, 1947–1957 folder, Suttles Papers; Biscoe to Harmon Caldwell, 6 October 1947, box 17, Proposal, 1944 folder, RG33–1–51.

228 William M. Randall to George Sparks, box 21, folder 264, Sparks to Alvin B. Biscoe, 11 August 1947, Biscoe to Sparks, 2 September 1947, box 20, folder 260, Sparks Papers, SCGSU; *University Signal*, 22 September 1947, 1.

229 Harmon Caldwell to Ed Bridges, 25 September 1947, box 32, Atlanta Division folder, Caldwell Papers; Alvin Biscoe to George Sparks, 29 September 1947, box 20, folder 260, Sparks Papers, SCGSU.

230 Report of conference, Athens College of Business Administration, 22 September 1947, box 21, folder 264, Sparks Papers, SCGSU; George Manners to John W. Hall, March 1961, draft, 7–9, box 15, folder 11, Manners Papers, SCGSU.

231 Report of conference, Athens College of Business Administration, 22 September 1947, box 21, folder 264, Sparks Papers, SCGSU; accounting conference, 11 October 1947, mimeographed, 1, box 42, folder 8, G73–8, SCGSU.

232 Report of conference, Athens College of Business Administration, 22 September 1947, box 21, folder 264, Sparks Papers, SCGSU.

233 George Manners, interview by Les Hough and Joe Constance, 24 March 1986, 57–58, George Manners, in discussion with the author and Gary M. Fink, 2 February 1989, 5–6, SCGSU. "Survey of the Atlanta Division of the University of Georgia," n.d. [January 1955], typescript, Exhibit "B," from fac. min., 17 October 1947, box 3, Atlanta Division, 1954–1955, folder, Aderhold Papers, UGAL.

234 George Manners, interview by Les Hough and Joe Constance, 24 March 1986, 58.

235 Ibid.; "Survey of the Atlanta Division of the University of Georgia," n.d. [January 1955], typescript, Exhibit "C," Alvin B. Biscoe to George M. Sparks, 19 December 1947, box 3, Atlanta Division 1954–1955 folder, Thomas Mahler, "Summary of

Thinking Regarding the Operations of the Atlanta Division," 1 September 1954, typescript, Atlanta Division, confidential, Aderhold Papers, UGAL; Sparks to Biscoe, 22 December 1947, box 69, Atlanta Division-Biology folder, RG 2, Records Management, UGA; Dyer, *University of Georgia*, 262.

236 Leon P. Smith to N. S. Herod, 5 March 1948, box 20, fold 259, Oscar J. Campbell to James Routh, 16 March 1948, Smith to Edwin M. Everett, 2 February 1948, Everett to Routh, 16 March 1948, Routh to Everett, 19 August 1948, box 11, folder 149, Sparks Papers, SCGSU.

237 Alvin Biscoe to George Sparks, 5 October 1948, Atlanta Division, box 32, Caldwell Papers; Sparks to Pope Brock, 1 October 1948, box 6, folder 65, Tomlinson Fort to V. V. Lavroff, 15 March 1949, box 20, folder 259, 15 February 1950, box 21, folder 264, Sparks to Harry T. Healy, 11 October 1948, box 20, folder 260, Sparks Papers, SCGSU; J. D. Bolton to George Manners, 18 June 1948, box 1, folder 2, gen. corres, "B," G82–10, SCGSU; Harmon Caldwell to Leon P. Smith, 17 April 1948, box 69, Atlanta Division-Biology folder, RG 2, UGA Records Management; George Manners, in discussion with the author and Gary M. Fink, 2 February 1989, 10, SCGSU.

238 George Sparks to Harmon Caldwell, 16 August 1948, box 33, folder 410, Sparks to Leon Smith, 16 August 1948, box 20, folder 259, Sparks Papers, SCGSU; Smith to Caldwell, 18 August 1948, box 69, Atlanta Division-Biology folder, RG 2, UGA Records Management; Caldwell to Smith, 19 August 1948, box 32, Atlanta Division folder, Caldwell Papers.

239 George Sparks to Leon P. Smith, 2 June 1948, box 20, folder 259, Edwin M. Everett to James Routh, 19 August 1948, Sparks to Frank R. Neuffer, 9 August 1949, box 11, folder 149, Sparks Papers, SCGSU; Smith to heads of departments, 18 August 1948, Smith to O. C. Aderhold et al., 2 February 1949, box 69, Atlanta Division-Biology folder, RG 2, UGA Records Management; Alvin Biscoe to S. Walter Martin, 29 July, 15 September 1949, Biscoe to Aderhold, 15 September 1949, Biscoe to James E. Gates, 29 July 1949, Analysis of Grades, Arts and Sciences, Bus. Adm., Summer Quarter, 1949, Winter Quarter, 1950, Atlanta Division folder, Rogers Papers, UGAL.

240 Lamar Dodd to Newton S. Herod, 3 October 1947, Herod to Dodd, 31 October 1947, box 20, folder 259, George Sparks to Dodd, 6 April 1948, Dodd to Sparks, 13 April 1948, Dodd to Hal Hulsey, 13, 17 August 1948, University of Georgia and the Atlanta Branch-Music Department, from Hugh Hodgson, n.d. [April 1948], Hodgson to Sparks, 30 April 1948, Hulsey to Hodgson, 29 April 1948, Sparks to Hodgson, 24 May 1948, Hodgson to Sparks, 5 July 1948, box 20, folder 259, Herbert D. Oliver to Harmon Caldwell, 1 November 1948, box 21, folder 266, Sparks Papers, SCGSU; *University Signal*, 21 October 1948, 1.

241 Hugh Hodgson to George Sparks, 25 May, 5 July 1948, Mrs. W. C. Cantrell to Hodgson, 29 May 1950, Hodgson to Sparks, 27 September 1951, Leighton M. Ballew to Sparks, 5 August 1948, box 20, folder 259, Sparks to Alvin Biscoe, 11 July 1949, box 20, folder 260, Sparks Papers, min., adm. council, 8 June 1965, box 19, folder 3, G73–8, SCGSU; *University Signal*, 6 October 1948, 1.

242 James E. Gates to G. H. Boyd, 20 June 1951, box 72, James Gates folder, RG 2, UGA Records Management; George E. Manners to George Sparks and Thomas Mahler, 22 June 1954, box 7, folder 88, John P. Gill to Mahler, 31 July 1954, box 26, folder 324, Sparks Papers, SCGSU.

283

243 James Gates to George Manners, 28 September 1948, box 12, folder 47, G73–8, George Sparks to Leon P. Smith, 11 June 1948, box 20, folder 259, Sparks Papers, SCGSU.

244 M. C. Huntley to Harmon Caldwell, 22 June 1948, box 15, SAC folder, RG33–1–51. For a lengthy analysis of this failure by a UGA faculty member, see M. C. Prunty, "Educational Operations in the Atlanta Division of the University of Georgia," 1950–1951, typescript, 29 August 1951, 3, Atlanta Division Report, box 3, Atlanta Division to 30 June 1952 folder, Caldwell Papers.

CHAPTER 14

245 Conference of joint committee...of adm. officers, 28 September 1948, box 6, folder 73, George Sparks to Pope Brock, 1 October 1948, box 6, folder 65, Sparks Papers, SCGSU.

246 "Atlanta Division-Procedures," 1 October 1948, Exhibit "E," in O. C. Aderhold, "A Progress Report Regarding the Integration of the Atlanta Division," n.d., [1955], box 3, Atlanta Division, 1954–1955, folder, Aderhold Papers, UGAL; conference of joint committee...of administrative officers, 28 September 1948, George Sparks to Pope Brock, 1 October 1948, box 6, folder 65, Sparks Papers, SCGSU; *University Signal*, 6 October 1948, 1; *Atlanta Constitution*, 6 October 1948, 18.

247 George Sparks to Carl Gray, Jr., 23 February 1949, Sparks to Dillard B. Lasseter, 24 February 1949, box 43, folder 521, Sparks Papers, SCGSU; J. Thomas Askew to Sparks, 13 November 1947, box 32, Atlanta Division folder, Caldwell Papers, UGAL; *Bulletin of the University of Georgia, General Catalog, 1947–1948*, 58.

248 J. Thomas Askew to George Sparks, 13 November 1947, box 32, Atlanta Division folder, Caldwell Papers; Askew to Alvin B. Biscoe, 5 April 1948, box 20, folder 260, John E. Sims to Harmon Caldwell, 8 January 1949, Sparks to M. D. Mobley, 1 March 1959, box 43, folder 521, Sparks Papers, SCGSU.

249 Anonymous to Drew Pearson, 24 January 1949, George Manners to Pearson, 25 Jan 1949, box 16, gen. file 1950–1956, folder, RG33–1–51, GDAH; George Sparks to Dillard B. Lasseter, 24 February 1949, box 43, folder 521, Sparks Papers, SCGSU.

250 *University Signal*, 6 December 1948, 1; mem., conversation between M. C. Huntley and E. A. Lowe, 17 February 1949, Atlanta Division, Rogers Papers, UGAL; Harmon Caldwell to A. M. Hoffar, 31 March 1950, gen. file, 1950–1956, folder, box 16, RG33–1–51; Thomas G. Dyer, *The University of Georgia: A Bicentennial History, 1785–1985* (Athens GA: UGA Press, 1985) 267–68.

251 Mem., conversation between M. C. Huntley and E. A. Lowe, 17 February 1949, Atlanta Division, Rogers Papers.

252 Ibid.; confidential report of Raymond Styles to L. R. Siebert, 4 January 1946, box 15, RG33–1–51; mem., conversation between M. C. Huntley and E. A. Lowe, 17 February 1949, Atlanta Division, Rogers Papers; George Sparks to J. C. Rogers, 21 March 1949, box 21, folder 266, Sparks Papers, George Manners, in discussion with the author and Gary M. Fink, 2 February 1989, Tape 1, 47–48, SCGSU; *Atlanta Constitution*, 9 January 1951.

253 Harmon Caldwell to J. C. Rogers, 1 March 1949, A&S, 1943–1954, folder, box 51, RG33–1–51; George Sparks to Rogers, 21 March 1949, box 21, folder 266, Sparks Papers, SCGSU.

254 George Sparks to J. C. Rogers, 21, 24 March 1949, Rogers to Sparks, 23 March 1949, box 21, folder, 266, Sparks Papers, SCGSU.

255 Regents resolution, 29 March 1949, quoted in J. C. Rogers to Harmon Caldwell, 21 February 1950, Atlanta Division folder, Rogers Papers; L. R. Siebert to Heads of All Units, 15 March 1949, box 34, folder 411, Sparks Papers, J. M. Goddard to Harmon Caldwell, 3 December 1959, box 30, Regents, 1949–1960, folder, Suttles Papers, SCGSU; *Atlanta Constitution*, 6 February 1949, 6; Dyer, *University of Georgia*, 294.

256 "Act to Create the University Building Authority," n.d. [spring 1949], box 24, folder 411, George Sparks to Francis Stubbs, 26 July 1949, box 37, folder 435, Sparks to Robert Arnold, n.d. [c. 1956], box 6, Folder 79, Sparks Papers, SCGSU; *University Signal*, 9 March 1949.

CHAPTER 15

257 George Sparks to Harmon Caldwell, 15 July 1949, box 34, folder 412, Sparks Papers, SCGSU; *Atlanta Constitution*, 8 December 1949, 4; Thomas G. Dyer, *The University of Georgia: A Bicentennial History, 1785–1985* (Athens GA: UGA Press, 1985) 269; Fincher, *University System of Georgia*, 35, 39.

258 J. C. Rogers to Mary Frances Ward, 21 July 1949, S. Walter Martin to George Sparks, 6 October 1950, box 21, folder 266, Sparks Papers, SCGSU; *University Signal*, 7 December 1949, 8.

259 S. Walter Martin to George H. Boyd, 3 March 1950, vice president for academic affairs, graduate school, dean's subject file, 1947–1954, box 1, S. Walter Martin Folder, UGA Records Management; Martin to James E. Gates, 9 June 1950, Atlanta Division folder, Rogers Papers, UGAL.

260 George Sparks to William K. Meadow, 21 July 1948, box 36, folder 433, Sparks Papers, SCGSU; *University Signal*, 18 February 1948; 8 April 1949, 1; 12 October 1949, 1; *Atlanta Constitution*, 6 February 1949, 6.

261 Regents, *Annual Report* (1948–1949): 26, 38, 57, 65, 76; instructional costs, box 9, series 1, University System misc., 1967–1974, Langdale Papers, SCGSU.

262 Leland Dean to Harmon Caldwell et al., 27 October 1949, box 34, folder 412, Sparks Papers, SCGSU.

263 George D. Strayer et al., *A Report of a Survey of the University System of Georgia* (1949) 26, 76, box 1, RG33–1–32, GDAH; Regents, *Annual Report* (1948–1949): 17; Scott, *Crisis Management*, 90–91; Winfred L. Godwin, "The Southern Regional Education Board—A Public Regional System," *Higher Education: From Autonomy to Systems*, ed. James A. Perkins (New York: International Council for Educational Development, 1972) 67; Dyer, *University of Georgia*, 269–70.

264 Strayer, *Report*, 75–76; J. M. Goddard to Harmon Caldwell, 8 December 1949, quoted in J. C. Rogers to Caldwell, 21 February 1950, Atlanta Division folder, Rogers Papers; Dyer, *University of Georgia*, 269–70.

265 J. C. Rogers to Harmon Caldwell, 12 January 1950, gen. adm., records of the chancellor, accreditation corres. and reports, box 16, 1944–1951, folder, RG33-1-51; Rogers to Caldwell, 21 February, 7, 10 March 1950, L. R. Siebert to Rogers, 22 March 1950, Atlanta Division folder, Rogers Papers; Sparks to Rogers, 10 March 1950, box 21, folder 266, Sparks Papers, George Manners, interview by Les Hough and Joe Constance, 24 March 1986, SCGSU.

266 L. R. Siebert to All Presidents, 3 April 1950, box 34, folder 413, Sparks Papers, SCGSU; J. C. Rogers to James R. McCain, Rogers to J. G. Stipe, Rogers to Sparks, all 27 March 1950, Atlanta Division folder, Rogers Papers; George Manners to Merl Reed, 5 March 1999, in possession of the author; *Atlanta Journal*, 22 March 1950, 1; *Atlanta Journal*, 3 April 1950, 1, 14, 18; *University Signal*, 1 April 1950, 5; 20 April 1950, 6–7.

267 J. C. Rogers to William S. Morris, 3 May 1950, Rogers to Hughes Spalding, 4 May 1950, Rogers to Harmon Caldwell, 5 May 1950, box 15, Director…1950, folder, RG33-1-51, GDAH; Rogers to R. L. Brantley, 13 June 1950, Atlanta Division directorship folder, Rogers Papers, O. C. Aderhold to Henry King Stanford, 29 May 1953, box 3, Atlanta Division to 30 June 1954, folder, Aderhold Papers, UGAL; *University Signal*, 17 May 1950, 1.

268 Dyer, *University of Georgia*, 278–82.

269 George Sparks to Wippert Stumpf, 3 December 1947, box 21, folder 264, report of survey, June 23–24, 1950, by F. W. Stamm [vice president, University of Louisville], report of a visit to the Atlanta Division, June 21–22, 1950, by Roger P. McCutcheon, [graduate school dean, Tulane University], report of visit to Atlanta Division of the University of Georgia, June 26–28, 1950, by R. L. Brantley [president, Virginia Intermont College], box 6, folder 73, Sparks Papers, hereinafter collectively cited as Atlanta Division Survey, 1950, SCGSU.

270 Atlanta Division Survey, 1950.

271 Ibid.

272 Ibid.

273 Ibid.; fac. min., 6 December 1950, box 16, fac. meeting min., 1951–1956, folder, RG31-1-51.

274 Typescript, draft, untitled, n.d. [c. July 1950], 2, box 6, folder 65, "Suggestions for the Operation of the Atlanta Division of the University of Georgia," typescript, draft, n.d. [c. August 1950], box 6, folder 73, Sparks Papers, SCGSU; Dyer, *University of Georgia*, 281.

275 James E. Gates to O. C. Aderhold, 11 August 1950, box 3, Atlanta Division folder, Aderhold Papers, UGAL.

276 James E. Gates to O. C. Aderhold, 5 September 1950, box 3, Atlanta Division folder, Aderhold Papers, UGAL.

277 "Notes on the Report of the Chancellor," typescript, confidential, n.d. [April 1955], Atlanta Division, Aderhold Papers, UGAL; L. R. Siebert to George Sparks, Siebert to O. C. Aderhold, 15 September 1950, box 34, folder 414, Sparks Papers, "Memorandum of Understanding Regarding the Atlanta Division of the University," 13 September 1950, box 46, folder 17, G73-8, George Manners to John W. Hall, March 1961, draft, 12–13, box 15, folder 11, Manners Papers, SCGSU.

278 "Memorandum of Understanding," 13 September 1950, box 6, folder 73, Sparks Papers, George Manners, interview by Les Hough and Joe Constance, 26 March 1986, 95–96, SCGSU.

CHAPTER 16

279 George D. Strayer et al., *A Report of a Survey of the University System of Georgia* (1949) 76, box 1, RG33–1–51, GDAH; George Manners to Alvin B. Biscoe, personal, 18 April 1950, box 38, folder 7, G73–8, SCGSU.

280 George Manners to Alvin B. Biscoe, personal, 18 April 1950, box 38, folder 7, G73–8, SCGSU.

281 Ibid.; George H. Boyd to James Gates, 28 September 1950, box 3, Atlanta Division to 30 June 1951, folder, Aderhold Papers, UGAL; Boyd to Gates, 23 March 1951, box 72, James Gates folder, RG2, UGA Records Management.

282 *Atlanta Alumnus* 1/1 (October 1950): 4, George Sparks to Mr. Hal Hulsey, Mr. George Manners, Mr. V. V. Lavroff, Mr. J. D. Blair, and Mr. J. C. Camp, 14 September 1950, box 6, folder 75, Sparks Papers, SCGSU; M. C. Prunty, Educational Operations in the Atlanta Division of the University of Georgia, 1950–1951, typescript, August 1951, 4, Atlanta Division Report folder, box 3, Atlanta Division to 30 June 1952, folder, Caldwell Papers, UGAL.

283 George Sparks to O. C. Aderhold, 28 September 1950, box 20, folder 257, Sparks Papers, SCGSU.

284 S. Walter Martin to George Sparks, 6 October 1950, box 21, folder 264, Martin to Sparks, 7 November 1950, box 20, folder 259, O. C. Aderhold to Sparks, 5 February 1951, box 20, folder 257, Sparks Papers, SCGSU; Martin to Aderhold, n.d. [November 1950], Aderhold to Alvin Biscoe, 18 October 1950, box 3, Atlanta Division folder to 30 June 1951, Aderhold Papers, UGAL; Merl E. Reed, "The Struggle for State-Supported Higher Education in a Southern Regional Center: Atlanta and the 'Mother Institution,' 1944–1955," *Georgia Historical Quarterly* 80 (Fall 1996): 575.

285 George Manners to George Sparks, 1 December 1953, box 7, folder 88, Sparks to O. C. Aderhold, 24 March 1951, box 20, folder 257, Sparks Papers, SCGSU.

286 O. C. Aderhold to George Sparks, 26 March 1951, box 20, folder 257, Sparks Papers, SCGSU; George Manners to Merl Reed, 5 March 1999, in possession of the author.

287 George Sparks to O. C. Aderhold, 29 March 1951, box 20, folder 257, Sparks Papers, SCGSU.

288 O. C. Aderhold to George Sparks, 6 April 1951, box 3, Atlanta Division to 30 June 1951, folder, Aderhold Papers, UGAL.

289 O. C. Aderhold to Frank D. Foley, 29 April 1954, Aderhold to Paul E. Pfuetze, 10 November 1954, box 3, Atlanta Division to June 30, 1954, folder, Aderhold Papers, UGAL; Aderhold to George Sparks, 5, 13 April, 1951, George Sparks to O. C. Aderhold, 18 May 1951, box 20, folder 257, Sparks Papers, SCGSU.

290 Mem., S. Walter Martin to O. C. Aderhold, 21 July 1951, Merle C. Prunty to Martin, 18 June 1953, Martin to Prunty, 29 June 1953, box 3, Atlanta Division to June 30, 1952, folder, Aderhold Papers, UGAL.

291 O. C. Aderhold to Paul E. Pfuetze, 10 November 1954, Harmon Caldwell to O. C. Aderhold, 27 June 1952, box 3, Atlanta Division 1954–1955, folder, T. W. Mahler to Aderhold, 13 September 1954, Atlanta Division, confidential folder, Aderhold Papers, UGAL; George E. Manners, "Reminiscences on the Building of Georgia State University," typescript, n.d. [1989], 155–58, SCGSU.

292 M. C. Prunty to Harmon Caldwell, 29 August 1951, Prunty, Educational Operations in the Atlanta Division, 1950–1951, 6, 9–17, box 3, Atlanta Division report folder, Caldwell Papers; J. C. Horton Burch to George Sparks, 1 June 1956, Sparks Papers, SCGSU; George Manners to Merl Reed, 5 March 1999, in possession of the author.

293 Prunty, "Educational Operations," 14–16, 20, 31–33, box 15, Chancellor's Records, GDAH. For a discussion of the class of 1936, see chapters 7 and 10.

294 Ibid., 17–25, 37, 39, 45.

295 Ibid., 48–49.

296 Ibid., 53–57.

297 Ibid., 71–72.

298 Ibid., 68–69.

299 Ibid.

300 "Special Study of the Atlanta Division of the University of Georgia," 2–5 March 1952, O. C. Aderhold to Frank D. Foley, personal and confidential, 24 March 1955, box 1, Atlanta Division folder, Aderhold Papers, UGAL; Educational and General Allotments, 1951–1952, box 34, folder 415, Sparks Papers, SCGSU.

301 "Special Study of the Atlanta Division," box 1, Atlanta Division folder, Aderhold Papers, UGAL.

CHAPTER 17

302 George Sparks to Robert Arnold, n.d. [c. January 1955], box 6, folder 79, Sparks Papers, SCGSU; *University Signal*, 6 June 1951, 4; 22 February 1952, 1; 6 March 1953, 1; *Atlanta Constitution*, 12, 17 June 1951.

303 James E. Gates to Alvin B. Biscoe, 1 October 1951, Biscoe to O. C. Aderhold, 4 October 1951, box 3, Atlanta Division to June 30, 1952, folder, Thomas Mahler, "Summary of Thinking Regarding the Operations of the Atlanta Division," 1 September 1954, typescript, 3, Atlanta Division, confidential, Aderhold Papers, UGAL; Gates to George E. Manners, 19 April 1948, box 42, folder 8, G73–8, SCGSU.

304 Mem., Ole S. Johnson to All Members of the Advisory Committee for the Fourth Annual Retailing Clinic, 20 June 1952, tentative program, Fourth Annual Atlanta Retailing Clinic, 15 October 1952, box 42, folder 8, G73–8; Merl E. Reed, "The Struggle for State-Supported Higher Education in a Southern Regional Center: Atlanta and the 'Mother Institution,' 1944–1955," *Georgia Historical Quarterly* 80 (Fall 1996): 579–80.

305 Jennings Randolph to George Sparks, 25 May 1950, James L. Campbell to Sparks, 23 May 1952, box 42, folder 8, G73–8; O. C. Aderhold to Thomas Mahler, 22 September 1952, box 3, Atlanta Division to June 30, 1952, folder, Aderhold Papers, UGAL; *University Signal*, 18 January 1952, 1; 25 January 1952, 1.

306 Community Services, Atlanta Division-University of Georgia, 1952–1953, box 3, folder 34, Sparks Papers, SCGSU; O. C. Aderhold to Henry King Stanford, 29 May 1953, Aderhold to Charles J. Bloch, 23 May 1953, box 3, Atlanta Division to June 30, 1954, folder, Aderhold Papers, UGAL.

307 E. J. Soop to Harmon Caldwell, 8 June 1955, box 15, Chancellor's Study…1955, folder, Emory A. Johnston to Herman Talmadge, 23 October 1952, box 17, Graduate School…1949–1955, folder, RG33–1–51, GDAH; George H. Boyd to James Gates, 28 September 1950, box 3, Atlanta Division to 30 June 1951, folder, Aderhold Papers, UGAL; Boyd to Gates, 23 March 1951, box 72, James B. Gates folder, RG2, UGA Records Management.

308 Herman Talmadge to R. O. Arnold, 23 May 1951, box 41, folder 505, O. C. Aderhold to Harmon W. Caldwell, 11 June 1951, box 20, folder 257, Sparks Papers, SCGSU; George Manners, interview by Les Hough and Joe Constance, 8 April 1986, 125, SCGSU.

289

309 O. C. Aderhold to Harmon W. Caldwell, 11 June 1951, box 20, folder 257, Sparks Papers, SCGSU.

310 Mrs. B. V. Wolfe to Herman Talmadge, 15 November 1951, box 41, folder 505, O. C. Aderhold to Harmon W. Caldwell, 11 June 1951, box 20, folder 257, Sparks Papers, SCGSU; George E. Manners to Aderhold, draft copy, 20 November 1951, box 35, folder 9, G73–8; Mary Elizabeth Smith to Board of Regents, 30 June 1953, box 17, Graduate School…1949–1955, folder, RG33–1–51.

311 Mem., George Manners to T. W. Mahler, 26 March 1952, box 49, folder 14, G73–8, Charles J. Bloch to Howard B. Harmon, 16 December 1952, box 6, folder 79, Sparks Papers, SCGSU; Emory A. Johnston to Herman Talmadge, 23 October 1952, Harmon Caldwell to Johnston, 24 November 1952, O. C. Aderhold to Caldwell, 4 July 1952, Henry King Stanford to Aderhold, 12 July 1952, Mary Elizabeth Smith to board of regents, 30 June 1953, Oren Warren to Talmadge, 24 September 1953, box 17, Graduate School…1949–1955, folder, RG33–1–51; the *University Signal* had already announced the program on 1 August 1952.

312 O. C. Aderhold to Thomas Mahler, 29 August 1952, box 3, Atlanta Division to June 30, 1954, folder, Aderhold Papers, UGAL; George Manners, in discussion with the author and Gary M. Fink, 2 February 1989, tape 1, 26–27, SCGSU.

313 S. Walter Martin to A. B. Biscoe, 11 September 1952, O. C. Aderhold to Charles J. Bloch, box 3, Atlanta Division to 30 June 1954, folder, Aderhold Papers, UGAL; George Manners to George Sparks, 1 December 1953, Manners to Thomas Mahler, 30 April 1953, box 7, folder 88, Sparks Papers, SCGSU.

314 Atlanta Division, annual report, 1952, 14–16, box 31, folder 389, Sparks Papers, SCGSU; John E. Drewry to O. C. Aderhold, 31 October 1953, box 3, Atlanta Division to 30 June 1954 folder, Aderhold Papers, UGAL; *University Signal*, 23 January 1953; Reed, "Atlanta and the 'Mother Institution,'" 576.

315 Henry King Sanford to O. C. Aderhold, 27 May 1952, Atlanta Division, hospital administration folder, Aderhold Papers, UGAL; Thomas Mahler to Aderhold, 25 July 1952, Aderhold to R. C. Williams, 20 August 1952, box 20, folder 258, Sparks Papers, SCGSU.

316 George Manners to R. Howard Dobbs, Jr., 23 July 1952, box 7, folder 88, Sparks Papers, SCGSU.

317 Ibid.

318 George Manners to I. M. Sheffield, Jr., 26 January 1953, Manners, "Proposal to Member Banks of Atlanta Clearing House," 22 July 1954, box 7, folder 88, Thomas W. Mahler to George M. Sparks, 30 June 1953, box 26, folder 323, annual president's report, School of Business Administration, 1955–1956, 45–49, Sparks Papers, George Manners, interview by Les Hough and Joe Constance, 26 March 1986, 92–94, SCGSU.

319 Untitled [Report for academic year, 1952–1953, by Thomas Mahler], typescript, n.d., 11–22, box 3, folder 34, Sparks Papers, SCGSU; Mahler, "Summary of Thinking Regarding the Operations of the Atlanta Division," 1 September 1954, 4, Atlanta Division, confidential folder, Aderhold Papers, UGAL; George Manners to Merl Reed, 5 March 1999, in possession of the author.

CHAPTER 18

320 L. R. Siebert to Tom Luck, Jr., 15 April 1954, Atlanta Division, confidential folder, Aderhold Papers, UGAL; Paul F. Clark to Board of Regents, 4 June 1954, box 49, folder 14, G73–8; College Park Woman's Club to state board of regents, 14 June 1954, [Swainsboro] *Forest Blade*, 1 May 1954, box 17, "Requests for Expansion…1954–1957," folder, RG33–1–51, GDAH; Merl E. Reed, "The Struggle for State-Supported Higher Education in a Southern Regional Center: Atlanta and the 'Mother Institution,' 1944–1955," *Georgia Historical Quarterly* 80 (Fall 1996): 582.

321 George Sparks to Ben T. Wiggins, 19 November 1954, box 21, folder 270, see also, Sparks to C. J. Broome, Jr., 17 December 1954, box 7, folder 89, Sparks Papers, SCGSU.

322 *Alma Times*, Georgia, 1 April 1954, 1; "Up from a Grease Pit," *Newsweek*, 7 December 1953, 93; George Sparks to C. J. Broome, Jr., 17 December 1954, box 7, folder 89, Sparks Papers, SCGSU; O. C. Aderhold to Frank D. Foley, 29 April 1954, Aderhold to Harmon Caldwell, 28 May 1954, box 3, Atlanta Division to 30 June 1954, folder, Aderhold Papers, UGAL.

323 James A. Blissit to Frank Foley, 22 April 1954, box 3, Atlanta Division folder, Aderhold Papers, UGAL; Merle Prunty, "Educational Operations in the Atlanta Division…1950–1951," 69, box 3, Atlanta Division to 30 June 1954, folder, Caldwell Papers, "Special Study of the Atlanta Division of the University of Georgia," 2–5 March 1952, 15, box 1, Atlanta Division folder, Aderhold Papers, UGAL; George Manners to Merl Reed, 5 March 1999, in possession of the author.

324 *Alma Times*, 1 April 1954; O. C. Aderhold to Robert O. Arnold, personal and confidential, 30 June 1954, box 1, Atlanta Division, confidential folder, Aderhold Papers, UGAL.

325 O. C. Aderhold to Robert O. Arnold, personal and confidential, 30 June 1954, box 1, Atlanta Division, confidential folder, Thomas Mahler, "Summary of Thinking Regarding the Operations of the Atlanta Division," 1 September 1954, typescript, 2–3, Atlanta Division, confidential, Aderhold Papers, UGAL.

326 O. C. Aderhold to Robert O. Arnold, personal and confidential, 30 June 1954, Arnold to Aderhold, 8 July 1954, mem., Frank Foley to O. C., 9 July 1954, box 1, Atlanta Division, confidential folder, Aderhold Papers, UGAL.

327 T. W. Mahler to O. C. Aderhold, 13 September 1954, box 3, Atlanta Division, confidential folder, Aderhold Papers, UGAL.

328 Thomas Mahler, "Summary of Thinking Regarding the Operations of the Atlanta Division," n.d. [1 September 1951], typescript, 10–14, Atlanta Division, confidential folder, Aderhold Papers, UGAL.

329 Ibid., 17–19.

330 Thomas Mahler, "Current Problems and Recommendations," n.d. [13 September 1954], typescript, 1–3, Atlanta Division, confidential folder, Aderhold Papers, UGAL.

331 Ibid., 3–4.

332 Ibid., 6–7, 8–10.

333 Ibid., 8–10.

334 Ibid., 18–19.

291

CHAPTER 19

335 Merle C. Prunty to O. C. Aderhold, 19 January 1955, box 3, Atlanta Division, confidential folder, Aderhold Papers, UGAL.

336 *Atlanta Journal*, 19 January 1955.

337 Mem., station WAGA to George Sparks, 4 April 1955, box 10, folder 128, Mrs. Harry Epstein to president, UGA, Atlanta, 25 April 1955, box 11, folder 155, Sparks Papers, SCGSU.

338 O. C. Aderhold to Harmon Caldwell, 1 February 1955, "A Progress Report Regarding the Integration of the Atlanta Division as a Part of the University of Georgia," n.d. [January 1955], 1–3, excerpt from "Proposed Changes in the Constitution and Standards of the Southern Association of Colleges and Secondary Schools," 2 December 1954, appended to "A Progress Report," Aderhold to Frank Foley, 2 February 1955, confidential, Atlanta Division, box 3, 1954–1955, folder, Aderhold Papers, UGAL; George Manners, interview by Les Hough and Joe Constance, 26 March 1986, 98, SCGSU; Merl E. Reed, "The Struggle for State-Supported Higher Education in a Southern Regional Center: Atlanta and the 'Mother Institution,' 1944–1955," *Georgia Historical Quarterly* 80 (Fall 1996): 583–84.

339 The report handled Division library appropriations in a similarly misleading manner. From a 1947 base of $16,302, it cited a 419.37 percent Division increase during six years compared with Athens' 22.35 percent. "A Progress Report," 2, 3–5, box 3, 1954–1955, folder, James E. Gates to O. C. Aderhold, 26 January 1955, box 3, Atlanta Division, confidential folder, Aderhold Papers, UGAL.

340 "A Progress Report," 2, 5–12, box 3, 1954–1955, folder, O. C. Aderhold to James A. Blissit, 18 March 1955, Atlanta Division, confidential folder, Aderhold Papers, UGAL; Mem., Blissit to Harmon Caldwell, 16 March 1955, gen. adm. records of the chancellor, "Chancellor's Study...1955," box 15, folder 2, RG33–1–51, GDAH; excerpts from auditor's report, year ending 1953, in mem., George Manners to George Sparks et al., 27 December 1954, box 7, folder 88, Sparks Papers, SCGSU.

341 Atlanta Division Survey, 1950, folder 73, box 6, Sparks Papers, clipping from the *Atlanta Journal*, 9 February 1955, in GSU Scrapbook, 1953–1954 [55], SCGSU.

342 George Sparks to O. C. Aderhold, 3 February 1955, box 20, folder 258, Thomas Mahler to Sparks, 7 February 1955, box 26, folder 325, Sparks Papers, SCGSU; min., 22 February 1955, box 29, gen. fac. min. 1952–1959, folder, RG33–1–51.

343 According to a survey by Division registrar J. D. Blair, nearly sixty percent of the students lived in the area, and the rest came from 143 Georgia counties. Less than one-fifth (day) had full time jobs, although almost half of them worked part-time. About ninety-four percent (evening) worked full-time. Over three-quarters affirmed that they must work to attend college, and the same number (night) and over a quarter (day) could not have attended any other college. Only about eight percent (day) and four percent (night) would have gone to UGA. Finally, over thirty-five percent wanted coursework not presently offered at the Division, primarily in A&S and education. Harmon Caldwell to O. C. Aderhold, 11 February 1955, box 17, chancellor's office 1954–1955, folder, RG33–1–51; Thomas R. Luck, Jr., to Caldwell, 7 February 1955, Frank Foley to Aderhold, 22 February 1955, box 3, Atlanta Division, confidential folder, Aderhold Papers, UGAL; Reed, "Atlanta and the 'Mother Institution,'" 584–85.

344 O. C. Aderhold to Frank D. Foley, 2 March 1955, box 3, Atlanta Division, confidential folder, Aderhold Papers, UGAL.

345 O. C. Aderhold to Frank D. Foley, 2, 24 March 1955, box 3, Atlanta Division, confidential folder, Aderhold Papers, UGAL; *Atlanta Constitution*, 9 March 1955, GSU Scrapbook, 1953–1954 [55], SCGSU.

346 The four members favoring separation came from semi-rural Carroll, Sumter, Baldwin, and Bacon Counties. "Report of University System of Georgia Sub-Committee of General Assembly," 3 March 1955, Aderhold to Ralph Mcgill, 12 April 1955, box 3, Atlanta Division, confidential folder, Aderhold Papers, UGAL; Frank Foley to Harmon Caldwell, 11 March 1955, box 15, chancellor's study 1955, folder 2, RG33–1–51; *University Signal*, 8 March 1955, 1; 11 March 1955, 1; *Atlanta Constitution*, 10 March 1955, 3, 20, see also editorials; 12 April 1955, 4; 14 April 1955, 4; 15 April 1955, 4; Reed, "Atlanta and the 'Mother Institution,'" 584–86; Fincher, *University System of Georgia*, 44.

347 S. Walter Martin to O. C. Aderhold, 7 March 1955, Ernest A. Lowe to Harmon Caldwell, 15 March 1955, Atlanta Division, confidential folder, Aderhold Papers, UGAL; W. LeRoy House to board of regents, 31 March 1955, box 17, excerpt from Georgia News Panorama, typescript, 6 April 1955, gen. adm. records of the chancellor, box 15, chancellor's study 1955, folder 1, RG33–1–51; Reed, "Atlanta and the 'Mother Institution,'" 586.

348 Margaret Shannon, clipping from the *Atlanta Journal-Constitution*, Section E, 27 March 1955, GSU Scrapbook, 1953–1954 [55], April 1955, box 11, public relations 1953–1959, folder, G73–4, Harmon Caldwell to members of the comm. on education, 8 April 1955, box 36, folder 423, Sparks Papers, SCGSU; George B. Brooks to Caldwell, 7 April 1955, Atlanta Division, confidential folder, Aderhold Papers, UGAL; Frank Foley to Robert Arnold et al., 14 May 1955, box 15, chancellor's study 1955, folder 2, RG33–1–51.

349 "Comments on Proposal That Atlanta Division Be Separated from University in Athens," 8 April 1955, 1–5 box 36, folder 423, Sparks Papers, SCGSU; Frank Foley to Robert Arnold et al., 14 May 1955, box 15, chancellor's study 1955, folder 2, RG33–1–51.

350 "Comments on Proposal that Atlanta Division Be Separated From University in Athens," 8 April 1955, 4–12, box 36, folder 423, Sparks Papers, SCGSU.

351 Ibid., 11–16.

352 Ibid., 17, 19–21; the state's five four-year "white" colleges were located in Athens, Dahlonega, and Milledgeville to the north and east of Atlanta, and in Statesboro and Valdosta in southern Georgia.

353 Ibid., 13, 21–23.

354 Notes on the report of the chancellor, typescript, n.d. [April 1955], 1–5, Atlanta Division, confidential folder, Aderhold Papers, UGAL.

355 Untitled, Questions and Answers, typescript, n.d. [April 1955], [O. C. Aderhold] to Dear Mac [G. A. Booth], 30 April 1955, the University of Georgia and the Atlanta Division, typescript, n.d. [30 April 1955], Booth to Aderhold, 12 May 1955, "Questions Regarding the Operations of the Atlanta Division as an Integral Part of the University of Georgia," typescript, n.d. [spring 1955], box 3, Atlanta Division, confidential folder, Aderhold Papers, UGAL; *Atlanta Constitution*, 14 April 1955, 4, GSU Scrapbook, 1953–1954 [55], SCGSU; Reed, "Atlanta and the 'Mother Institution,'" 588, 590.

356 Untitled, typescript, carbon, n.d. [April 1955], with "Memo of Mr. C. J. Bloch" penciled at top, Frank Foley to Robert Arnold et al., 14 May 1955, Bloch to Foley, 16 May 1955, box 15, chancellor's study, folder 2, RG33–1–51; Clive Webb, "Charles Bloch, Jewish White Supremacist," *Georgia Historical Quarterly* 83/2 (Summer 1999): 267–92.

357 O. C. Aderhold to Frank Foley, 2 June 1955, Atlanta Division, confidential folder, Aderhold Papers, UGAL.

358 Ibid.; Frank Foley to O. C. Aderhold, n.d. [June 1955], Aderhold to Foley, 28 June 1955, Atlanta Division, confidential folder, Aderhold Papers, UGAL.

359 Frank Foley to O. C. Aderhold, n.d. [June 1955], Aderhold to Foley, 28 June 1955, Atlanta Division, confidential folder, Aderhold Papers, UGAL; regents resolution, n.d. [11 July 1955], box 19, folder 246, Sparks Papers, SCGSU, George Manners to John W. Hall, March 1961, draft, 15, box 15, folder 11, Manners Papers; *University Signal*, 15 July 1955, 1; *Atlanta Constitution*, 14 July 1955, 1.

360 *University Signal*, 15 July 1955, 1.

CHAPTER 20

361 Called fac. meeting, 14 July 1955, box 8, folder 97, Sparks Papers, George Manners, interview by Les Hough and Joe Constance, 24 March 1986, 79–80, SCGSU; *Georgia State Signal*, 27 July 1956, 2.

362 George Sparks to Harmon Caldwell, 15, 19 July 1955, AAUP Executive Committee to Caldwell, 15 July 1955, box 35, folder 419, excerpt from regents min., 12 October 1955, folder 420, J. C. Horton Burch to Sparks, 10 November 1955, box 4, folder 47, Report of a Study of the New State College of Business Administration, 1–3 August 1955, box 22, folder 282, Sparks Papers, SCGSU, Caldwell to O. C. Aderhold, 18 July 1955, box 30, Regents 1959–60 folder, Suttles Papers, George Manners to John W. Hall, Mqr. 1961, draft, 16–18, box 15, folder 11, Manners Papers, SCGSU; Arthur A. Haynes to Sparks, 29 July 1955, and other letters from graduating seniors, Charles Bloch to Caldwell, 2 August 1955, box 15, folder 3, RG33–1–51, GDAH; *Atlanta Constitution*, 13 September 1955, 19; 14 October 1955, 1; *GSC Signal*, 24 February 1956, 4.

363 Report of a "Study of the New State College of Business Administration," 1–3 August 1955, Report on "Examination of the GSCBA," 14–16 October 1956, box 22, folder 282, 1955–1956 annual president's report, SBA, box 3, folder 37, George Sparks to Harmon Caldwell, 19 July 1955, box 35, folder 419, Sparks Papers, Sparks to J. D. Blair, 6 October 1955, G73–8, box 57, folder 15, untitled, unsigned [George Manners], handwritten comments, n.d. [c. March 1961], box 15, folder 11, Manners papers, George Manners, interview by Les Hough and Joe Constance, 24 March 1986, 81, 104, SCGSU; *University Signal*, 27 July 1956, 2; 30 October 1956.

364 Charles Bloch to Harmon Caldwell, 10 August 1955, Caldwell to Bloch, 15 August 1955, box 15, folder 3, RG33–1–51; George Sparks to M. C. Huntley, 12 October 1955, box 22, folder 282, Sparks Papers, George Manners, interview by Les Hough and Joe Constance, 24 March 1986, 83, SCGSU.

365 Charles Bloch to Gordon Brown, 24 September 1955, Brown to Bloch, 28 September 1955, box 15, folder 3, Bloch to Robert O. Arnold, 7 December 1955, box 16, gen. file, folder, RG33–1–51; Brown to George Sparks, 13 December 1956, box 30, Regents, 1959–1960, folder, Suttles Papers; Marjorie Smith, *University Signal*, 18 January 1957, 1.

366 George Sparks to Harmon Caldwell, 1 September 1955, box 35, folder 420, min., SBA fac. meeting, 12 September 1955, box 7, folder 89, 1955–1956 annual report, J. C. Horton Burch to J. D. Blair, 20 January 1956, Planning and Curriculum Committee to SBA faculty, 13 April 1956, George Manners to Blair, 23 April 1956, Blair to George Sparks, 27 April 1956, 1955–1956 SBA Annual Report, 5, box 3, folder 37, Sparks Papers, SCGSU; *Atlanta Constitution*, 13 September 1955, 19; 15 September 1955, 33; *University Signal*, 16 September 1955, 1; 14 October 1955, 1; *Georgia State Signal*, 27 January 1956, 12.

367 George Manners to John E. Drewry, 7 October 1955, Drewry to Manners, 2 December 1955, box 7, folder 89, Sparks Papers, SCGSU, Manners to George Sparks, 16 August, 6 December 1955, box 64, folder 4, G73–8.

368 Harmon Caldwell to George Sparks, 31 October 1955, box 35, folder 420, M. Gordon Brown to O. C. Aderhold, 27 June 1956, folder 421, J. C. Horton Burch to

Sparks, 4 November 1955, box 4, folder 47, Sparks Papers, SCGSU; Lamar Dodd to S. Walter Martin, 26 May 1956, box 27, Art, 1944–1964, folder, RG33-1-51.

369 J. D. Blair to George Sparks, 26 September 1956, Sparks to Harmon Caldwell, 4 October 1956, box 35, folder 421, Sparks Papers, SCGSU; *Georgia State Signal*, 28 September 1956, 1.

370 George Sparks to Harmon Caldwell, 24 August 1956, box 3, folder 37; Report on Examination of the GSCBA, 14–16 October 1956, 3, 12–22, box 22, folder 282, Sparks Papers, SCGSU; *Georgia State Signal*, 18 January 1957, 1.

371 Report on "Examination of the GSCBA," 14–16 October 1956, 3, 12–13, box 22, folder 282, Donald C. Agnew to George Sparks, 14 December 1956, box 40, folder 479, Sparks Papers, SCGSU; fac. min., SBA, 31 October 1956, box 16, 1956–1958 folder, RG33-1-51.

372 Harmon Caldwell to M. M. "Muggsy" Smith, 1 March 1957, box 35, folder 421, George Manners to J. C. Horton Burch, 27 May 1957, min., SBA fac., 29 May 1957, box 7 folder 89, Sparks Papers, SCGSU; SBA fac. petition, n.d. [May 1957], box 16, gen. file 1957–1958, RG33-1-51; *Georgia State Signal*, 1 February 1957, 4; 31 May 1957, 2.

373 SBA fac. min., 8 February 1957, box 16, min., 1956–1958, folder, RG33-1-51; Sparks to Harmon Caldwell, 29 March 1957, box 35, folder 421, Sparks Papers, SCGSU, Manners to L. R. Siebert, 16, 20 May 1957, box 57, folder 14, Sparks to Manners and J. C. Horton Burch, 1 April 1957, box 64, folder 4, G73-8.

374 John P. Dyer to Harmon Caldwell, 3 December 1956 and other letters, box 17, president...1957, folder, RG33-1-51; fac. resolution, n.d. [fall 1956], box 13, folder 174, Report of the "Ad Hoc Committee on Naming a Successor to Dr. Sparks," n.d. [10 December 1956], box 11, folder 161, Sparks Papers, SCGSU.

375 Rufus C. Harris to Harmon Caldwell, 18 January 1957, Caldwell to W. R. Knight, 5 March 1957, Caldwell to Harris, 15 March 1957, meeting, gen. fac., 16 May 1957, corres., box 17, president...1957, folder, RG33-1-51; Report of the ad hoc comm. of the fac. council, 20 May 1957, box 11, folder 161, Sparks Papers, SCGSU.

376 Rufus Harris to Harmon Caldwell, 20 May 1957, box 17, president...1957, folder, RG33-1-51.

377 Malcolm Peabody to L. R. Siebert, 6 June 1957, Hugh C. Carney to Roy V. Harris, 31 May 1957, box 17, president...1957 folder, RG33-1-51; Caldwell to J. D. Blair, 1 July 1957, Blair Papers, George Manners, interview by Les Hough and Joe Constance, 26 March 1986, 104–106, SCGSU; clipping from the *Atlanta Constitution*, 27 June 1957; *Atlanta Journal*, 11 July 1957, 11; 12 July 1957, 11; *Georgia State Signal*, 12 July 1957, 5.

378 Harmon Caldwell to Horace B. Brown, 12 July 1957, box 17, president... 1957 folder, RG 33-1-51.

CHAPTER 21

379 Eugene Cook to M. D. Collins, 6 October 1954, Marvin Griffin to Dear Friend, 22 October 1954, box 21, folder 240, Sparks Papers, SCGSU; *Atlanta Constitution*, 9 February 1956, 1; Paul E. Mertz, "Mind Changing Time Over Georgia: HOPE, Inc. and School Desegregation, 1958–1961," *Georgia Historical Quarterly* 77 (Spring 1993): 42;

Thomas G. Dyer, *The University of Georgia: A Bicentennial History, 1785–1985* (Athens GA: UGA Press, 1985) 305–13.

380 *Atlanta Constitution*, 9 February 1956, 1; Ronald H. Bayor, "A City Too Busy To Hate: Atlanta's Business Community and Civil Rights," in *Business and Its Environment*, ed. Harold Sharlin, (Westport CT: Greenwood, 1983) 146–47; Robert C. McMath, Jr., Ronald M. Bayor, James E. Brittain, Lawrence Foster, August W. Giebelhaus, and Germaine M. Reed, *Engineering the New South: Georgia Tech, 1885–1985* (Athens GA: UGA Press, 1985) 313; Mertz, "Mind Changing Time Over Georgia," 47; Dyer, *University of Georgia*, 316; Bradley R. Rice, "If Dixie Were Atlanta," in *Sunbelt Cities: Politics and Growth Since World War II*, eds. Richard M Bernard and Bradley R. Rice (Austin TX: University of Texas Press, 1983) 46.

381 Cross examination of Charles Bloch, 747–52, regents resolution on admissions, Exhibit I, folder 1, findings of fact, 14–17, folder 2, testimony of L. R. Siebert, 114–15, folder 4, *Barbara Hunt et al. v. Robert Arnold et al.*, Case 5781, box 18, Record Group (RG) 21, National Archives Southeast Region (NASR); excerpt from regents min., 9 May 1956, box 35, folder 421, Sparks Papers, SCGSU, *Atlanta Constitution*, 13 March 1956, 1, 6, box 7, folder 1272/2, Blair Papers, SCGSU; *Atlanta Daily World*, 24 March 1956, 4, box 7, folder 1272, Blair Papers, SCGSU; David Wayne Nunnery, "The Attempted Integration of Georgia State College of Business Administration in 1956, A Significant Step Toward the Withdrawal of Georgia from the Massive Resistance Stance," (senior paper, GSU History Department, 1995) 5–6, in possession of the author; Dyer, *University of Georgia*, 107–08, 316–17.

382 The others included Myra Elliot Dinsmore, Virginia McChee Weems, Charlie Mae Knight, and Russell Thomas Roberts, all Atlanta Life employees. Eugene Gumby to L. R. Siebert, 22 March 1956, box 35, folder 421, Sparks Papers, SCGSU; Paul E. X. Brown, *Courier Georgia*, n.d. [March 1956); clippings from *Atlanta Daily World*, 24 March 1956, box 7, folder 1272/2, Blair Papers, SCGSU; testimony of J. D. Blair, 866–68, folder 7, Complaint 3, case 5781, findings of fact, 9–10, folder 1, 2, box 18, RG21, NASR; *University Signal*, 6 April 1956, 5; Nunnery, "Attempted Integration," 6–8.

383 George Sparks to Obey T. Brewster, "Sparks: College Will Follow the Law," 29 May 1956, box 43, folder 92, Sparks Papers, SCGSU; *Macon* (GA) *Telegraph*, 24 March 1956; *Atlanta Constitution*, 26 March 1956, 9 and 27 March 1956, box 7, folder 1272/2, clipping in Blair Papers, SCGSU; Nunnery, "Attempted Integration," 9–10.

384 George Sparks to Harmon Caldwell, 4 April 1956, Caldwell to Sparks, 13 April 1956, box 35, folder 421; William P. Layton to Sparks, 2 May 1956, box 25, folder 313, Sparks Papers, SCGSU.

385 In this attempt, Myra Elliot Dinsmore and Russell Thomas Roberts were joined by Iris Mae Welch, Barbara Pace Hunt, and Marian McDaniel. Findings of fact, 10–13, box 187, folder 2, complaint, 9–13, box 18, folder 1, testimony of Marian McDaniel, 10–11, box 18m, folder 2, testimony of Barbara Hunt, 195, 198–99, box 18, folder 4, RG 21, NASR; E. E. Moore, Jr., to George Sparks, 15 June 1956, Sparks to Moore, 22 June 1956, box 28, folder 357, Sparks Papers, SCGSU; *Georgia State Signal*, 5 October 1956, 4; Nunnery, "Attempted Integration," 11–13, 15.

386 Ian Macauley et al. to Al Haskell, 18 July 1956, box 40, folder 474, Sparks Papers, SCGSU; *Georgia State Signal*, 5 October 1956, 4; 30 October 1956, 16; 13 November 1956, 16.

387 Motion to dismiss, 6 February 1957, box 18, folder 1, RG 21, NASR; *Atlanta Journal*, 25 February 1957, 17, GSU press book, 1955–1956, SCGSU; *Atlanta Constitution*, 19 February 1958, 18; Nunnery, "Attempted Integration," 17–18; Alton Hornsby, Jr., "Black Public Education in Atlanta, Georgia, 1954–1973, From Segregation to Segregation," *Journal of Negro History* 76 (1991): 21–47; Dyer, *University of Georgia*, 309.

388 Meeting, fac. council, 28 January 1958, SBA dean's office, box 46, folder 17, G73–8, SCGSU; min., gen. fac., 19 February 1958, box 16, faculty meetings min., 1956–1958, folder, George Manners to Noah Langdale, 10 October 1958, box 17, folder, RG33–1–51, GDAH.

389 Testimony of J. D. Blair, 15–16, folder 4, testimony of Charles Bloch, 734–36, 738, 778, folder 7, testimony of Howard Calloway, 142, testimony of L. R. Siebert, 79–81, 102–104, 114–15, folder 4, box 18, Case 5781, RG21, NASR; *Atlanta Daily World*, 8 December 1958, scrapbook, 1957–1958, SCGSU; Dyer, *University of Georgia*, 316–19.

390 Testimony of Barbara Hunt, 211–14, 236–37, folder 7, testimony of Myra Elliot Dinsmore, 388, folder 5, box 18, case 5781, RG21, NASR.

391 Testimony of J. D. Blair, 863–64, 866–68, box 18, folder 7, RG 21, NASR; *Atlanta Constitution*, 8 December 1958, 1; 9 December 1958, 1; 10 December 1958, 1; 13 December 1958, 1; Nunnery, "Attempted Integration," 19.

392 Findings of Fact, 14–17, box 18, folder 2, RG21, NASR; *Atlanta Journal*, 10 January 1959, 1; *Atlanta Daily World*, 11 January 1959, 1.

393 *Atlanta Journal and Constitution*, 11 January 1959, 1; *Atlanta Journal*, 12 January 1, 21; *Atlanta Journal*, 13 February 1959; Dyer, *University of Georgia*, 319–21.

394 Fac. min., 19 February 1958, box 16, 1956–1958 folder, RG33–1–51; Mrs. Ruth G. DeKinder to the *Atlanta Constitution*, 26 Jan 1959, 9, *Atlanta Constitution*, 14 February 1958, 9, 11 January 1, 16, 21 February, 1, 26 January, 1, 4, 2 February, 4, 1959, *Atlanta Journal*, 12 January 1, 21, *Atlanta Journal*, 13 January 1959, 1.

395 *Atlanta Constitution*, 12 February 1959, 30; Dyer, *University of Georgia*, 319–20.

396 Noah Langdale to Harmon Caldwell, 14 November 1958, box 15, President Langdale, Noah, Jr., 1957–1966 folder, RR33–1–51, GDAH.

397 Ibid.

398 Ibid.; V. V, Lavroff to Noah Langdale, 25 May 1959, box 16, gen. file 1959–1966, Harmon Caldwell to Langdale, 19 December 1958, box 17, President Langdale, Noah, Jr., 1957–1966, folder, RG33–1–51, GSAH; Dyer, *University of Georgia*, 310–21.

399 William Patrick to O. R. Siebert, 6 March 1959, box 17, Patrick William, director of admissions, 1959–1962, folder, RG33–1–51.

400 *Atlanta Journal*, 6 May 1959, 1; *Atlanta Journal*, 7 May 1959, 1; *Atlanta Journal*, 8 May 1959, 1; *Atlanta Journal*, 10 May 1959, 4; *Atlanta Journal*, 11 May 1959, 1; Dana F. White, "The Black Sides of Atlanta: A Geography of Expansion and Containment, 1870–1970," *Atlanta Historical Journal* 26 (Summer–Fall 1982): 220.

401 The three included Mary Evelyn Rogers, age 20, Ernestine Brown, 25, and Alice Wyche, 24. *Atlanta Journal*, 12 May, 1; Melvin Ecke, in discussion with the author, 29 July 1999, 2, 7; *Georgia State Signal*, 5 May 1959, 1.

402 Mini [Mrs. William T. Newman] to Uncle Bob [Robert O. Arnold], 20 October 1959, box 9, folder 181, G84–24, SCGSU; William Patrick to Chappell Mathews, 30 January 1962, box 16, GSU internal enrollment, 1981 folder, Langdale Papers, *Atlanta Journal*, 9 March 1960, in GSU scrapbook, 1957–1960, SCGSU; Manners, "Reminiscences," 314–41; Dyer, *University of Georgia*, 320.

403 George Manners to Noah Langdale, 6 April 1960, Langdale to Harmon Caldwell, box 17, 1957–1966, folder, RG33–1–51, GDAH.

404 *Atlanta Journal,* 8 December 1959, GSU scrapbook, 1957–1960, SCGSU; *Atlanta Constitution*, 7 January 1959, 3; 7 January 1960, 1; Dyer, *University of Georgia*, 322–24.

405 *Atlanta Constitution,* 21 February 1960, 3E, dean of students records, 1930–1970, box 11, promotions folder, G73–4, Noah Langdale to deans, 25 February 1960, box 10, folder 196, G84–24, SCGSU; *Atlanta Constitution*, 26 January 1960, 5; *Atlanta Journal*, 31 January 1960, 7A; *Atlanta Journal*, 10 February 1960, 10; Dyer, *University of Georgia*, 324.

406 *Atlanta Constitution,* 22 February 1960, 16.

407 *Atlanta Constitution,* 23 February 1960, 14; 24 February 1960.

408 *Atlanta Journal,* 9 March 1960, GSU scrapbook, 1957–1960, SCGSU; *Atlanta Constitution*, 13 December 1960, 9; 7 January 1961, 1; Pratt, *We Shall Not Be Moved*, 67–110; Numan V. Bartley, *The Creation of Modern Georgia* (Athens GA: UGA Press, 1990) 197; Dyer, *University of Georgia*, 324–29; Calvin Trillin, *An Education in Georgia: Charlayne Hunter, Hamilton Holmes, and the Integration of the University of Georgia* (Athens GA: UGA Press, 1991) xi, 3, 12.

409 Harmon Caldwell to presidents, 16 March 1962, box 30, regents 1961–1963 folder, Suttles Papers; *Atlanta Constitution*, 26 July 1966, 5 February 1968, GSU scrapbook 1966, Noah Langdale to Abraham S. Venable, 6 August 1968, box 21, reading files, 1966–1970, Langdale Papers, SCGSU; *Georgia State Signal*, 27 June 1962, 1; *Atlanta Journal*, 3 October 1962, box 17, President Langdale, Noah, Jr., 1957–1966 folder, "Report on Status of Negro Admissions and Applications," 1 October 1963, box 15, Georgia State College folder, RG33–1–51, GDAH; McMath, Jr., et al., *Georgia Tech*, 317; David Smith, Jr., "Georgia State University: A Historical and Institutional Perspective, 1913–2002," (Ph.D. diss., GSU, 2005) 131–32.

410 Noah Langdale to Abraham S. Venable, 6 August 1968, box 21, reading files 1966–1970, Langdale to George Simpson, 10 June 1969, reading files May to September 1969 folder, box 21, Langdale Papers, *Atlanta Constitution*, 26 July 1966, GSU scrapbook 1966, SCGSU; *GSC Signal,* 20 June; 20 November 1968; 26 June 1969; Roger L. Geiger, *Research and Relevant Knowledge: American Research Universities since World War II* (New York: Oxford University Press) 157–58.

CHAPTER 22

411 J. D. Blair to Noah Langdale, 11 July 1957, Blair to Ralph Thaxton, 10 July 1957, Langdale to Blair, 20 April 1959, box 10, corres. 1954–1970, folder, Blair Papers, Langdale to William Suttles, 25 July 1969, box 1 folder 19, Manners Papers, min., box 85, adm. council folder, GSU printed material, SCGSU; Joe B. Ezell, in discussion with the author, 13 January 2000, 2; Manners, "Reminiscences," 283.

412 Gen. fac. meeting, 2 August 1957, box 16, min., 1956–1958, folder, RG33–1–51, GDAH; George Manners, interview by Les Hough and Joe Constance, 26 March 1986, 105; Manners, "Reminiscences," 294.

413 Summary of informal meeting of Langdale with the SBA ex. comm., 23 July 1957, box 46, folder 13, G73–8, Harmon Caldwell to Nell Trotter, 18 July 1957, box 11, pub. Rel., 1954–1959, folder, G73–4, mem., Paul G. Blount to Langdale, 21 August 1957, box 40, assoc. dean, A&S folder, Langdale Papers, SCGSU; Caldwell to M. M. Smith, 16 October 1957, box 16, gen. file, 1957–1958, folder, RG33–1–51; Manners, "Reminiscences," 285.

414 Noah Langdale, Jr., to Harmon Caldwell, 14 September, 16 October 1957, box 16, gen. file, 1957–1958, folder, J. D. Blair to Langdale, 18 June 1958, box 15, fac. apmts. Folder, Caldwell to Langdale, 27 May 1960, gen. file, 1959–1966 folder, min., SBA fac., 11 September 1961, fac. min., 1959–1964, folder, box 16, RG33–1–51, GDAH; summary of informal meeting of Langdale with SBA ex. com., 23 July 1957, box 46, folder 13, G73–8, Langdale office diary, 29 August 1957, box 6 series 3, Langdale Papers, George Manners to John W. Hall, March 1961, draft, 32, box 15, folder 11, Manners Papers, Manners to Langdale, 26 June 1959, box 9, folder 161, G84–24, SCGSU; *Georgia State Signal*, 13 November 1956, 1, 4; 23 January 1959, 1.

415 Noah Langdale, Jr., to Harmon Caldwell, 14 September, 16 October 1957, box 16, gen. file., 1957–1958, folder, 9 Jan 1958, box 17, ROTC, 1958–1961, folder, RG33–1–51.

416 Harmon Caldwell to Noah Langdale, 24 September 1957, box 40, A&S folder, Langdale Papers, L. R. Siebert to Langdale, 21 October 1957, folder 14, Langdale to Caldwell, 12 December 1957, dean's office folder, box 57, G74–8, report, comm. on academic growth, 6 December 1967, box 17, folder 1, G76–18; Langdale to L. M. Lester, 23 October 1957, 7 November 1957, box 16, gen. file 1957–1958, folder, visitation report, 22–4 January 1958, 1–3, box 15, AACSB folder, RG33–1–51; *Atlanta Journal*, 21 September 1957, 2; 10 October 1957, 34; *Georgia State Signal*, 6 December 1957, 1; 11 October 1957; 2 May 1958, 1.

417 Visitation report, 22 January 1958, 4–5, 8–10, 18, box 15, AACSB folder, RG33–1–51.

418 Ibid., 12; George Manners to John W. Hall, March 1961, draft, 24, box 15, folder 11, Manners Papers; min., SBA fac., 16 October 1959, box 16, fac. min., 1959–1964, folder, SCGSU; membership comm. of the AACSB, n.d. [November 1959], box 17, AACSB, 1959 visitation folder, RG33–1–51; Manners, "Reminiscences," 295–302, 314–25, George Manners, interview by Les Hough and Joe Constance, 26 March 1986, 116–17, SCGSU.

419 Noah Langdale to Harmon Caldwell, 16 October, 7 November 1957, box 16, gen. file, 1957–1958, folder, RG33–1–51; Langdale to Freeman Strickland, 22 October 1957, box 5, Freeman Strickland folder, Langdale Papers; *Georgia State Signal*, 8 November 1957, 1; 18 January 1957, 1; 1 February 1957, 1; 14 February, 4; 18 April; 31 October 1958; 22 November 1960; *Atlanta Constitution*, 30 January 1958, 4.

420 Three professors in 1959 received grants: George R. Ridge (French) author of a book on French romantic literature, researched at the Sorbonne; Harley J. Walker (geography and geology) did naval research in the Indian Ocean; and Raymond

Carter Sutherland (English) edited a fifteenth century manuscript at Oxford and the British Museum. In addition, Henry Malone (history) authored a book on the Cherokee Indians, and John Alexander (history) on classical Greek inscriptions. Noah Langdale to Harmon Caldwell, 24 February 1958, gen. file, 1957–1958, folder, fac. min., SBA, 3 January 1961, fac. min., 1959–1964, folder, George Manners to Noah Langdale, 5 February 1959, fac. appointments, 1959–1962, folder, box 16, RG33–1—51; James Lemly to Langdale, 15 March 1960, box 10, folder 196, G84–24; Report to adm. council, 17 March 1965, box 19, folder 3, G73–8, J. C. Horton Burch to Harmon Caldwell, 27 June 1962, box 9, folder 181, G84–24, SCGSU; *Georgia State Signal*, 31 January 1958, 5; 25 November 1958; 10 July 1959; Geiger, *Research and Relevant Knowledge*, 285.

421 George Manners to John W. Hall, March 1961, draft, 18–19, box 15, folder 11, Manners Papers, Manners to Noah Langdale, box 4, Manners folder, Langdale Papers, Langdale to Harmon Caldwell, 19 August 1958, box 15, faculty appointments, 1958, folder, RG33–1–51; *Georgia State Signal*, 2 May 1958, 4–5.

422 Report, comm. on academic growth, 6 December 1967, box 17, folder 1, G76–18, Harmon Caldwell to Noah Langdale, 20 March 1961; Langdale Papers, clipping from *Atlanta Constitution*, 13 November 1958, scrapbook, 1956–1958; John E. Drewry to O. C. Aderhold, 24 November 1958, box 32, journalism school, gen. file 1956–1960, folder, Lamar Dodd to Aderhold, 23 February 1959, Joe Perrin to Dodd, 24 May 1961, box 27, art 1944–1964, folder, RG33–1–51; *Atlanta Journal*, 9 October 1958, 21.

423 O. C. Aderhold to Harmon Caldwell, 19 May 1961, 2 June 1961, Lamar Dodd to John O. Eidson, 1 June 1961, box 27, Art, 1944–1963 folder, RG33–1–51; S. Walter Martin to Langdale, 13 December 1962, box 8, Regents-curricula changes 1963–1967, folder, Martin to Langdale, 14 December 1965, box 40, visual arts folder, Langdale Papers.

424 John E. Drewry to O. C. Aderhold, 24 November 1958, box 32, journalism school, gen. file, 1956–1960, folder, RG33–1–51; Allen Woodall to Langdale, 21 March 1960, Langdale to Woodall, box 6, Allen Woodall folder, Langdale papers; *Georgia State Signal*, 4 April 1958, 4.

425 *Georgia State Signal*, 1 February 1957, 1; 1 March 1957, 1; 17 April 1959; Report, sub-comm., House University System comm., n.d. [1959–1960], 16–17, box 58, folder 5, G73–8; *Macon Telegraph*, 19 July 1959; clipping from *Macon*(GA) *News*, 8 October 1959, scrapbook 1959–1960; Harmon Caldwell to Noah Langdale, 22 September 1960, box 15, Buildings, 1957–1966, folder, RG33–1–51.

426 Arthur M. Gignilliat to Harmon Caldwell, 9 January 1960, box 17, President Langdale folder, RG33–1–51.

427 Ibid.

428 Noah Langdale to Harmon Caldwell, 5 December 1960, Senate res. 50, House res. 196, n.d. [January 1961], box 17, President Langdale folder, RG33–1–51; James Lemly to adm. council, 11 May 1960, box 14, James Lemly folder, Langdale Papers, min., adm. council, 10 May 1960, box 11, adm. advisory council folder, Suttles Papers, J. C. Horton Burch to Langdale, 17 May 1960, box 10, folder 196, G84–24, SCGSU; Geiger, *American Research Universities*, 211.

429 Noah Langdale to Harmon Caldwell, 5 December 1960, unsigned letter [Arthur M. Gignilliat] to the chancellor, January 1961, box 17, President Langdale, 1957–1966, folder, [L. R.] Siebert to Edgar Blalock, n.d. [c. January 1961], Langdale to Caldwell, 27, 30 November 1961, 1 December 1961, Caldwell to Langdale, 14 December 1961, box 16, gen. file, 1959–1966, folder, RG33-1-51; Caldwell to Langdale, 15 June 1961, box 40, College of Allied Health Sciences folder, Langdale Papers, organizational meeting, 16 July 1962, box 23, folder 325, G73–4, report, comm. on academic growth, 6 December 1967, box 17, folder 1, G76–18.

430 William Patrick to Chappelle Mathews, 20 January 1962, box 16, GSU internal enrollment, 1982, folder, Langdale Papers, Noah Langdale to J. D. Blair, 22 January 1962, box 10, folder 196, G84–24, *Atlanta Constitution*, 21 December 1961, publicity clippings, July 1961–June 1962, Manners, "Reminiscences," 326–27, SCGSU.

431 Senate Bill, 168, 3 March 1962, box 58, folder 5, G73–8, Harmon Caldwell to the presidents, 16 March 1962, box 30, Regents, 1961–1963, folder, Suttles Papers, *Atlanta Journal*, 7 December 1961, pub. clippings, July 1961–June 1962, SCGSU.

CHAPTER 23

432 George Sparks to O. C. Aderhold, 30 December 1952, box 20, folder 258, Sparks Papers, SCGSU; Malcolm B. Knowles, *A History of Adult Education* (Huntington NY: R. E. Krieger Publishing Co., 1977) 84–85; James W. Wilson and Edward H. Lyons, *Work-Study College Programs*, (Westport CT: Greenwood Press, 1977) 7–8.

433 *University Signal*, 6 December 1948, 3.

434 Gen. adm. bull. 1.1, 2.2, September 1953, announcement from N. H. Trotter, n.d. [c. 1945], Sparks Papers, min., council of deans, 14 April 1969, box 3, folder 26, G80–24, Trotter to William Suttles, 5 December 1957, box 13, Suttles, 1956–1959, folder, G73–4, SCGSU.

435 Thomas Mahler to O. C. Aderhold, 14 May 1952, box 20, folder 258, Sparks Papers, SCGSU; *University Signal*, 7 March 1953, 1; 30 September 1955; 14 October 1955, 1; *Georgia State Signal*, 6 December 1955, 2; 14 February 1957, 1; 5 April 1957; 31 January 1958, 5.

436 Letter signed Phantom, n.d. [c. 1955], attached to mem. to President Langdale from George Manners, 22 September 1958, box 14, Manners folder, Langdale Papers, Nell Trotter to William Suttles, 2 May 1960, box 13, folder 156, G73–4; George Sparks to Harmon Caldwell, 31 October 1955, James Blissit to Sparks, 16 November 1955, box 35, folder 420, Sparks Papers, SCGSU; Langdale to Caldwell, 23 April 1962, box 16, gen. file, 1959–1966, folder, RG33-1-51, GDAH. Robert C. McMath, Jr., Ronald M. Bayor, James E. Brittain, Lawrence Foster, August W. Giebelhaus, and Germaine M. Reed, *Engineering the New South: Georgia Tech, 1885–1985* (Athens GA: UGA Press, 1985) 346.

437 Notice to council members, 28 December 1955, campaign, n.d. [January 1956], box 2, clean-up campaign, 1955–1956, folder, Nell Trotter to William Suttles, 13 May 1957, box 13, William Suttles, 1956–1959, folder, G73–4; letter from Phantom, n.d. [c. 1955], attached to mem. to President Langdale from George Manners, 12 September 1958, box 4, Manners folder, Langdale Papers, SCGSU; *Atlanta Journal*, 9 May 1959, 4.

438 George Sparks to AAUP Atlanta chapter, draft, n.d. [June 1955], AAUP ex. com. to Sparks, 20 June 1955, Ian Macauley et al., to Al Haskell, 18 July 1956, box 40, folder 474, Sparks Papers, SCGSU; *University Signal*, 2 February 1949; 26 July 1954; 4 May 1956.

439 *University Signal*, 14 October 1955, 16; 27 January, 4; 18 May 1956; *Georgia State Signal*, 28 September, 5; 23 October 1956; 1 February 1957.

440 Lee Secrest to Noah Langdale, 24 April 1968, box 5, Secrest folder, Langdale Papers; *University Signal*, 6 December 1948.

441 *University Signal*, 3 June 1949; Harold Davis to George Simpson, 3 March 1966, box 17, President Langdale folder, RG 33–1–51; Noah Langdale to Kenneth England, 21 September 1962, box 44, folder 558, G73–4, Langdale to Martin Roberts, personal and confidential, 9 September 1968, box 5, Roberts, Martin, folder, Langdale Papers, Jack E. Johnson et al., 26 October 1966, box 13, folder 2, G76–18, *Oconee Enterprise*, 24 February 1965, GSC scrapbook, 1965, SCGSU; *Georgia State Signal*, 2 May 1958, 5; telephone conversation with Harold Davis by Gary M. Fink, 20 February 1988, Gary M. Fink to file, in possession of the author; Manners, "Reminiscences," 422–23.

442 Nell Trotter to sororities, n.d. [March 1958], box 13, folder 155, Kenneth England to Trotter, 30 January 1964, Trotter to England, 16 March 1964, Ralph Munster to England, 25 October 1968, box 8, folder 126, G73–7; Martin Klotsche, *The University of Wisconsin-Milwaukee, an Urban University* (1972) 98–101.

443 Nell Trotter to Kenneth England, 14 October 1963, box 8, folder 127, England to Jimmy Anderson, 26 July 1961, England to Marion Woodman, 17 July 1962, box 28, folder 377, G73–4, George Manners to George Sparks and J. D. Blair, 12 April 1956, box 7, folder 43, Sparks Papers, Noah Langdale to Francis Bridges, 28 February 1969, box 21, reading file, January–April 1969, folder, Langdale Papers, SCGSU; *University Signal*, 6 December 1955, 1.

444 Nell Trotter to J. C. Camp, 20 August 1954, newspaper clipping with picture, n.d., unidentified, box 2, housing, nonresident women students, 1956–1962, folder, Trotter to William Suttles, 21 February 1957, 28 December 1960, box 13, folder 157, Trotter to Suttles, 12 June 1958, box 13, William Suttles, 1956–1959, folder, G73–4, Trotter to Kenneth England, 14 October 1963, box 8, folder 127, G73–7, SCGSU; clipping from *Georgia State Signal*, 29 September 1966.

445 Nell Trotter to William Suttles, 27 February 1957, 13 April, 15 August, 1960, box 13, folder 156, Trotter to Mrs. E. R. Foster, 10 October 1960, box 2, housing, 1956–1962, folder, G73–4, SCGSU; Thomas G. Dyer, *The University of Georgia: A Bicentennial History, 1785–1985* (Athens GA: UGA Press, 1985) 346.

446 Nell Trotter to William Suttles. 25 June 1957, 18 November 1957, 12 June, 19, 20 November 1958, Trotter to Miss Carolyn Reed, 23 April 1958, box 13, Suttles, 1956–1959, folder, Trotter to Kenneth England, 9 December 1966, 31 January 1967, 30 August 1967, box 8, folder 125, 12 April 1963, folder 127, clipping from *Atlanta Constitution*, 12 January 1967, box 51, folder 661, G73–4, Noah Langdale to England, 24 June 1963, Suttles to George Manners, 21 October 1966, box 15, folder 4, G76–18, *Atlanta Constitution*, 15 January 1962, publicity clippings, 1961–1962, SCGSU; Dyer, *University of Georgia*, 345–46.

447 Thomas A. Hathcock, Jr. to Kenneth England, 12 January 1967, folder 276, Eugene H. Methvin, "SDS: Engineers of Campus Chaos," *Readers Digest* (October 1968) 103–108, England to Richard Judson Brown, 17 January 1969, folder 275, box 21, G73–4; Bok, *Beyond the Ivory Tower*, 7–9; John Brubacher and J. Willis Rudy, *Higher Education in Transition*, (New York: Harper & Row, 1976) 349–50; Nell Trotter, "Memoir," 28, 32.

448 Assorted COSI flyers, fact sheet on compulsory ROTC, flyer, n.d. [March 1968], box 21, folder 276, clipping from *Atlanta Constitution*, 6 November 1967, 6, box 51, folder 661, G73–4, SCGSU; faculty petition, 22 April 1968, "Altus" flyer, n.d. [April 1968], report of the Standards Committee to the college faculty, n.d. [June 1968], in possession of Gerald H. Davis; "Altus," 17 April, 1 May 1968, box 5, Secrest, Lee, folder, Noah Langdale to William Suttles, important and personal, 21 November 1968, box 21, reading file, Langdale Papers, min., adm. council, box 85, adm. council folder, GSU printed material, SCGSU; email, Gerald H. Davis to Merl Reed, 1 September 2000, in possession of the author; *Georgia State Signal*, 10 August 1967, 2; 2 May 1968, 2; 9 May 1968, 2; Dyer, *University of Georgia*, 348; McMath, Jr., et al. *Georgia Tech*, 347.

449 COSI to dear friend, 22 April 1968, flyer to faculty, folder 276, "REVOLT AT COLUMBIA UNIVERSITY," flyer, n.d. [May 1968], "A Burning for the Right to be Human," flyer, n.d. [spring 1968], folder 275, box 21, G73–4; "Altus," 15 August, 8 October 1968; McMath, Jr., et al., *Georgia Tech*, 348.

450 M. J. Goglia to membership, 10 November 1967, min., com. on student affairs, 15 April 1968, box 28, folder 425, regents statement on disruptive and obstructive behavior, October 1968, box 51, folder 661, G73–4, SCGSU.

451 "Altus," 2 January 1968, folder 276, Kenneth England to Robert J. Sullivan, 28 February 1968, folder 276, England to Noah Langdale and every top administrator, 26 September 1968, folder 275, box 21, G73–4, SCGSU; Philip Gailey, *Atlanta Constitution*, 6 November 1967, 6; Geiger, *American Research Universities*, 254–55.

452 Noah Langdale to Jack Rollow, personal and confidential, 1 August 1968, box 21, reading files 1966–1970, Langdale to Ralf Munster, 1 August 1968, box 4, Munster folder, Langdale Papers, list of anti-war publications, "Dean of Men Singleton Asked to Leave COSI Meeting," COSI, 31 October 1968, clipping, box 21, folder 275, G73–4, SCGSU.

453 Eugene H. Methvin, "SDS: Engineers of Campus Chaos," *Readers Digest* (October 1968) 103–108, box 21, folder 275, G73–4, Noah Langdale to V. V. Lavroff, 6 March 1969, Langdale to Milton H. Gorman, 5 November 1968, W. Armstrong Smith to Langdale, 25 February 1969, Langdale to Smith, 27 February 1969, box 21, reading files, 1966–1970, Langdale Papers, SCGSU; Gary M. Fink to file, n.d. [winter 1988], in possession of the author; oral interview with Joe B. Ezell, in discussion with the author, 13 January 2000, 23.

454 Clinton E. Male to Kenneth Black et al., n.d. [winter 1969], box 21, folder 275, G73–4, SCGSU; *Georgia State Signal*, 22 February 1968, 1.

455 Min., 19 August 1969, box 85, adm. council folder, GSU printed material, George Greaves to Nell Trotter, 3 March 1969, box 1, folder 11, G73–7, E. L. Secrest, Jr., to V. V. Lavroff, 14 May 1969, box 21, folder 275, G73–4, SCGSU; "Altus," 12 February

1969; *Georgia State Signal*, 10 August, 21 September, 5 October 1967, 11, 23, 25 January, 17 October 1968, 30 January, 20 November 1969; *Atlanta Constitution*, 6 January 1968; Richard Freeland, *Academia's Golden Age* (New York: 1992) 97–100.

456 Geiger, *American Research Universities*, 218, 236; Brubacher and Rudy, *Higher Education*, 214–15; Pusy, *American Higher Education 1945-1970, a Personal Report* (Cambridge: Harvard University Press, 1978) 2–7, 95–97; Levi, "Influence of Environment," 137.

457 Faculty Facts, 8 May 1964, printed material, misc., Blair papers, G78–21, SCGSU; fac. min., 23 April 1956, box 16, fac. meetings, 1956–1958 folder, fac. appointments, leaves, promotions, 1966–1967, folder, box 16, RG33–1–51, GDAH.

458 M. Gordon Brown to George Sparks, 23 August 1956, box 35, folder 421, Sparks Papers, SCGSU; Garland T. Byrd to Fred C. Tallant, 29 June 1959, box 16, gen. file, 1959–1966, folder, RG33–1–51, GDAH.

459 George Manners to Noah Langdale, 6 February 1959, box 15, Black, Kenneth, 1955–1960, folder, Manners to Langdale, 5 February 1959, box 16, fac. apmts, leaves, 1959–1962, folder, min., 1 May 1963, fac. min., 1959–1964, folder, box 16, RG33–1–51; James Lemly to Manners, n.d. [September 1956], box 46, folder 15, G73–8, Langdale to George Simpson, 3 December 1968, box 14, folder 6, G76–18, Michael Mescon to Langdale, 6 March 1963, box 4, Mescon folder, Langdale Papers; *Macon Telegraph*, 19 July 1959, GSC scrapbook, 1957–1960, *Atlanta Constitution*, 6 August 1962, GSC scrapbook, 1962–1963, clipping from *Atlanta Journal*, 15 January 1968, GSU scrapbook, 1968, SCGSU; *University Signal*, 11 November 1955, 1; *Georgia State Signal*, 31 May 1957, 1.

460 J. C. Horton Burch to William Suttles, 14 July 1965, box 10, folder 205, G84–24, min., adm. council, 14 November 1960, box 53, folder 686, G73–4, George Manners to Suttles, 8 July 1965, box 65, folder 2, G73–8, SCGSU.

461 Special mem. to Vice President William Suttles from George Manners, 10 January 1967, mem. to Vice President Suttles, personal and confidential, 19, 31 January, 17 March, 8 October 1967, box 15, folder 3, G76–18, SCGSU.

462 J. C. Horton Burch to Noah Langdale, 5 January 1962, box 9, folder 164, G84–24, George Manners to John W. Hall, 13 March 1961, box 15, folder 11, Report of the visiting comm., n.d. [1967], box 34, folder 2, G73–8, mem. to Vice President Suttles, personal and confidential, 19, 31 January, 8 October 1967, box 15, folder 3, G76–18, SCGSU.

463 William P. Fidler to Dear Colleague, n.d. [March 1966], AAUP ex. com. min., 13 January 1966, executive committee, AAUP, fall, 1963, Vincent C. Watson to William Suttles, 13 May 1965, box 15, folder 174, G73–4, min., 28 October 1964, 5 April 1965, box 85, adm. council folder, GSU printed material, Institutional Self-Study Report (1967) 64–65, SCGSU; Harmon Caldwell to Noah Langdale, 20 February 1964, box 17, Langdale, 1957–1966, folder, RG33–1–51, GDAH; Merl Reed to file, 8 September 2000, in possession of the author.

464 Min., 14 April 1965, box 85, adm. council folder, GSU printed material, min., AAUP executive committee, 13 January 1966, min., AAUP meeting, 27 January 1966, 21 February 1967, Arthur Waterman to Kenneth England, 16 February 1967, box 15, folder 174, G73–4, min., council of deans, 28 February 1969, box 3, folder 26, G80–24,

Gerald Davis to Noah Langdale, 1 May 1969, box 21, reading file, May–September 1969, Langdale Papers, SCGSU.

465 Min., AAUP meeting, 21 February 1967, Arthur E. Waterman to Noah Langdale, 7 April 1967, box 15, folder 174, G73–4, V. Avery to J. C. Horton Burch and George Manners, 2 February 1965, box 9, folder 164, G84–24; min., adm. council, 22 January 1969, box 85, adm. council folder, GSU printed material, SCGSU.

466 Ralph Munster to William Suttles, 28 September 1967, box 4, Munster folder, Langdale Papers, SCGSU.

467 Arthur E. Waterman to Noah Langdale, 7 April 1967, box 15, folder 174, G73–4, "SAC Visiting Committee Report" (1967) 21, box 34, folder 2, G73–8, SCGSU.

468 "SAC Visiting Committee Report" (1967) 20, box 34, folder 2, G73–8, George Manners to William Suttles, 16 January 1968, box 15, folder 1, G76–18, min., adm. council, 22 January 1969, box 85, adm. council folder, GSU printed material, "Institutional Self-Study Report" (1967) 22–23, SCGSU.

469 Min., AAUP special meeting, 23 February 1967, box 15, folder 174, clipping from *Atlanta Journal*, 24 February 1967, box 35, folder 459, "COSI" flyer, n.d. [February 1967], box 21, folder 276, G73–4, statement by J. C. Horton Burch, 24 February 1967, box 4, A&S folder, G73–4, SCGSU.

470 Karl O'Lessker and Vincent Watson to Dear Colleague, 18 November 1966, box 51, folder 661, Thomas G. Croker et al., to Noah Langdale, 17 February 1967, press release of O'Lessker statement at rally, 24 February 1967, "We Protest," flyer, n.d. [May 1967], box 35, folder 459, G73–4; *Georgia State Signal*, 16 February 1967; *Atlanta Journal and Constitution*, undated clipping [August 1966], GSC scrapbook, 1966, SCGSU.

CHAPTER 24

471 T. A. Hartshorn, "Getting Around Atlanta: New Approaches," in *Urban Atlanta: Redefining the Role of the City*, ed. Andrew Marshall Hamer (Atlanta: GSU College of Business Administration, Publishing Division, 1980) 168, 170–71; David Marshall Smith, *Inequality in an American City, Atlanta, Georgia, 1960–1970*, (London: Department of Geography and Earth Science, Queen Mary College, University of London, 1981) 5.

472 Hartshorn, "Getting Around Atlanta," 169; Bradley R. Rice, "If Dixie Were Atlanta," in *Sunbelt Cities: Politics and Growth Since World War II*, eds. Richard M Bernard and Bradley R. Rice (Austin TX: University of Texas Press, 1983) 40; Truman A. Hartshorn, S. Davis, G. E. Dever, P. R. Allen, and S. Bederman, *Metropolis in Georgia: Atlanta's Rise as a Major Transaction Center* (Cambridge MA: Ballinger, 1976) 1, 4–5.

473 Rice, "If Dixie Were Atlanta," 38–39, 44; Hartshorn et al., *Metropolis*, 9–11, 14, 61.

474 Noah Langdale to Harmon Caldwell, 16 October 1957, box 16, gen. file 1957–1958 folder, Langdale to William B. Hartsfield, 14 October 1960, box 16, Urban Renewal program, 1959–1964 folder, Langdale to Caldwell, 22 September 1959, Some advantages of inclusion of south side of Decatur Street in the Georgia State Urban Renewal expansion project, n.d. [1959], box 15, building, urban renewal program, 1959–1966 folder, Langdale to Caldwell, 5 February 1964, Caldwell to Langdale, 12 March 1964, box 15, Langdale to Robert O. Arnold, 14 June 1961, box 17, President

Langdale 1957–1966 folder, RG33–1–51, GDAH; clipping from *Atlanta Journal*, 27 May 1967, box 12, folder 1, G76–18; Langdale to Francis Bridges, 28 February 1969, box 21, reading files, January to April 1969 folder, Langdale Papers, Langdale to J. D. Blair, 22 January 1960, J. C. Horton Burch to Langdale, 20 June 1962, box 10, folder 196, G84–24, SCGSU; Richard Freeland, *Academia's Golden Age* (New York: Oxford University Press, 1992) 88; Martin Klotsche, *The University of Wisconsin-Milwaukee, an Urban University* (Milwaukee: University of Wisconsin, 1972) 73–75.

475 Report, House sub-committee, n.d. [c. 1959], 18–19, box 58, folder 5, George Manners to Noah Langdale and William Suttles, 30 December 1964, box 47, folder 15, Manners to Suttles, 12 January 1965, box 65, folder 3, G73–8, min., adm. council, 14 February 1962, box 85, adm. council folder, GSU printed material, Manners to Langdale, 26 October 1961, box 10, folder 196, G84–24, *Atlanta Journal*, 7 December 1961, 4, pub. clippings, July 1961–June 1962, regents min., 16 December 1964, box 43, school of gen. studies folder, mem., William Patrick to Langdale, 25 May 1964, box 4, William Patrick folder, Langdale Papers, min., adm. council, box 85, adm. council folder, GSU printed material, SCGSU; Langdale to Harmon Caldwell, 29 November 1961, gen. studies folder, Langdale to Caldwell, 1 December 1961, box 16, gen. file 1959–1966 folder, RG33–1–51, GDAH.

476 Noah Langdale to George Simpson, 12 July 1967, box 40, A&S, communications folder, mem., George Manners to William Suttles, 28 July 1965, box 8, regents-curricula changes, 1962–1967 folder, Langdale Papers, Langdale to Harmon Caldwell, 17 October 1963, box 6, folder 13, G76–18; resolution, annual assembly, Georgia Hospital Association, 1 March 1963, box 15, degree programs, graduate, 1957–1963 folder, RG33–1–51; Manners, Reminiscences, 302–303.

477 George Manners to Noah Langdale, 5 September 1957, box 15, EDP center, 1957, folder, RG33–1–51; report to the president by William Wells, n.d. [c. 1963], box 56, folder 16, G73–8, Manners to Wells, 31 July 1968, Wells to all faculty, 24 September 1968, computer comm. min., 14 April 1969, box 18, folder 4, G76–18, Langdale to Mario Goglia, 12 August 1966, box 8, Regents-Goglia folder, Langdale Papers; *Atlanta Journal*, 16 December 1964, GSU scrapbook, 1964–1965; Manners, "Reminiscences," 304–13, AG 16.

478 Meeting, adm. council, 29 July 1965, box 65, folder 2, G73–8, GSU min., 2 January 1964, box 85, adm. council folder, GSU printed material, report, 1965–1966, box 30, "Role & Scope Study" folder, Suttles Papers, Noah Langdale to George Simpson, 2 December 1965, box 7, regents-chancellor Simpson folder, Langdale Papers; min., SBA fac. meeting, 21 March 1964, box 16, fac. min., 1959–1964, folder, RG33–1–51; *Georgia State Signal*, 11 May 1967, 5.

479 V. V. Lavroff to Harmon Caldwell, 23 March 1962, Lavroff to L. R. Siebert, 24 April 1962, Noah Langdale to S. Walter Martin, 19 January 1965, Langdale to Caldwell, 15 February, 12 April 1963, box 15, building, urban renewal program, 1957–1966, folder, William R. Pullen to J. H. Dewberry, 24 May 1963, box 17, library, gen. file, 1963, folder, Langdale to Caldwell, 30 December 1963, Caldwell to William T. Snaith, 17 January 1964, James A. Dunlap to Philip Weltner, 21 January 1964, box 16, fine arts, proposed center, 1961–1964, folder, RG33–1–51; Langdale to J. D. Blair et al., 28 March 1963, box 30, Regents, 1963–1965, folder, J. H. Dewberry to Langdale, 13 Jan 1966, box 30, regents, 1966–1967, folder, Suttles Papers, min., 18 September 1963, box 85, adm. council folder, GSU printed material, Langdale to Charles Weltner, 13 June 1966, box 6, Weltner, Charles, folder, progress reports, 8 September 1965, box 9, University System building program folder, Langdale Papers, *Atlanta Journal*, 5 April 1968, box 12, folder 1, G76–18; *GSU Signal*, 20 November 1969, 2A, 9A; see also, Harvey K. Newman, "Decatur Street: Atlanta's African American Paradise Lost," *Atlanta History* 44/2 (Summer 2000): 16–18.

480 Noah Langdale to Harmon Caldwell, 12 February 1964, box 16, gen. file, 1957–1958, folder, RG33–1–51; Progress reports, 8 September 1965, box 9, University System building program folder, Langdale to George Simpson, 6 May 1966, box 21, reading file, Langdale Papers, Langdale to S. Walter Martin, 2 November 1964, box 9, folder 181, min., fac. council, 5 November 1964, box 46, folder 17, G73–8; *GSC Signal*, 13 July 1967, 1.

481 Fac. min., 14 Jan 1964, fac. min., 1959–1964 folder, "Proposed campus site plan...as directed by the Regents," 10 September 1958, 59, box 15, RG33–1–51; mem., Joseph Perrin to Noah Langdale, 20 November 1964, box 14, Perrin folder, Alex Lacy to York Willbern, 16 August 1968, box 44, urban observatory, 1968, folder, Langdale Papers, Langdale to William Suttles, 28 March 1966, box 9, folder 164, G84–24, min., box 85, adm. council folder, GSU printed collection, Manners, "Reminiscences," 399.

482 Noah Langdale to Mrs. Nadine Penney Moor, 20 January 1969, Langdale to Andrew E. Steiner, 20 September 1966, Langdale to Albert Bows, 11 October 1968, Langdale to J. H. Dewberry, 21 October 1966, Langdale to Carl Sanders, 18 November 1968, Langdale to Frank Dunham, 2 May 1969, Langdale to V. V. Lavroff, 17 June, 31 October 1969, box 21, reading files, 1966–1970, folder, Langdale Papers.

483 Statement by Noah Langdale to the regents, 15 September 1964, box 15, buildings, gen., 1957–1966 folder, RG33–1–51; Langdale to George Simpson, 24 June 1966, box 21, reading files, 1966–1970, folder, Langdale to Simpson, 9 July 1968, box 21, reading file, January to April 1969, folder, Langdale to William Suttles, 20 December 1968, box 8, regents, re: budgets folder, Langdale Papers, GSU min., 20 January 1968, box 85, adm. council folder, GSU printed material; *GSC Signal*, 19 October 1967, 1, 5; Freeland, *Academia's Golden Age*, 88.

484 The term "urban life" first appeared in a System document in the early 1950s, when Merle Prunty, in his study for the chancellor, suggested "an 'urban life' type of major program leading to the A.B. degrees" as a solution to Athens' opposition to senior A&S courses at the Atlanta Division. See chapter 15, fn. 19. Karl O'Lessker and Vincent Watson to Dear Colleague, 18 November 1966, box 51, folder 661, G73–4, Noah Langdale to George Simpson, 15 August 1966, box 8, regents-curricula changes, 1962–1967, folder, regents min., box 40, AHS folder, Langdale to Simpson, 26 September 1966, BS in urban life folder, Simpson to Langdale, 17 November 1966, regents min., 11 January 1967, BS in urban life, September 1, 1967, folder, Fred Davison to Langdale, 10 May 1967, school of urban life, Lacy, dean Alex, folder, Langdale to Leonard Robinson, 3 August 1967, criminal justice folder, box 44, Langdale Papers, report, CAD, 6 December 1967, box 17, folder 1, *GSC Signal*, 22 May 1967, box 12, folder 1, G76–18; *Atlanta Constitution*, 22 March 1967, clipping.

485 Thomas P. Murphy and James Zarnowiecki, "The Urban Observatory: A University-City Research Venture," in *Universities in the Urban Crisis*, ed. Thomas P.

Murphy, (New York: Dundlen Publication Co. Inc., 1975) 16–18, 19, 21–22; Klotsche, *Urban University*, 40, 43, 52; Freeland, *Academia's Golden Age*, 111–12; Geiger, *Research and Relevant Knowledge*, 165; Bok, *Beyond the Ivory Tower*, 6–7, 236; John Brubacher and J. Willis Rudy, *Higher Education in Transition*, (New York: Harper and Row, 1976) 235–36.

486 John B. Hall to George Manners, 17 November 1967, box 17, folder 1, report, committee on academic growth, n.d. [1967], 1, box 1, folder 12, G76–18, excerpts from min., Regents, 13 September 1967, George Simpson to Noah Langdale, 19 September 1967, box 29, folder 7, G73–8, Langdale to Simpson, 13 August 1966, box 8, Regents-curricula change, 1962–1967 folder, Langdale Papers.

487 John B. Hall to George Manners, 17 November 1967, box 17, folder 1, G76–18; clipping from *GSC Signal*, 20 June 1968.

488 *Atlanta Constitution*, 27 March, 7 May 1968, GSU scrapbook, 1968, report, CAD, 6 December 1967, box 17, folder 1, John B. Hall to George Manners, 17 November 1967, box 17, folder 1, notes on meeting, CAG, 22 April 1968, box 16, folder 7, G76–18, George Simpson to Noah Langdale, 15 February 1968, box 8, regents-curricular changes, 1968, folder, Langdale Papers; Melvin Ecke, in discussion with the author, 10, Atlanta, "Regents Committee on Academic Growth (CAG)," 29 July 1999, in possession of the author, 1, 5.

489 *GSC Signal*, 15 August 1968, 8; Noah Langdale to George Simpson, 23 May 1968, box 16, folder 7, G76–18, meeting of internal members, CAG, 19 June 1968, box 16, folder 7, G76–18, Langdale Papers.

490 Report of the academic growth committee, n.d. [summer 1968], 2–3, box 1, folder 12, proposal for establishment of an urban life center, n.d. [June 1968], Noah Langdale to George Simpson, 1 July 1968, box 16, folder 7, G76–18.

491 Alex Lacy to Noah Langdale, 27 August 1968, box 44, urban observatory, 1968, folder, routing slip and attached material, Dan Sweat to Lacey, n.d. [4 September 1968], Lacy to Langdale, 27 August 1968, press release by Ivan Allen, Jr., n.d. [December, 1968], school of urban life, urban observatory, 1968 folder, box 44, Langdale Papers; *Atlanta Constitution*, 15 November 1968, clipping from *Christian Science Monitor*, 18 January 1969; *Georgia State Signal*, 16 January 1969, 1.

492 Letter to George Simpson, 26 November 1968, rough draft prepared by Lacy for Noah Langdale's signature, box 4, Alex Lacy folder, Langdale to Simpson, 3 March 1969, box 21, reading files, 1966–1970, grants received by the Urban Life Center, 1969–1970, school of urban life, gen. corres., May 1970, folder, Dan E. Sweat, Jr., and Lacy to York Willbern, 27 February 1969, urban observatory, 1968, folder, Kenneth M. Gregor to Langdale, 29 August 1969, Langdale to Milton G. Farriss, 24 September 1969, urban observatory, 1968, folder, box 44, Langdale Papers, Manners, "Reminiscences," 431–35.

493 Noah Langdale to Alex Lacy, 21 November 1968, Langdale to George Simpson, 23 May 1969, box 21, reading files, 1966–1970, folder, Langdale Papers, Lacy to Langdale, 10 July 1969, box 28, folder 377, G73–4; Clarence N. Stone, *Regime Politics: Governing Atlanta, 1946–1988*, (Lawrence KS: University of Kansas Press, 1989) 51–78.

494 Noah Langdale to Paul C. Broun, 13 March 1969, box 21, reading file, January to April 1969, folder, Langdale Papers.

495 Charles B. Vail to Noah Langdale, 1 April 1969, box 19, GSU internal-Southern Labor Archives folder, Langdale Papers.

496 Noah Langdale to George Simpson, 9 July 1969, box 21, reading file, May to September 1969, folder, Langdale Papers.

INDEX

Arcade (1918) and Murphy building (1921), 7; during World War I, 7–8; first woman graduate (1919), 8; enrollment (1920s), 12; student activities (1920s), 16; reorganization (1925), 15; move to Forsyth Street building (1926), 16; permanent domicile sought, 19–22; move to Sheltering Arms (Luckie-Walton Street building) in 1931, 24; removed from Tech tutelage, 24–25; placed under chancellor and regents, 29; named University System of Georgia Center (also Atlanta Center and University System of Georgia Evening School [USGES]) in 1932, x-xi, 56; mentioned, 9, 10, 11, 13, 14, 19

Extension service, *see* Adult Education

F

Faculty Affairs, faculty governance, 23–24, 236–37; pressure for higher professional and recruiting standards, 237; recognition of faculty achievement, 237–38; disparate teaching loads, 238; rise of A&S, 238–39; faculty involvement in non-academic matters, 239–241; departmental versus administration judgment of faculty competence, 241–42; mentioned, 4–5, 14, 15, 17–18, 23, 37, 51, 53, 60, 72, 80–86, 88, 89, 109, 122–26, 137, 141, 142, 154, 155, 158, 166, 167, 173, 176, 186, 189, 194, 195–96, 201, 203, 210, 212, 216, 218–19

Federal Emergency Relief Administration (FERA), student scholarships, 45, 77

Financial affairs, mentioned, ix, 4, 15, 19, 21, 22, 23, 24, 27–28, 36, 42, 45, 46–48, 52, 61–63, 66, 77, 88–89, 90, 95–95, 98–99, 100–105, 112, 128–30, 131–33, 135–36, 138, 139, 143,

155–57, 170, 179, 184, 193, 221, 248, 250, 256

Fink, Gary M., vii

Flambo, 72, 75

Foley, Frank D., 164, 170, 172, 181, 182, 183, 187, 188

Forward Atlanta Movement (FAM), 10

Frank, Leo, 3

G

Gateway, name changed to *Rampway,* 225

Gates, James, 125, 126, 128, 131, 143, 144, 148, 151, 160, 218

General Education Board (GEB), 27–28, 29, 30, 89

General Extension Division, see Adult Education

Georgia Institute of Technology, x, 1, 2, 4, 11, 12, 13, 18, 19, 27, 29, 31, 33, 40, 41, 45, 47, 85, 89, 92, 100, 147, 150, 151, 172, 192, 196, 205, 207, 209, 210, 212, 218, 221, 234, 238, 247, 248, 256, 257

Georgia Tech School of Commerce, creation and curriculum, x, 1, 4; enrollment and degrees, 5; move from Tech to UGA and opposition thereto, 29–33; mentioned, 6, 7, 8, 10, 13, 14

Georgia State College (GSC), name authorized in 1962, 222; student activities, 225–33; arrival of student activism, 233–36; faculty affairs, 236–42; AAUP involvement, 239–41; 1960s physical expansion, 244–45, 247–50; school of general studies, 245–46; degree programs, 246–47, 252, 253; A&S programs lag, 250; Urban Life (UL) concept, 250–51, 252–53; new graduate degrees recommended, 253–54; GSC's urban observatory, 254; Urban Life pro-

315

ROTC, 233

Routh, James, 82, 83

S

Sanford, S. V., 40, 52, 54, 55, 56, 57, 66, 92, 93, 94, 95

Savannah Branch (UGA), 116, 122, 123

Servicemen's Readjustment Act of 1944 ("GI Bill"), 97, 115, 122, 129

Shannon, Margaret, 183, 208

Siebert, Leonard R., 15, 102, 109, 110, 111, 164, 201, 205, 222

Signal (also *Evening Signal, University Signal* and *GSC Signal*) 37, 40, 47, 60, 74, 75, 79, 80, 128, 137, 140, 188, 191, 194, 202, 218, 220, 226, 230, 236

Simpson, George, GSC to emphasize teacher training, 250; intrigued with Urban Life (UL), 251; mentioned, 234, 247, 250, 252, 256

Sloan, William Boyd, 203, 204–205

Smith, Leon P., 123–24, 126

Smith, M. M. "Muggsy," 194, 199

Smith, Marion, 32, 48, 95

Snelling, Charles M., director of General Extension, 36; mentioned, 28, 35, 42, 54, 56, 61, 75

Sopkin, Henry, 125

Southern Association of Colleges (SAC), challenges Evening School expansion, 38, 40, 41, 43; suspension of System "white" colleges, 87; mentioned, 23, 33, 51, 52, 53, 54, 56, 88, 89, 90, 92, 93, 94, 96, 105, 108, 109, 110, 111, 116, 121, 126, 130, 131, 132, 135 137, 138, 139, 142, 143, 148–49, 153, 157, 158, 159, 178, 180, 181, 182, 185, 193–94, 217, 218, 225, 236, 240, 241, 248

Southern Labor Archives, 256

Spalding, Hughes, 36, 41, 43, 44, 49, 72

Spalding, Jack, 183–84

Sparks, George M., profile, 16; management techniques, 17–18, 24, 108; search for permanent Evening School home, 19–20; faculty governance, 23–24; embraced Works's report, 31–32, 33, 41; moves to expand Evening School into a state college, 35–43, 51–57; seeks larger quarters and PWA funding, 46–47, 61; permits B.C.S. majors in any field, 60; overcrowded Luckie-Walton building, 60–61; acquisition of old Baptist Hospital (Nassau Hotel), 61–63; wartime promotion of Atlanta Center, 65–67; post-war expansion and need for new building, 67–68; recognizes accreditation problem, 88–89, 108, 109, 110, 111; case for expansion to Ivy Street garage, 98–101; renovation of the garage, 101–103, 104; preparations for UGA merger, 111–12; appointed assistant chancellor, 139, 140; retirement in 1957, 195, 197; mentioned, x, xii, 9, 14, 15, 45, 53, 59, 64, 65, 71, 75, 76, 77, 78, 80, 81, 82, 83, 84, 85, 87, 95–96, 97, 105, 109, 116, 117, 118, 119, 123, 127, 128, 129, 131, 132, 133, 135, 138, 139, 142–43, 144, 148, 149, 150, 151, 153, 156, 157, 158, 159, 170, 171, 173, 176, 177, 178, 180, 181, 182, 183, 189, 190, 193, 194, 200, 201, 211, 215, 225, 227, 229, 237, 240, 246, 257

Spencer, W. H., transfer Tech Commerce School to UGA, 30, 31–32; mentioned, 51

State College of Business Administration (SCBA), name rejected by GSC faculty and public, 189; mentioned, 188

Strayer, George D., 1949 System study, 135, 136–39; mentioned, 3, 141, 180

Student Activity fee, 227–28

School colors, 228–29